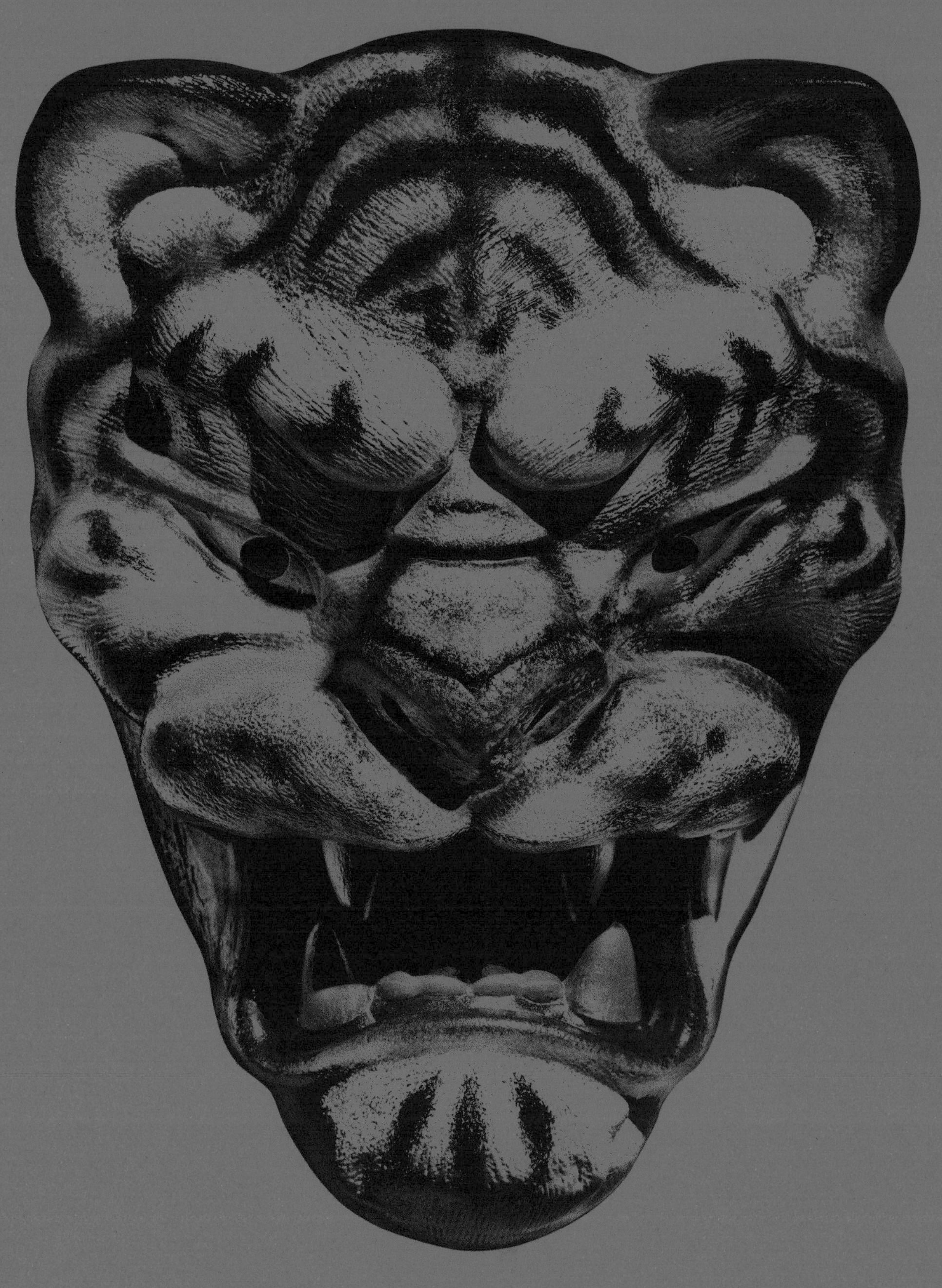

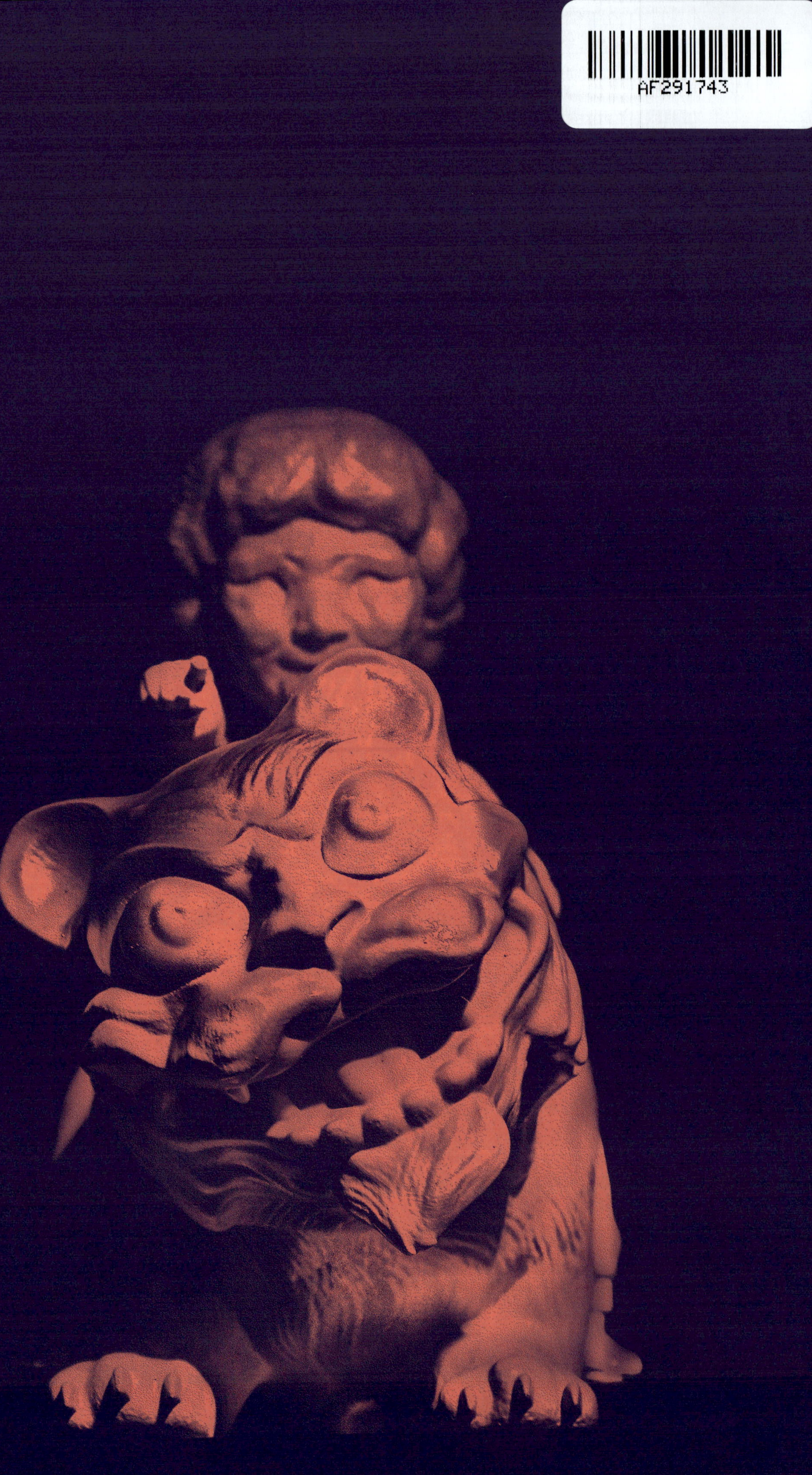

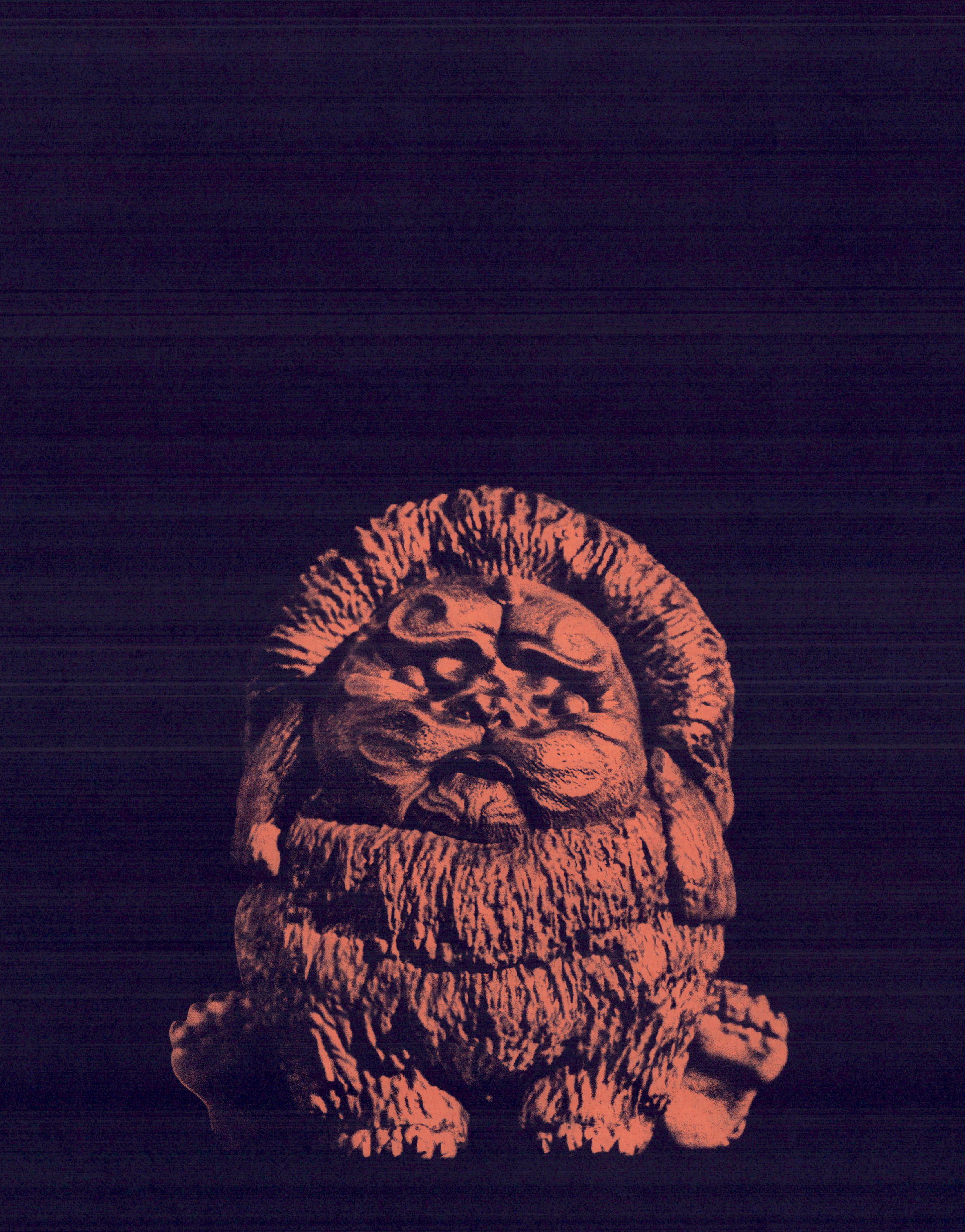

南無佛法僧
日日日月月月
天天天鬼鬼鬼

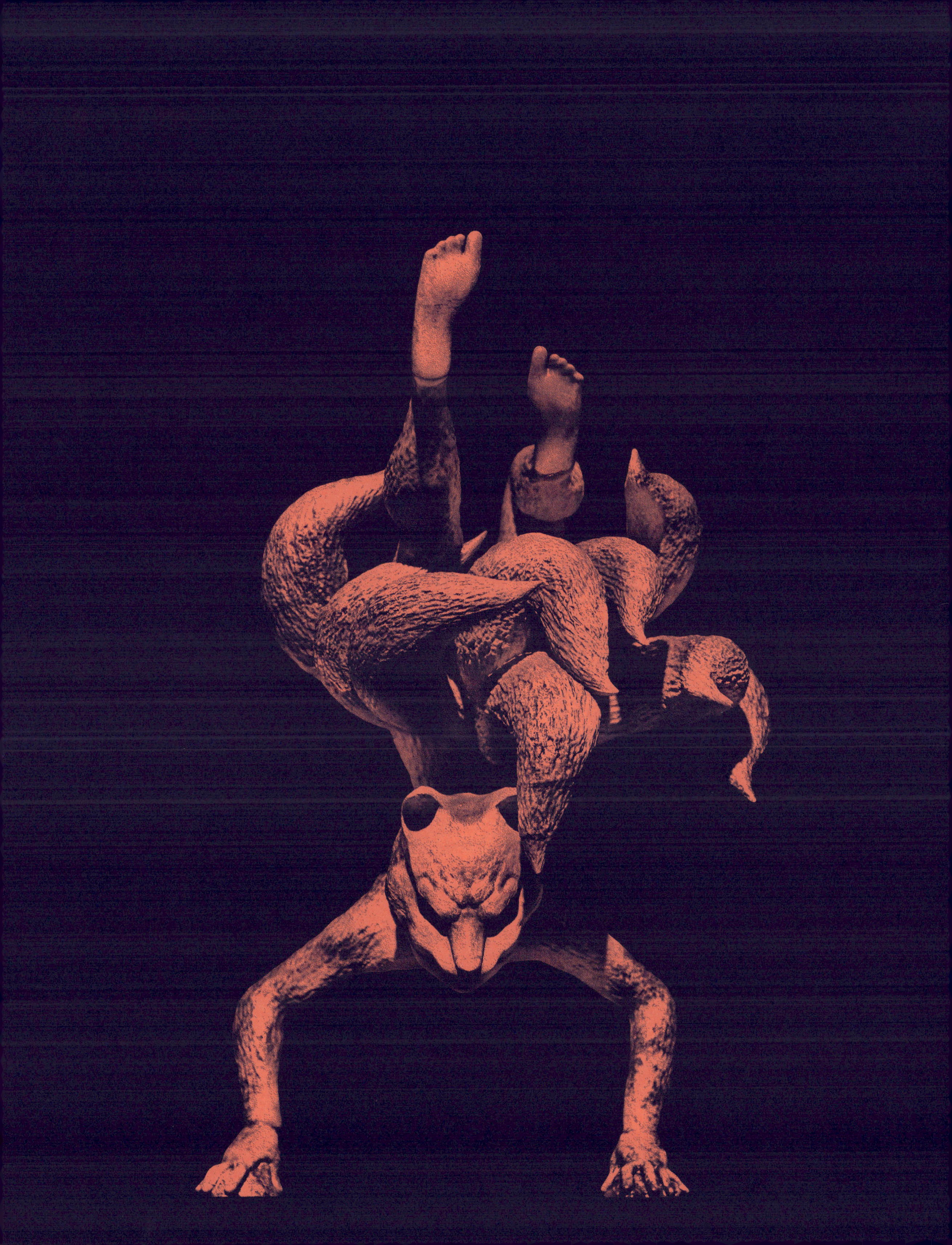

Zadie Xa

*House Gods,
Animal Guides
&
Five Ways
2 Forgiveness*

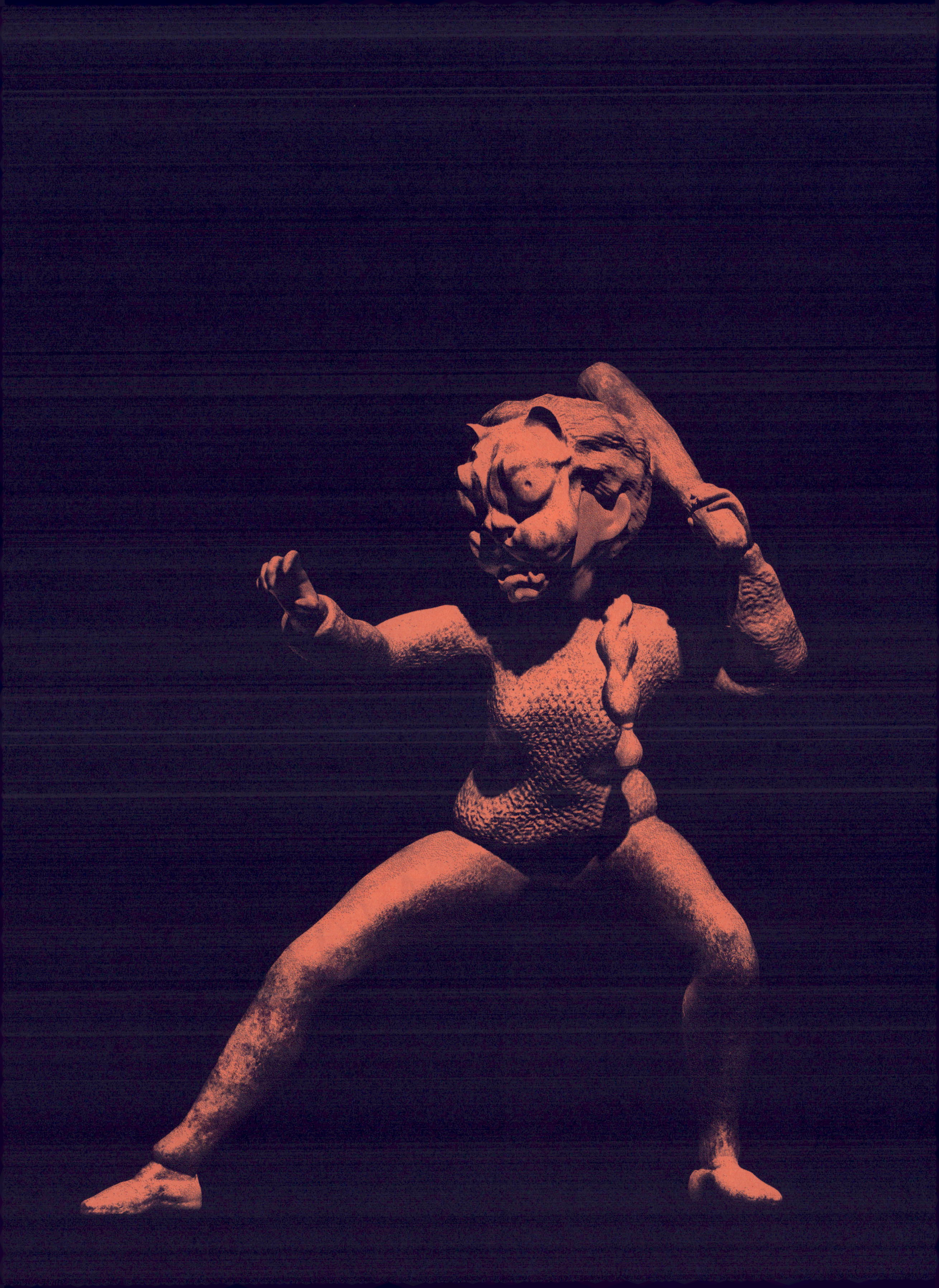

Words

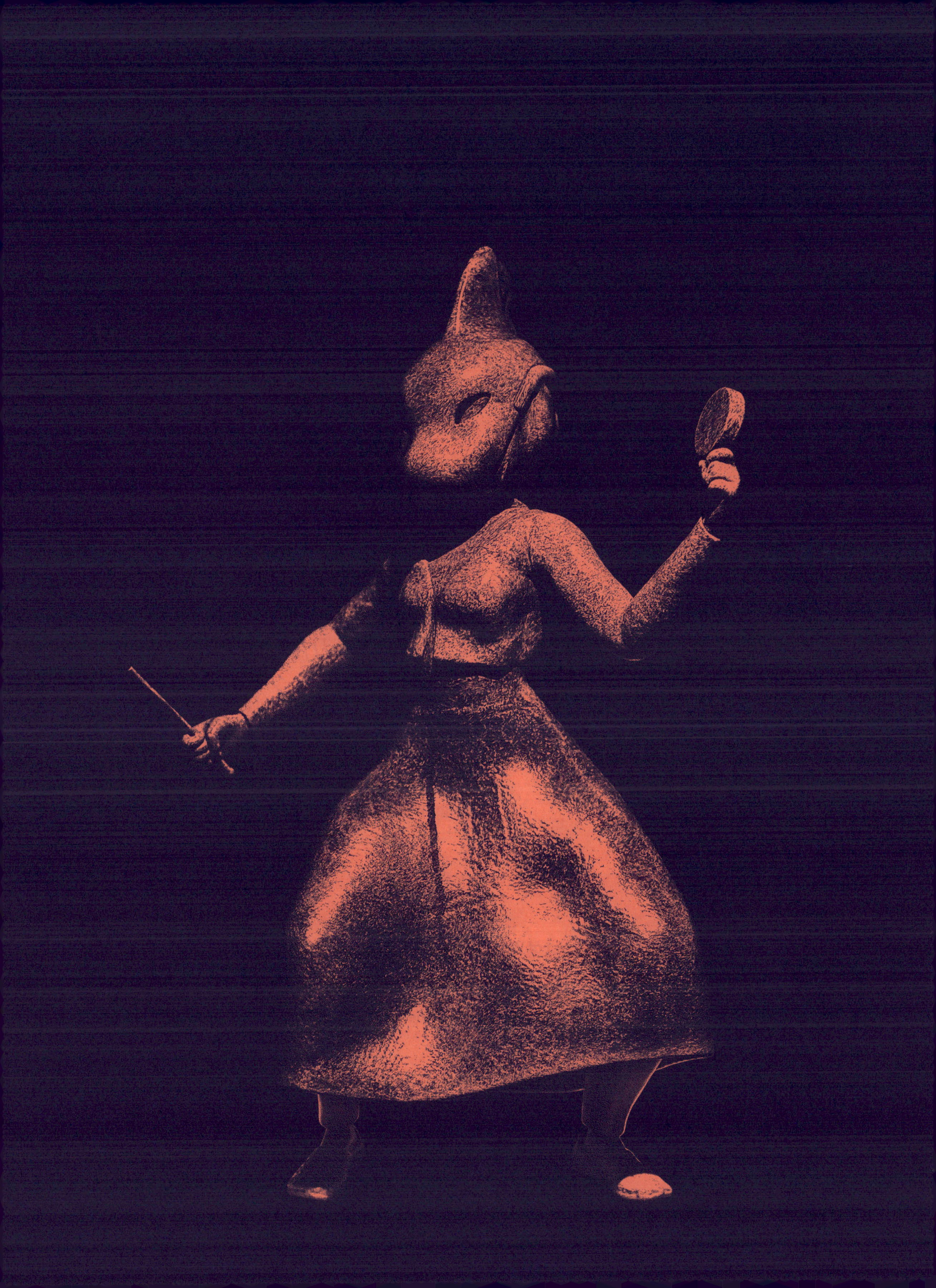

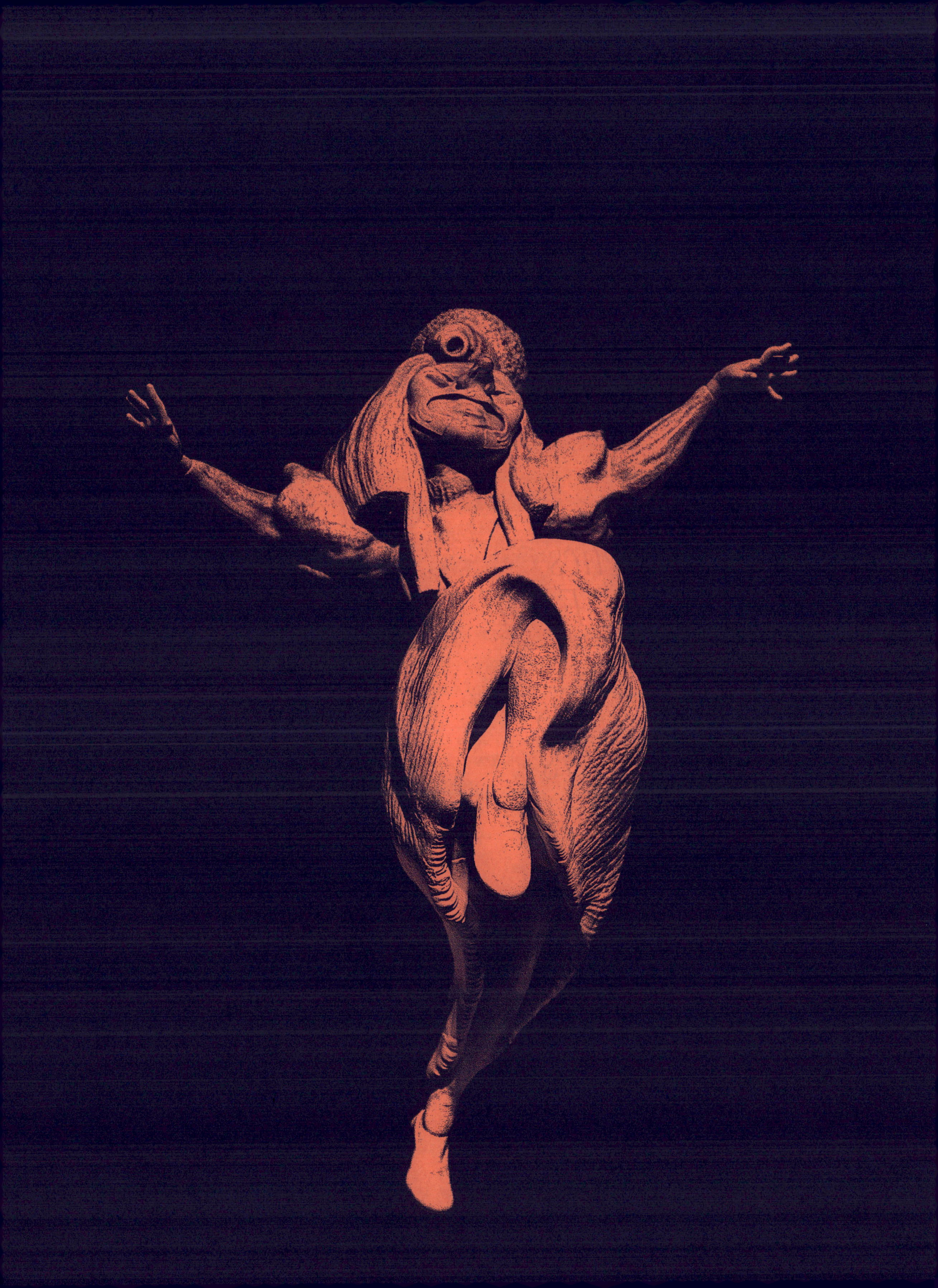

Foreword

'Museum and mausoleum are connected by more than phonetic association,' notes the German philosopher Theodor Adorno in his essay 'Valéry Proust Museum'. 'Museums are like the family sepulchres of works of art. They testify to the neutralisation of culture.' Like Adorno, Zadie Xa recognises the connection between the museum and the mausoleum. When invited to realise a new work for Whitechapel Gallery, she drew a connection between the brick-lined gallery (the former reading room of the Whitechapel Public Library) with the architecture of a mausoleum. In stark contrast to the gloomy stillness of the family sepulchres that embalm and neutralise works of art, Xa's commission reimagines the gallery as a Korean ancestral shrine in a vibrant installation comprising of sculptures, paintings, sound and light – animated by deities, tricksters, guardians and animal spirits who guide visitors on a journey between the worlds of the living and the dead.

The artist's commission has been brought to life by the creativity, care and kindness of many people. An enormous and heartfelt thank you is due to Zadie Xa herself for the many months of hard work, boundless imagination and meticulous planning that went into conceiving this project for Whitechapel Gallery. True to the collaborative nature of her practice, Xa brought together an exceptional team of individuals in order to realise this body of work. Artist Benito Mayor Vallejo supported on the exhibition's design and collaborated closely on the production of a number of key works. Working tirelessly in Xa's studio were Lin Sheng, Tang Hong and Xiao Xia who helped produce many of the textile components of the installation. In addition, Manuel Vadillo generously provided the patterns for the two jacket works in the exhibition. Tom Slater designed and engineered the installation's sound elements and Jihye Kim lent her vocals for the piece. The exhibition's immersive and theatrical lighting was designed and installed by Liam Cahill and Tom Johnson of Sanford Lighting Design, and the brilliant team at Sam Forster Ltd were responsible for the installation's build elements.

In reality every single member of the Whitechapel Gallery's team plays a key and necessary role in the realisation of the exhibitions we host and, as such, I am hugely grateful to all staff for their commitment to the Gallery's programme, as well as the passion and drive they demonstrate on a daily basis in supporting artists. Special thanks are due to the curators of Xa's commission: Curator Tarini Malik and Assistant Curator Inês Costa who worked incredibly hard to manifest the artist's vision and in managing all aspects of the project. The Gallery's technical team, led by Christopher Aldgate and Alejandro Ball, displayed expectational skill in planning and producing this installation.

Sophie Demay and Maël Fournier-Comte of In the shade of a tree have designed this beautiful catalogue, demonstrating a highly considered engagement with the artist's work. Many thanks are due to the publication's contributors: Tarini Malik and Inês Costa, Lucia Pietroiusti, Ana Teixeira Pinto, Wong Binghao and Daniella Valz Gen who have provided new and exciting insights into Xa's practice, as well as to outstanding copy editor Novuyo Moyo whose editorial oversight is greatly appreciated.

Lastly, an ambitious exhibition and publication of this kind would not be possible without the generosity of our supporters. A very sincere thank you is due to Whitechapel Gallery's Commissioning Council (Dorota Audemars, Erin Bell, Emilie De Pauw, Heloisa Genish, Leili Huth, Irene Panagopoulos, Nicole Saikalis Bay) and Dior for making this exhibition a reality, as well as to The High Commission of Canada to the United Kingdom, Nicoletta Fiorucci Foundation and Sanghee Kim. Additional support in the production of the installation was made possible by Abbotts Flooring and J&C Joel Ltd. The artist also gratefully acknowledges the support of the Canada Council for the Arts.

Lydia Yee, Chief Curator,
Whitechapel Gallery

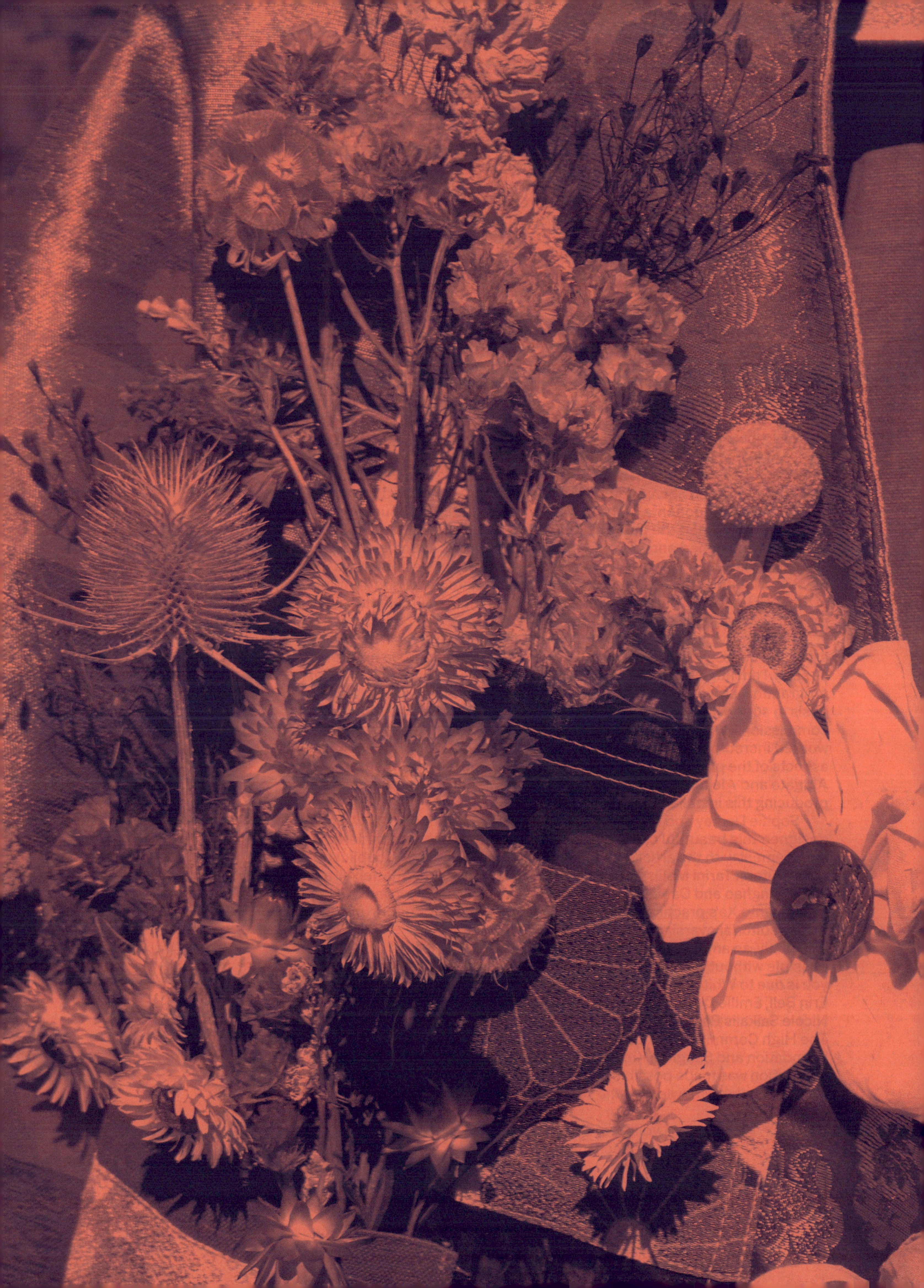

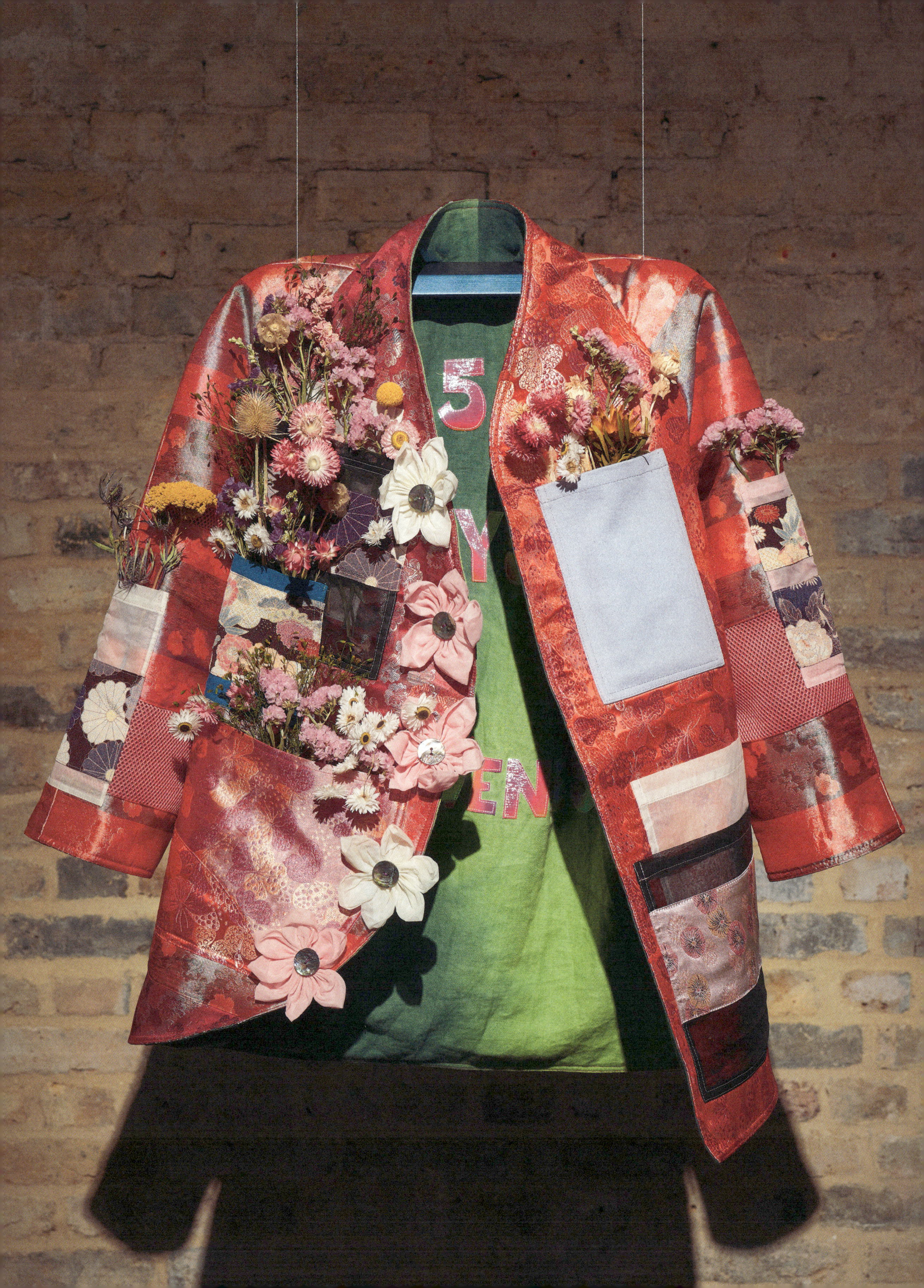

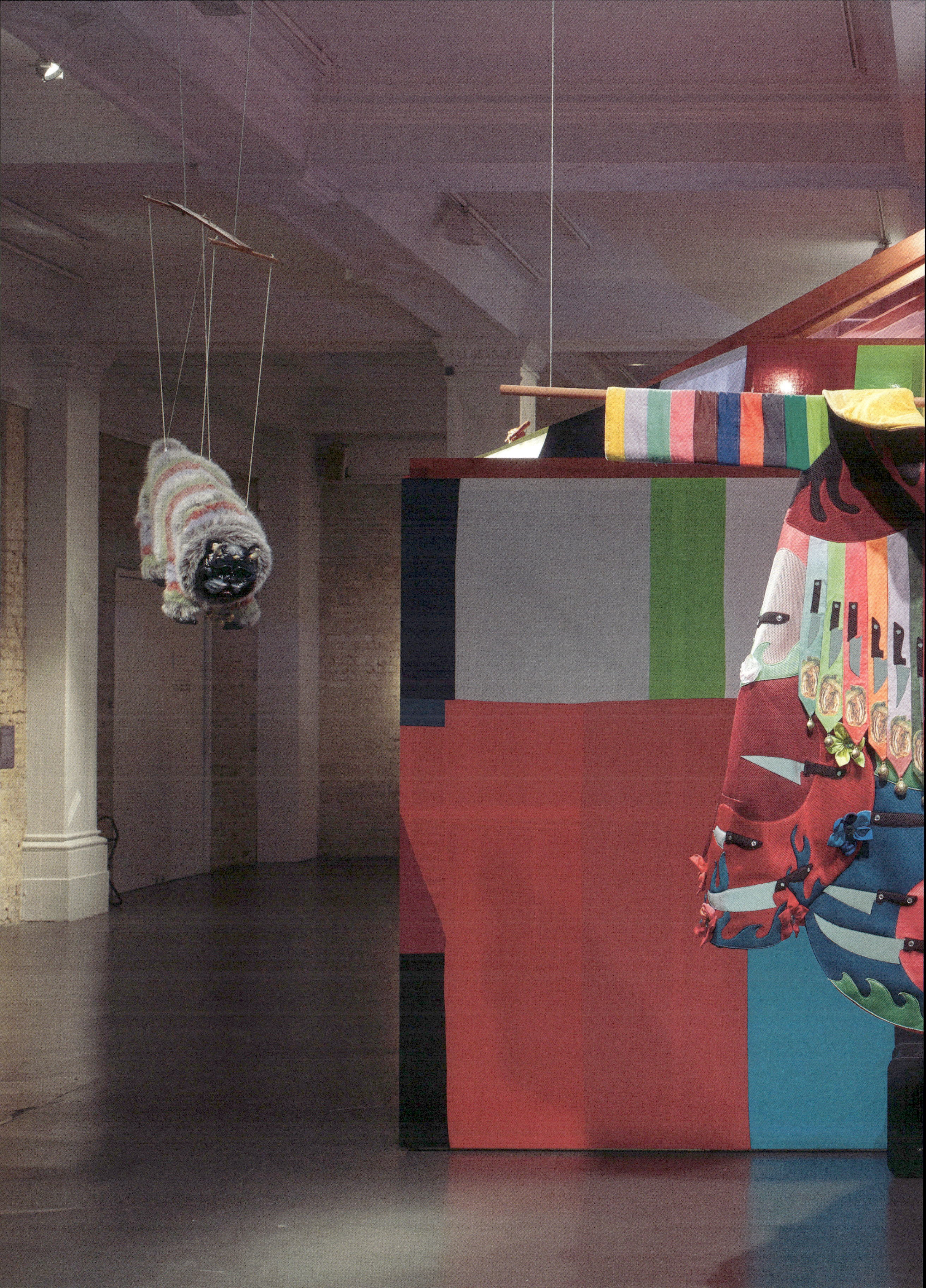

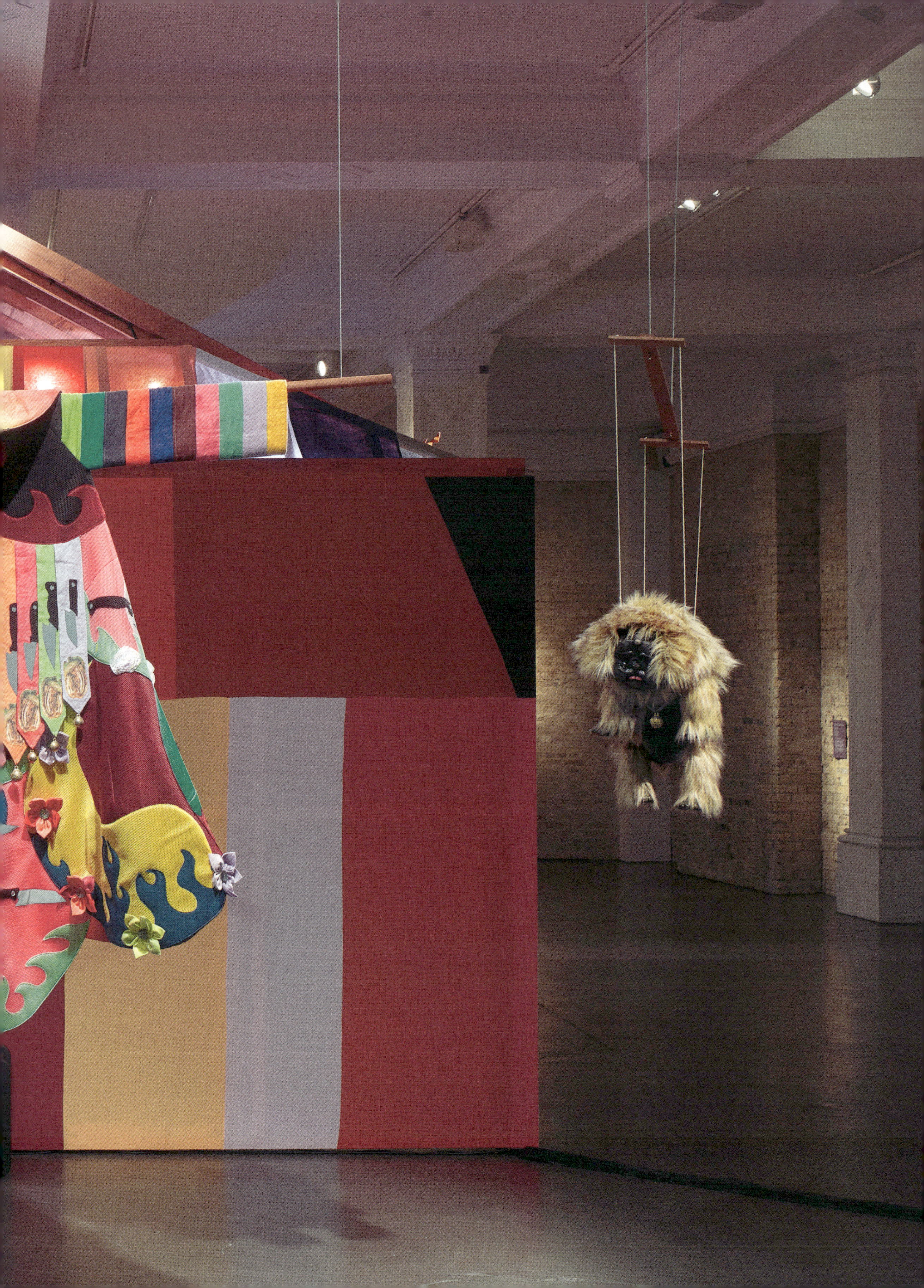

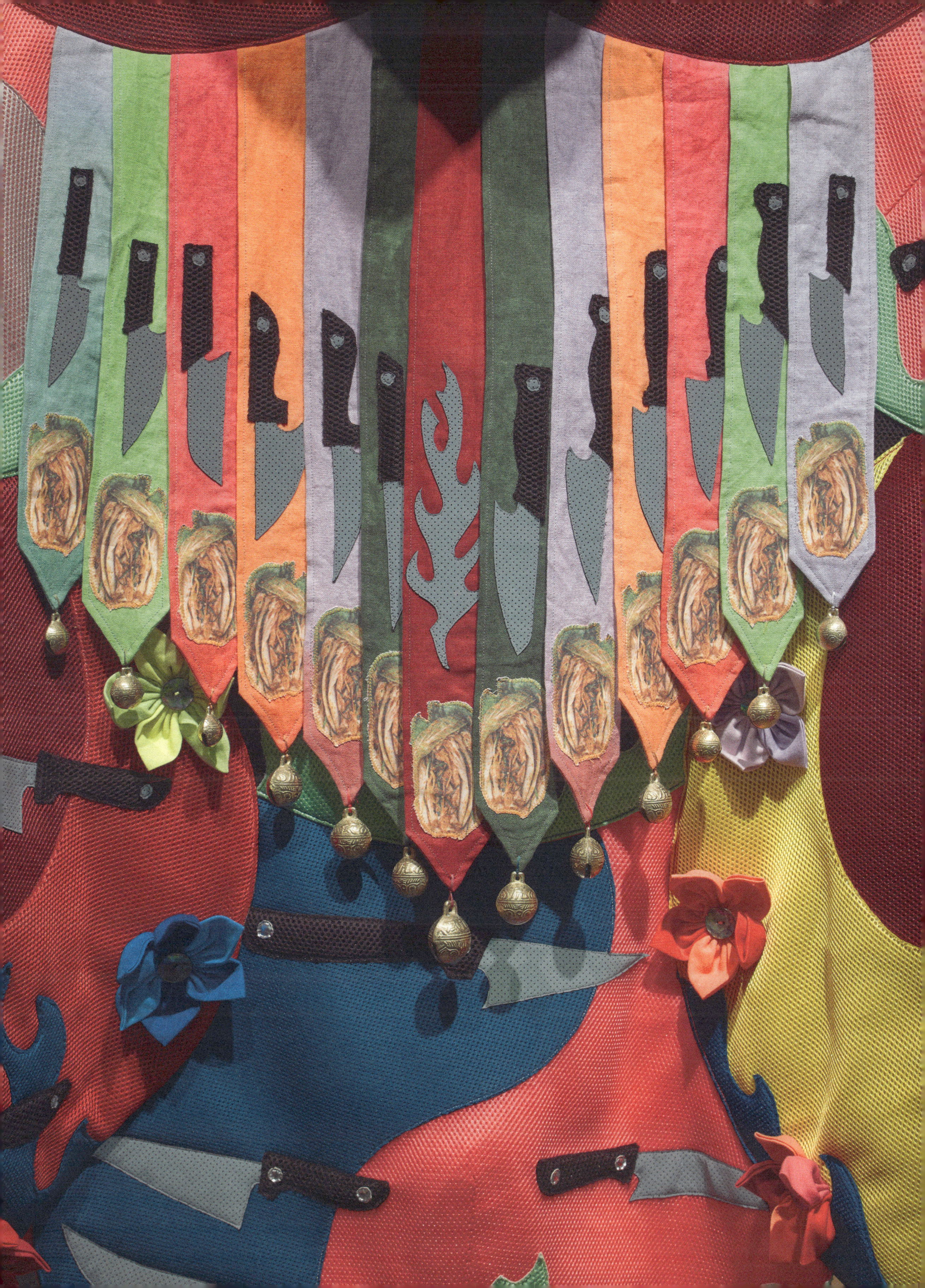

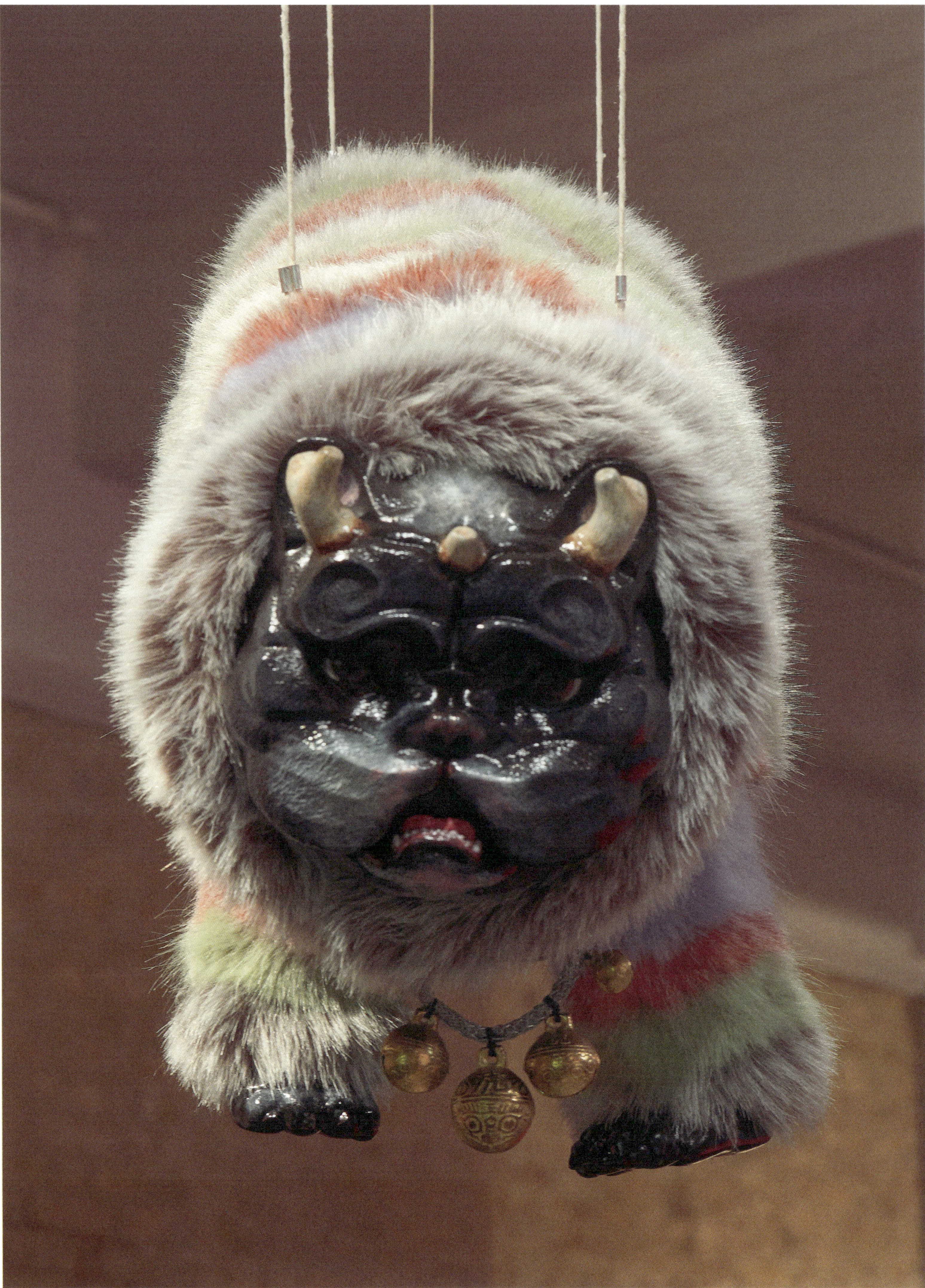

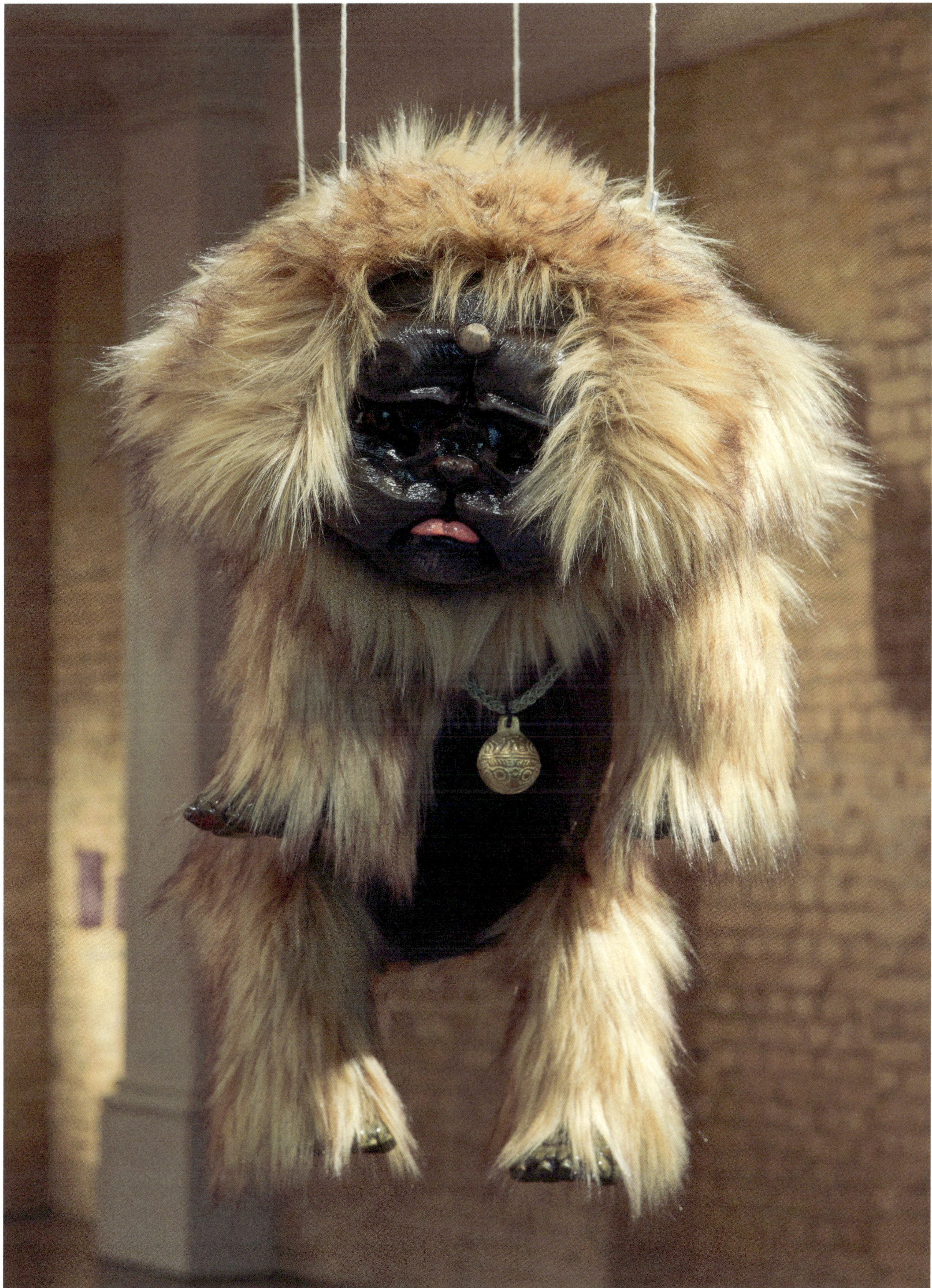

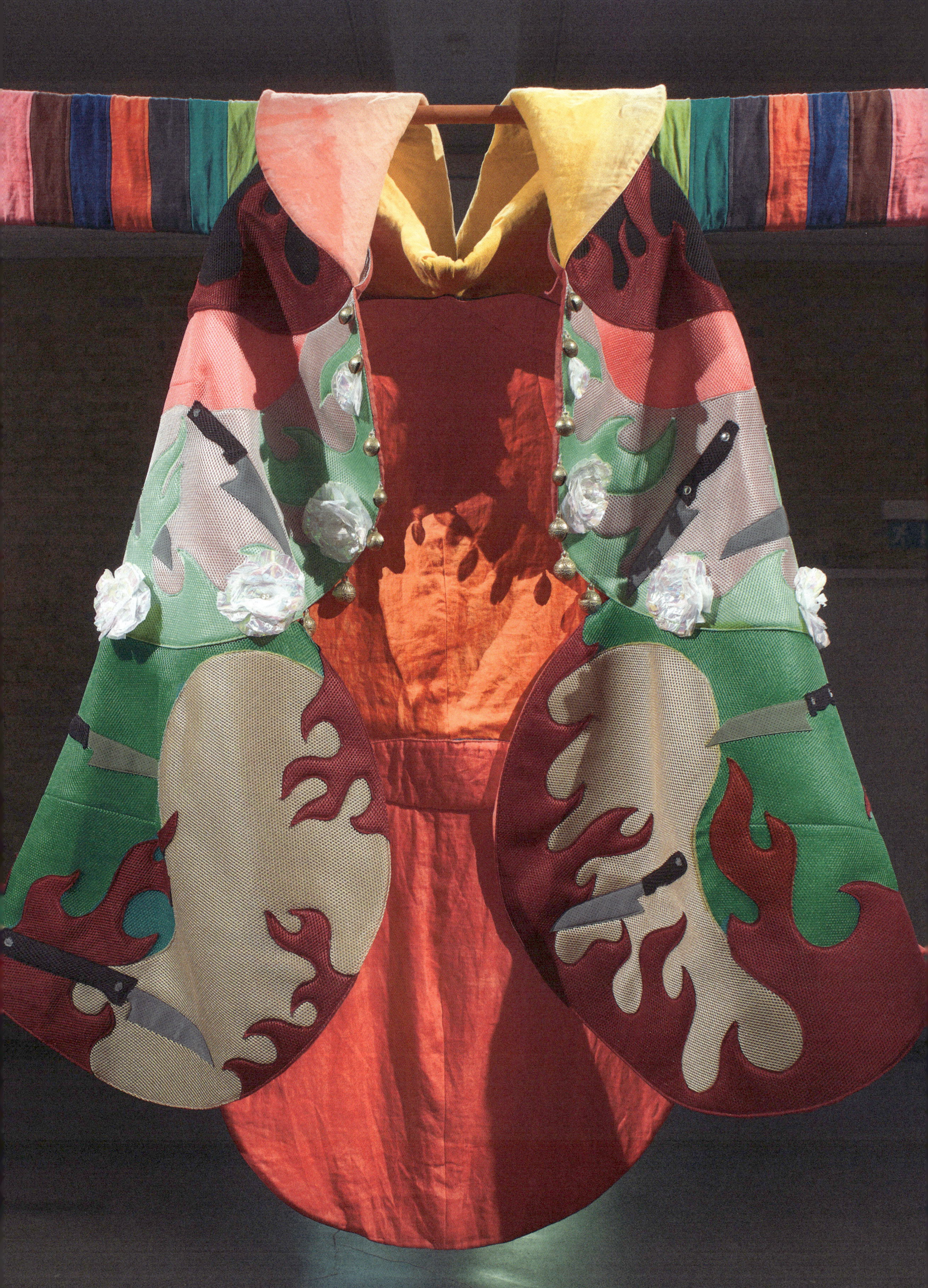

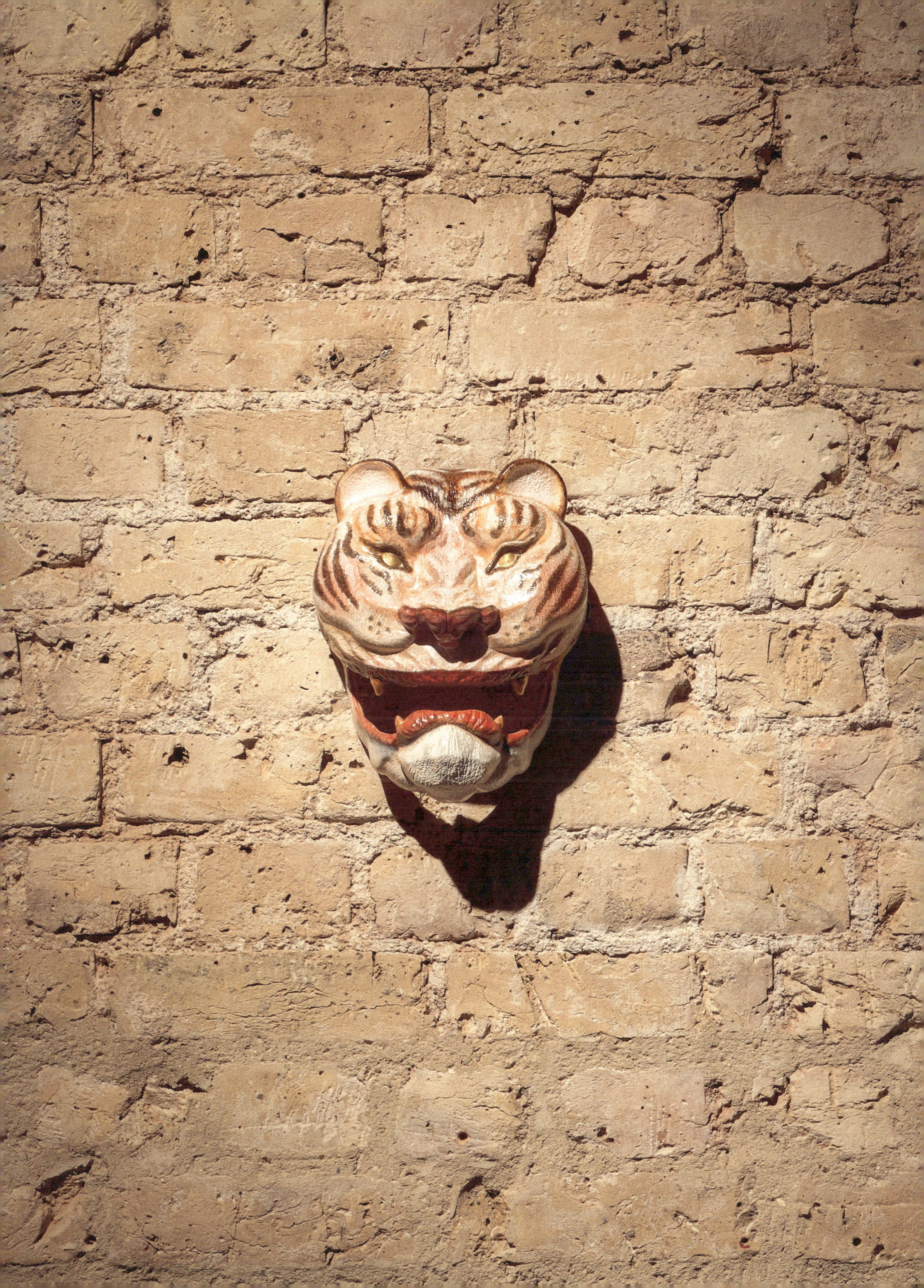

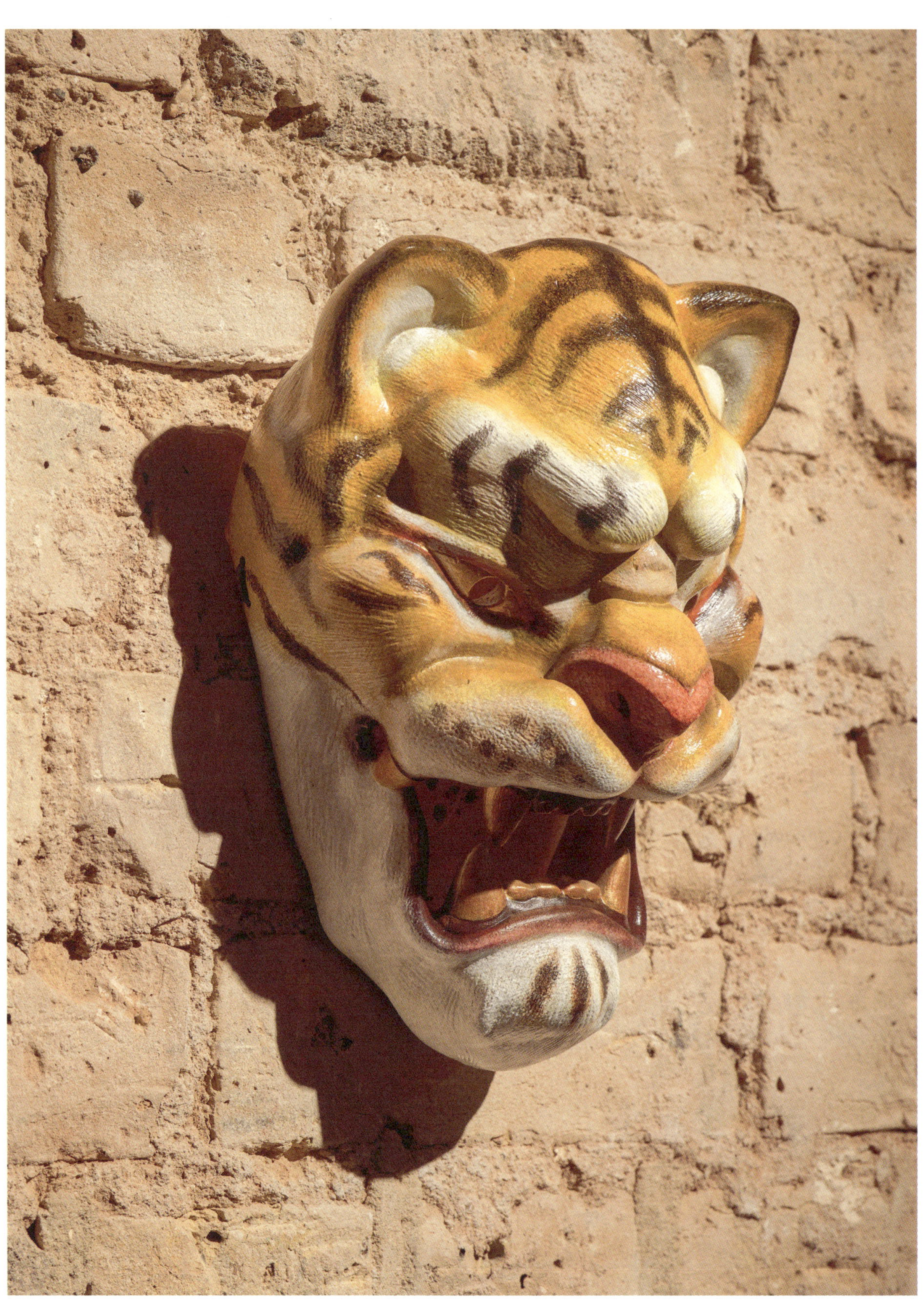

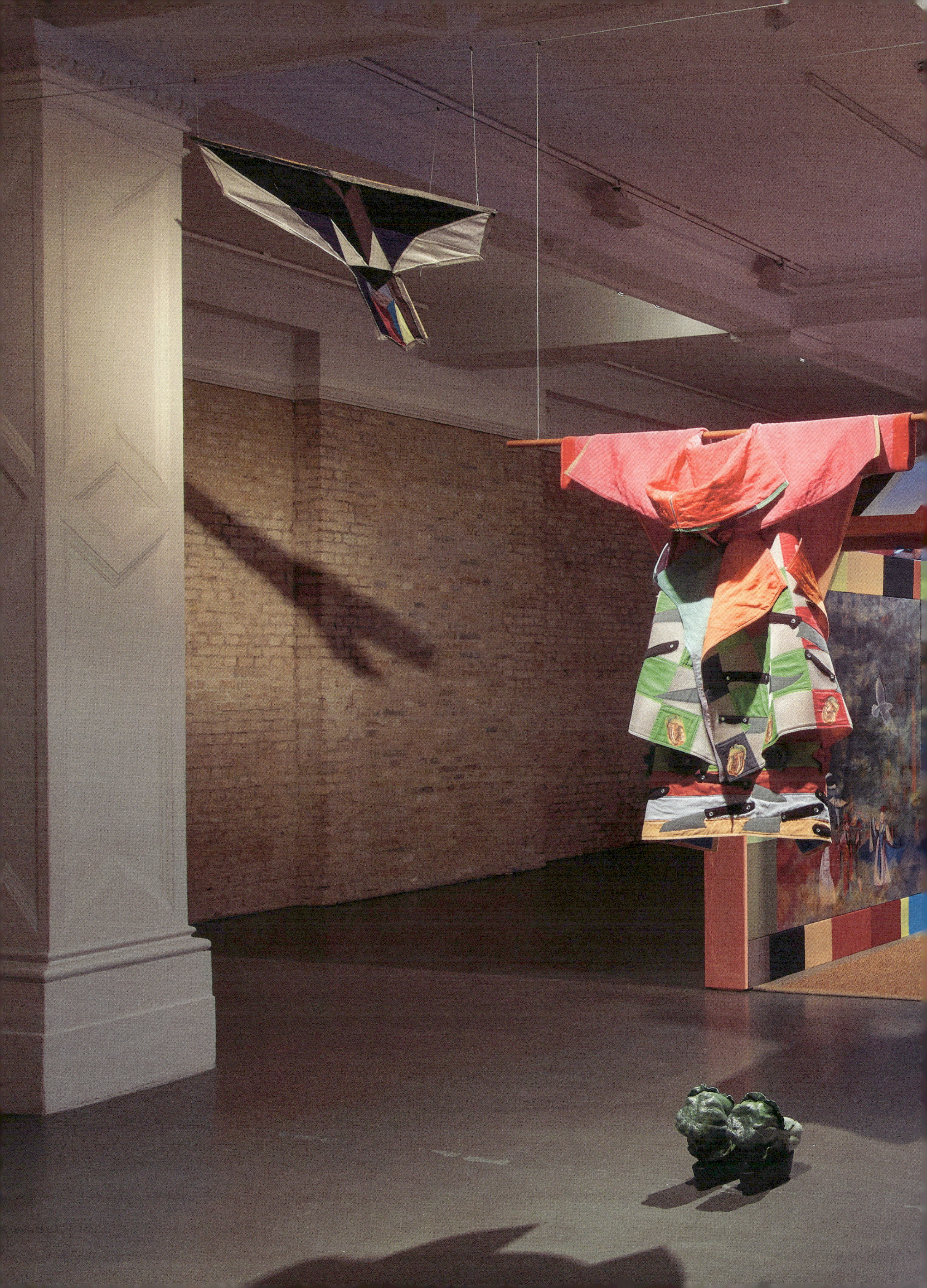

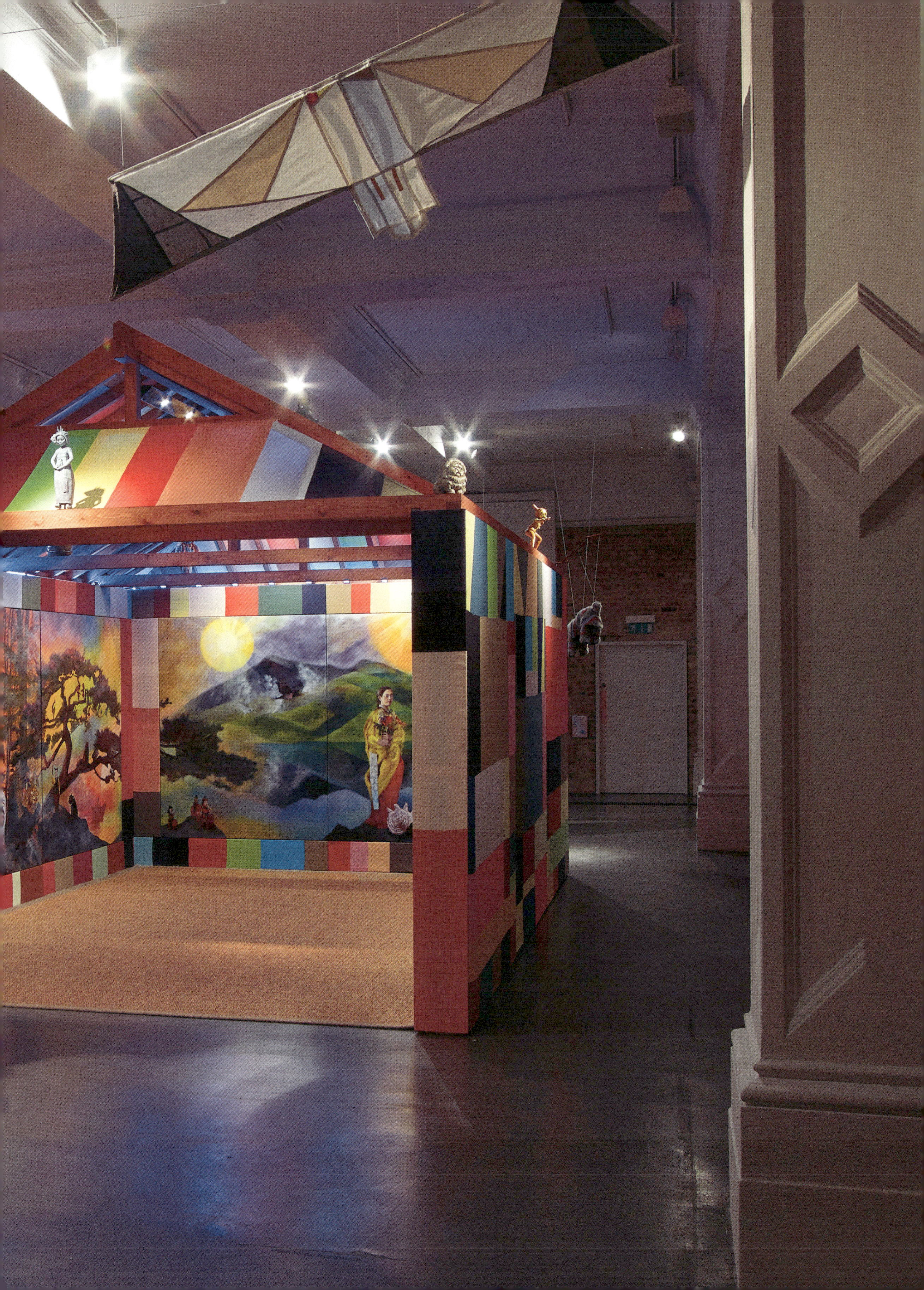

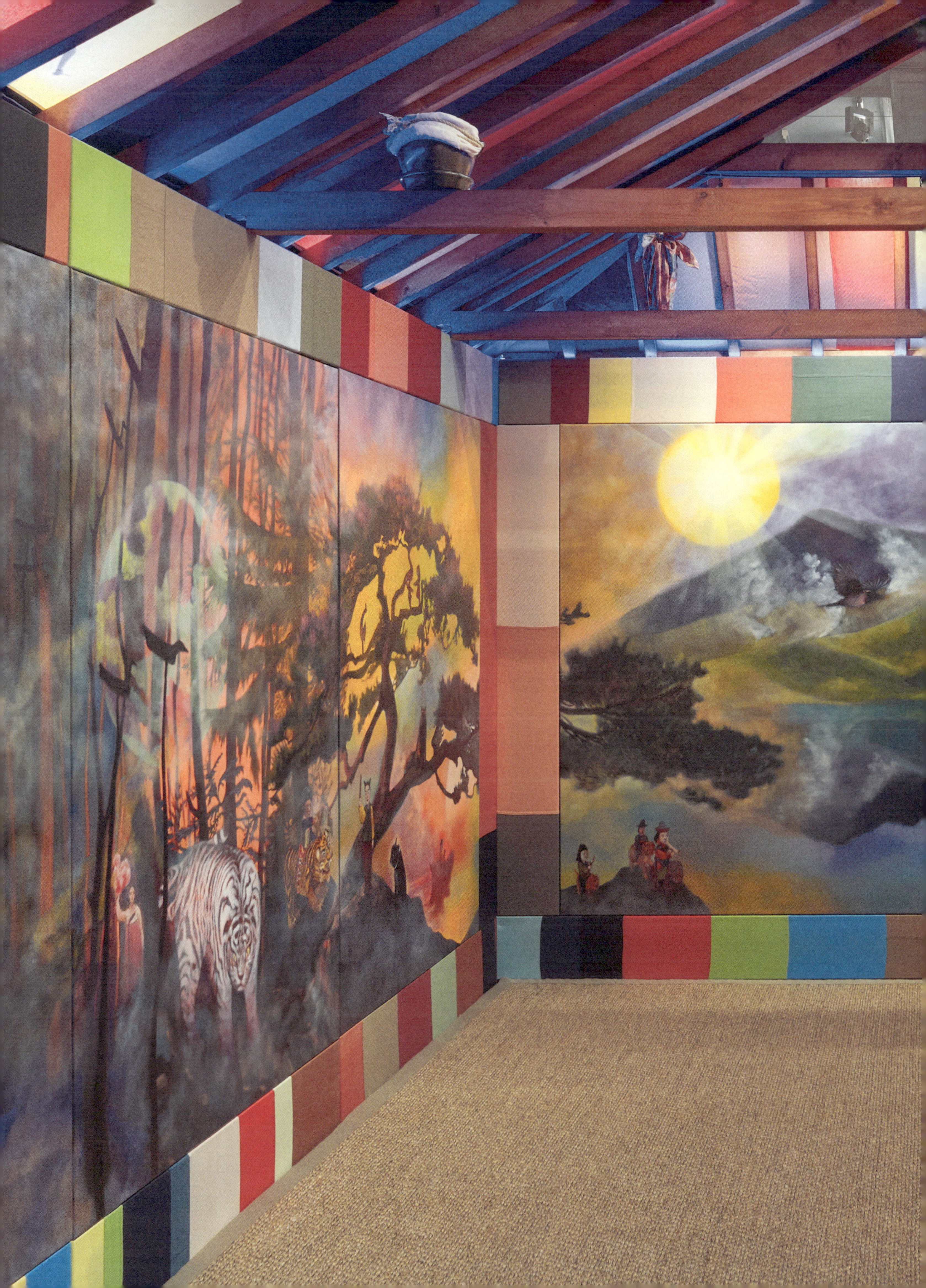

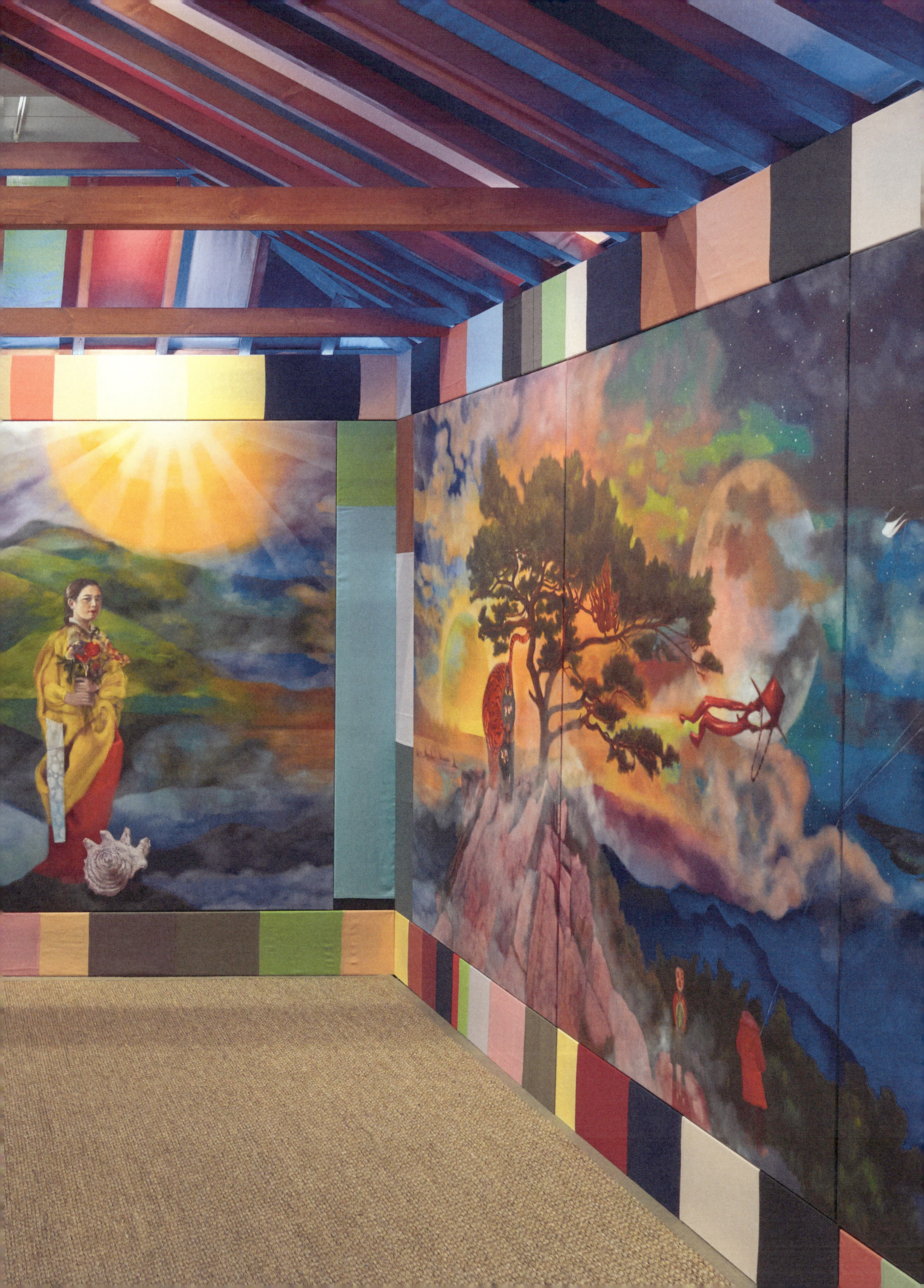

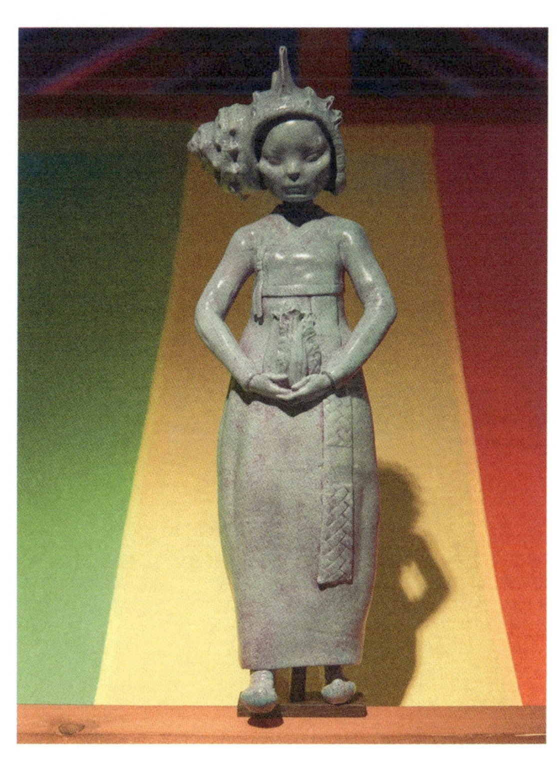

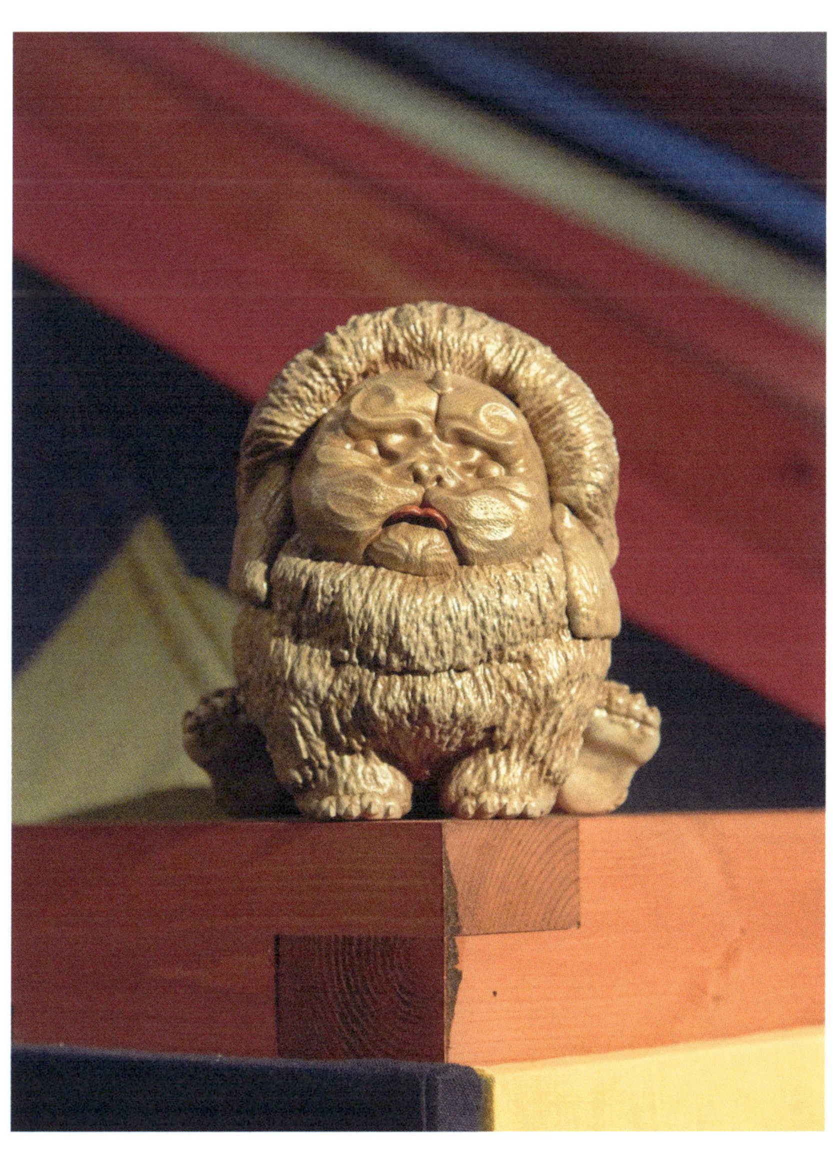

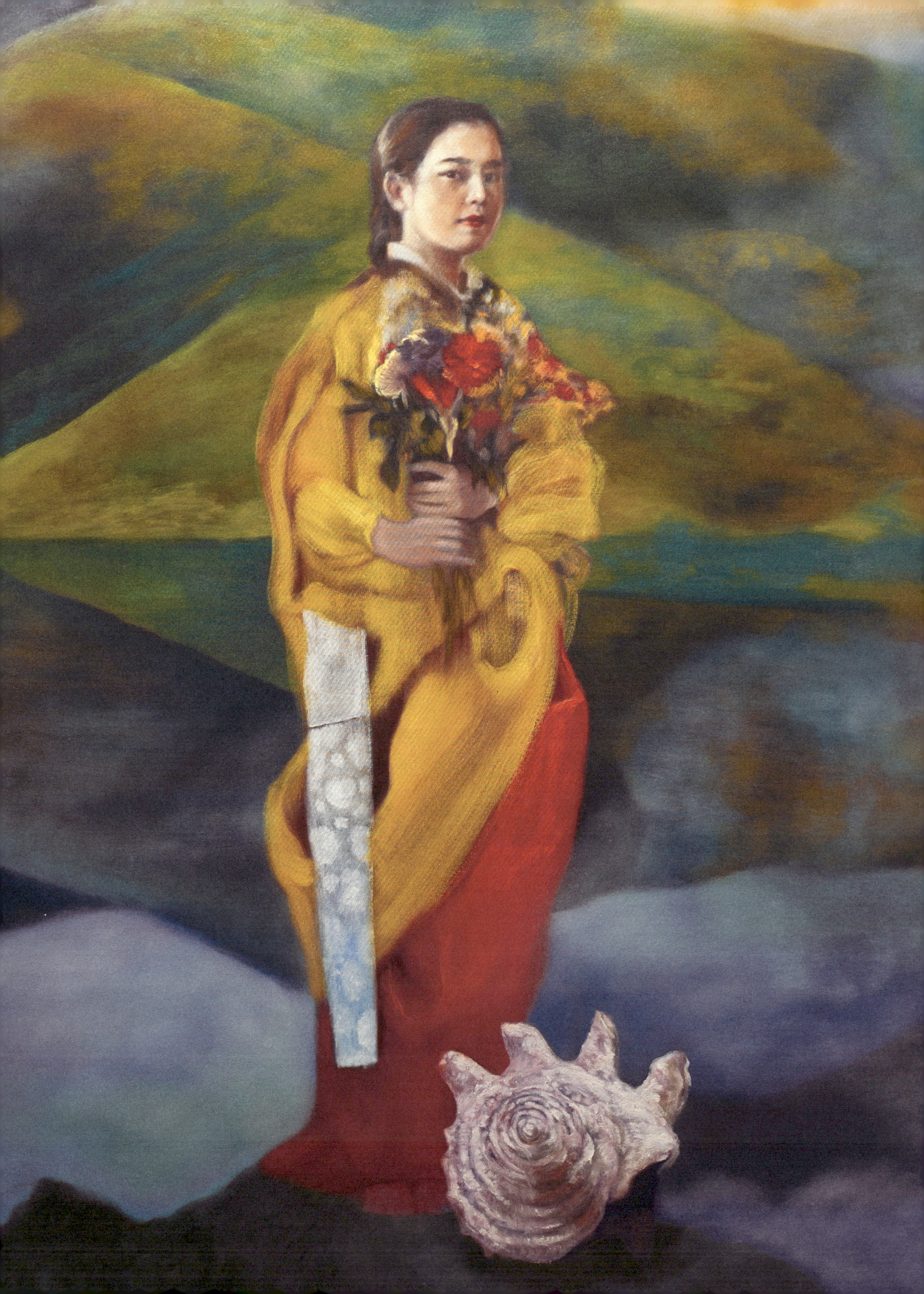

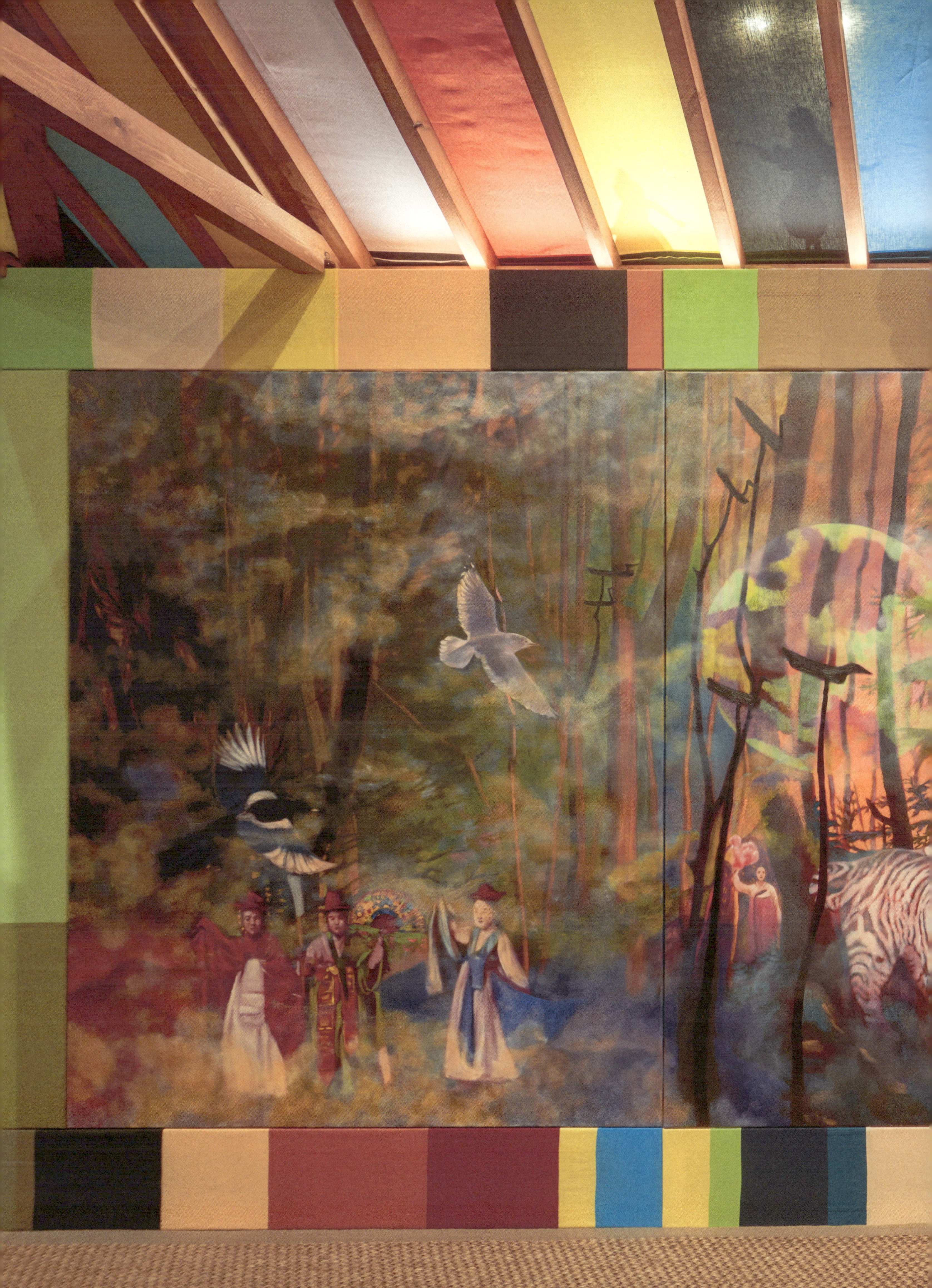

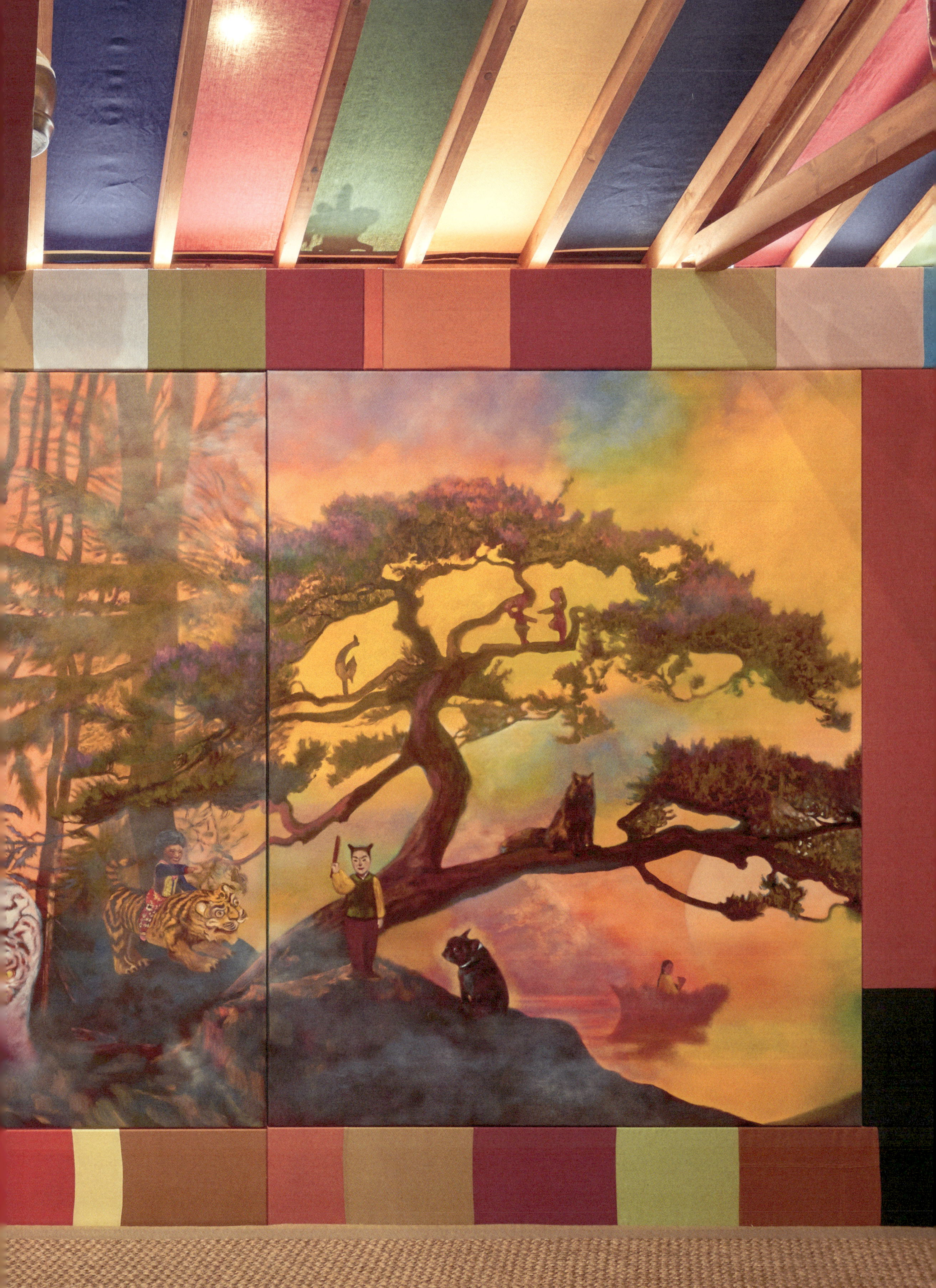

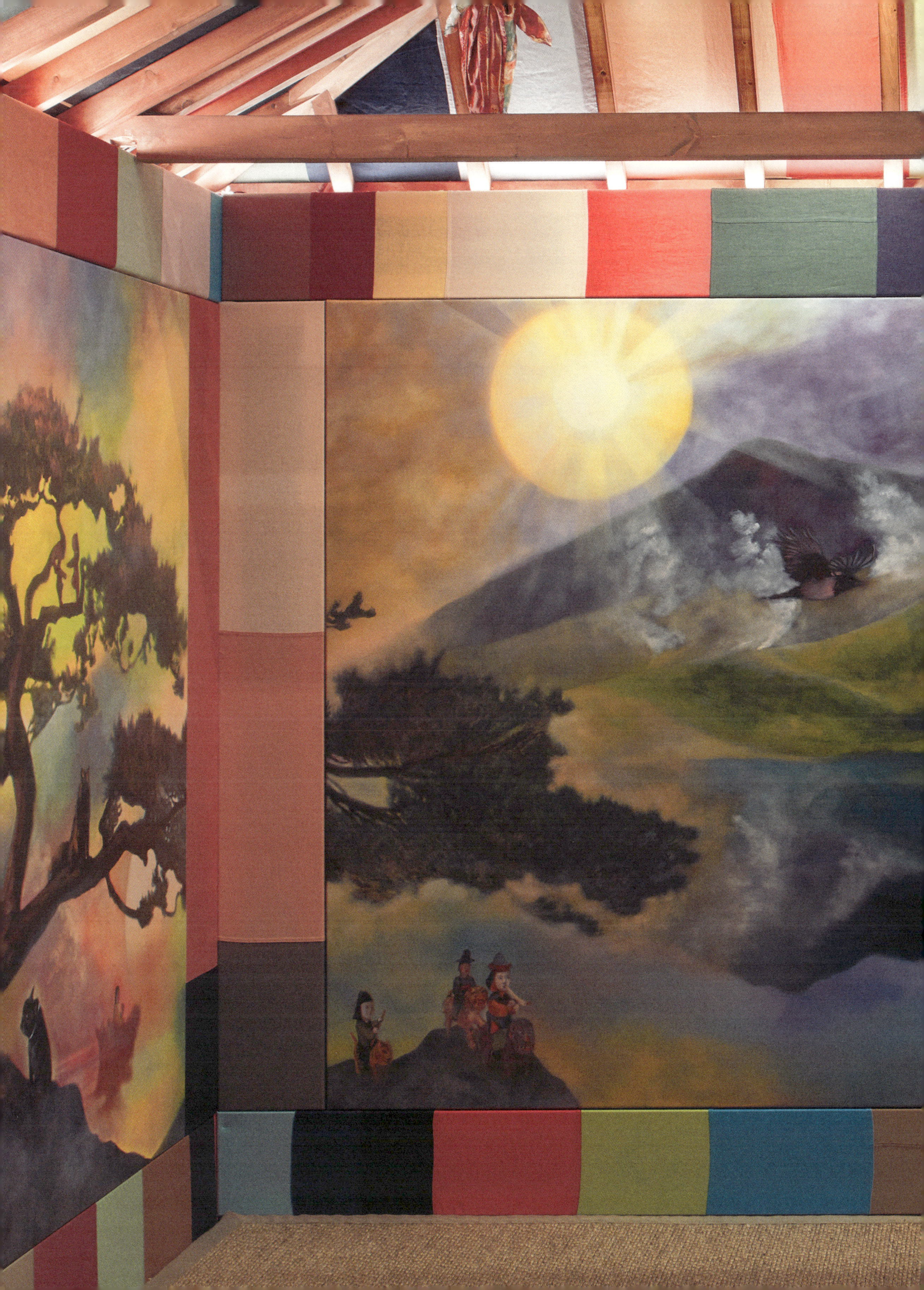

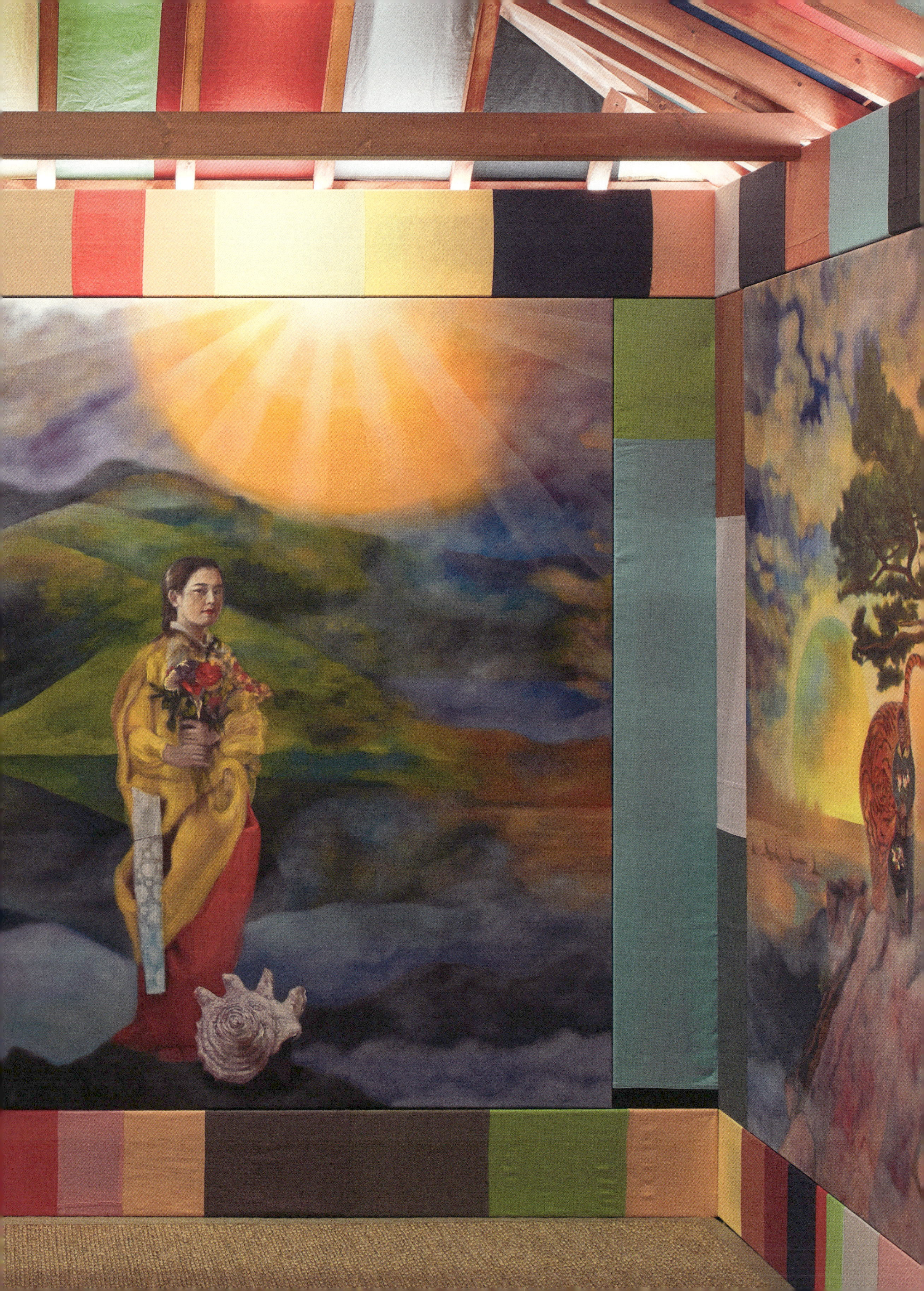

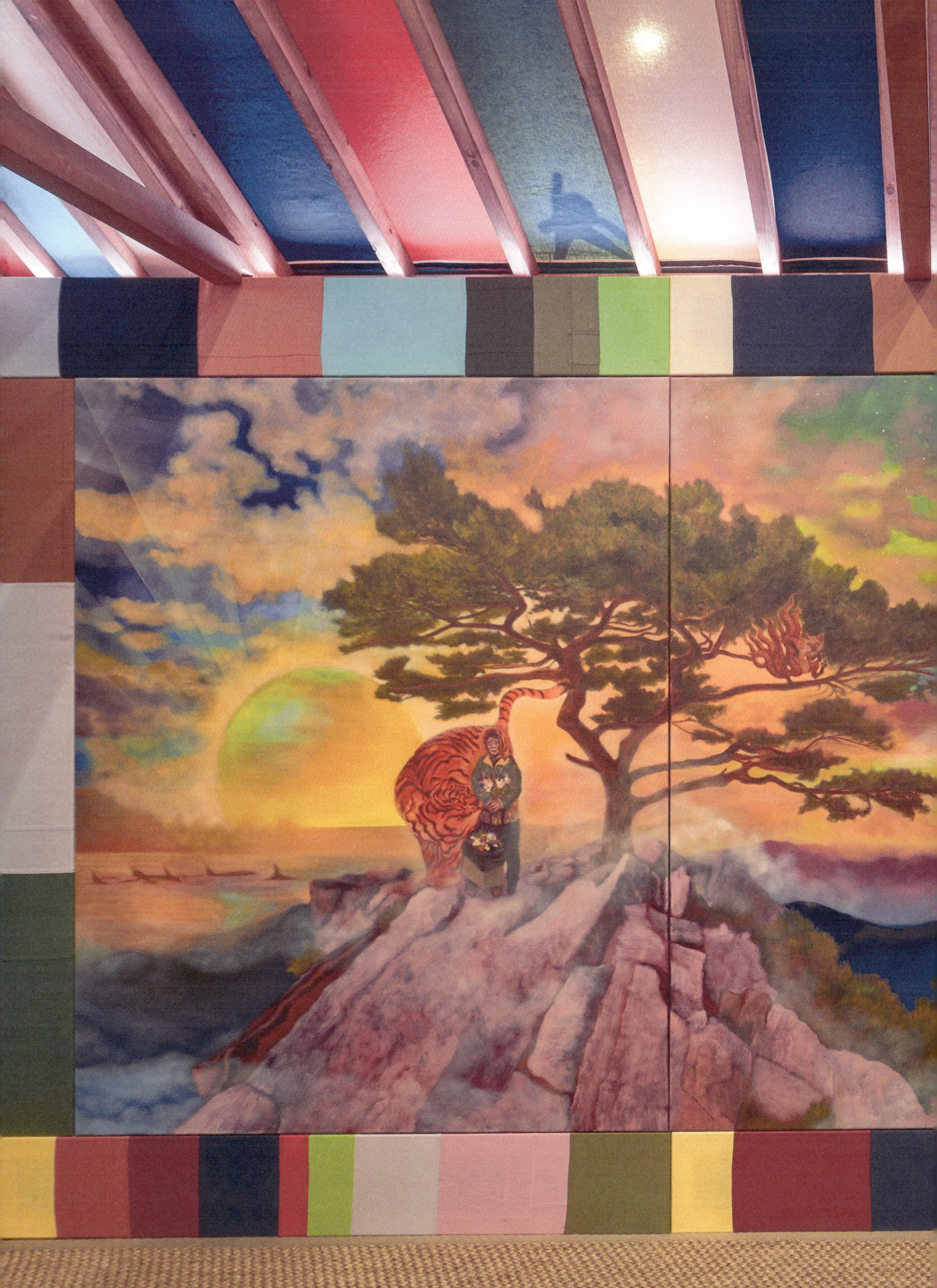

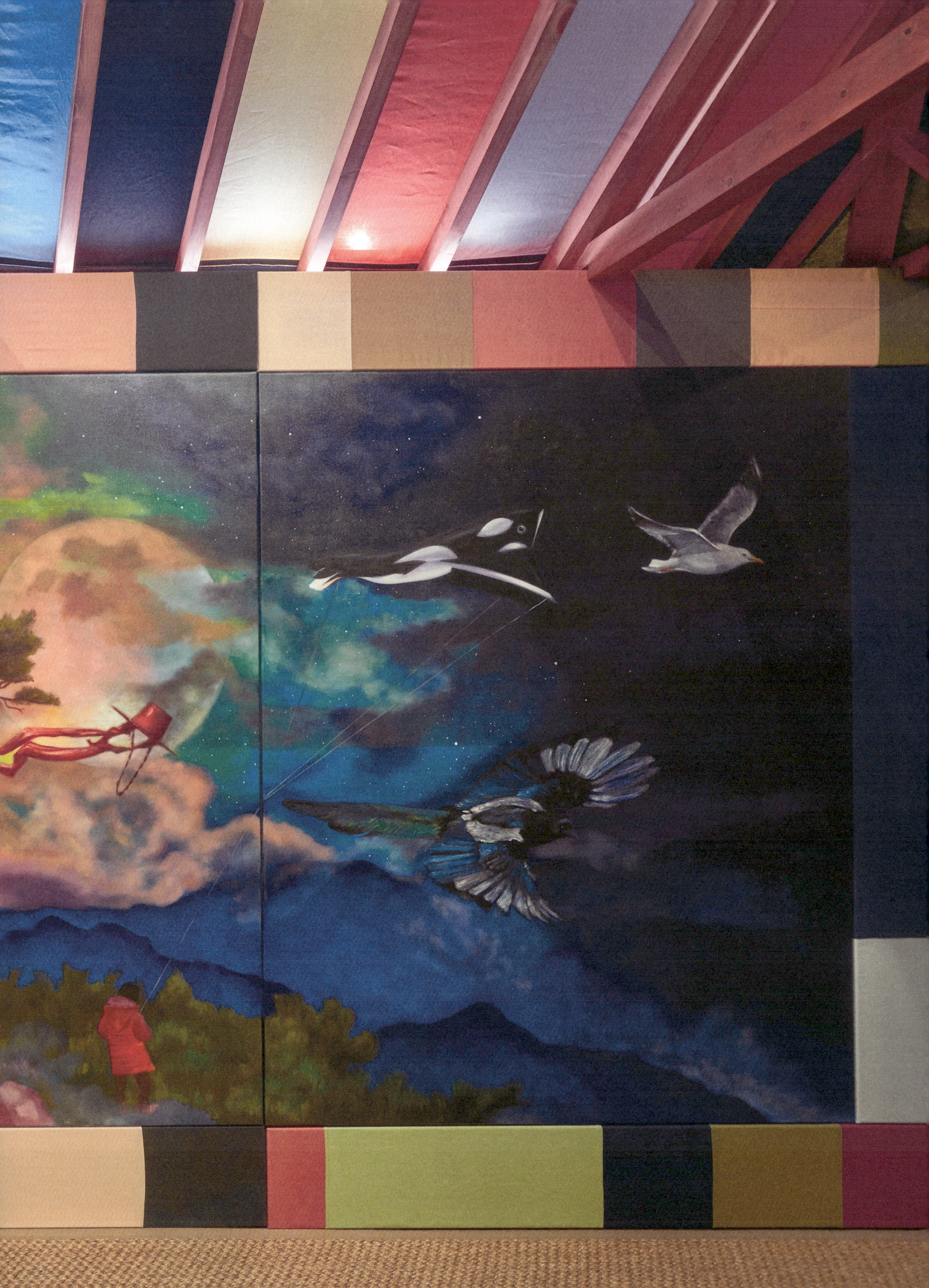

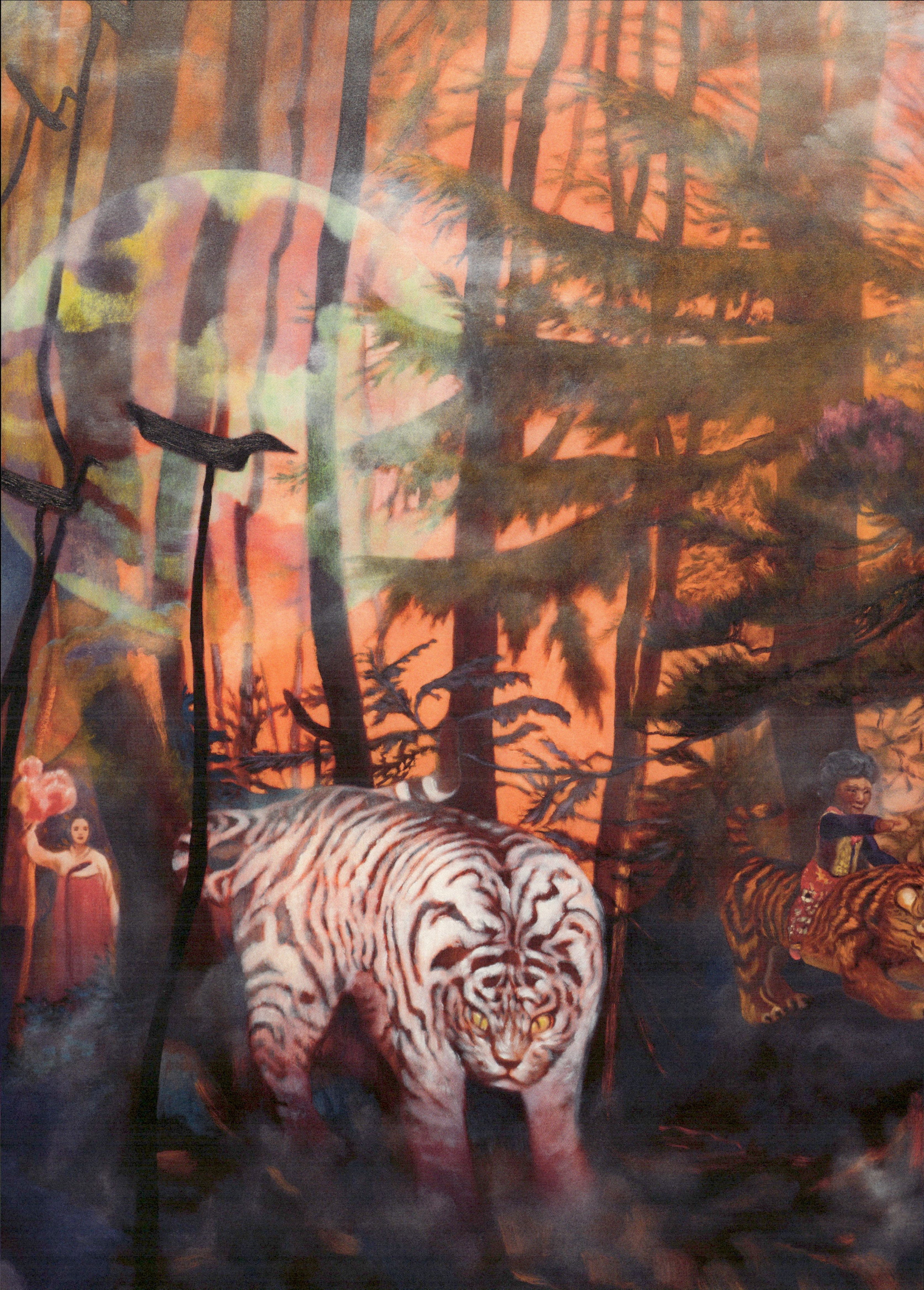

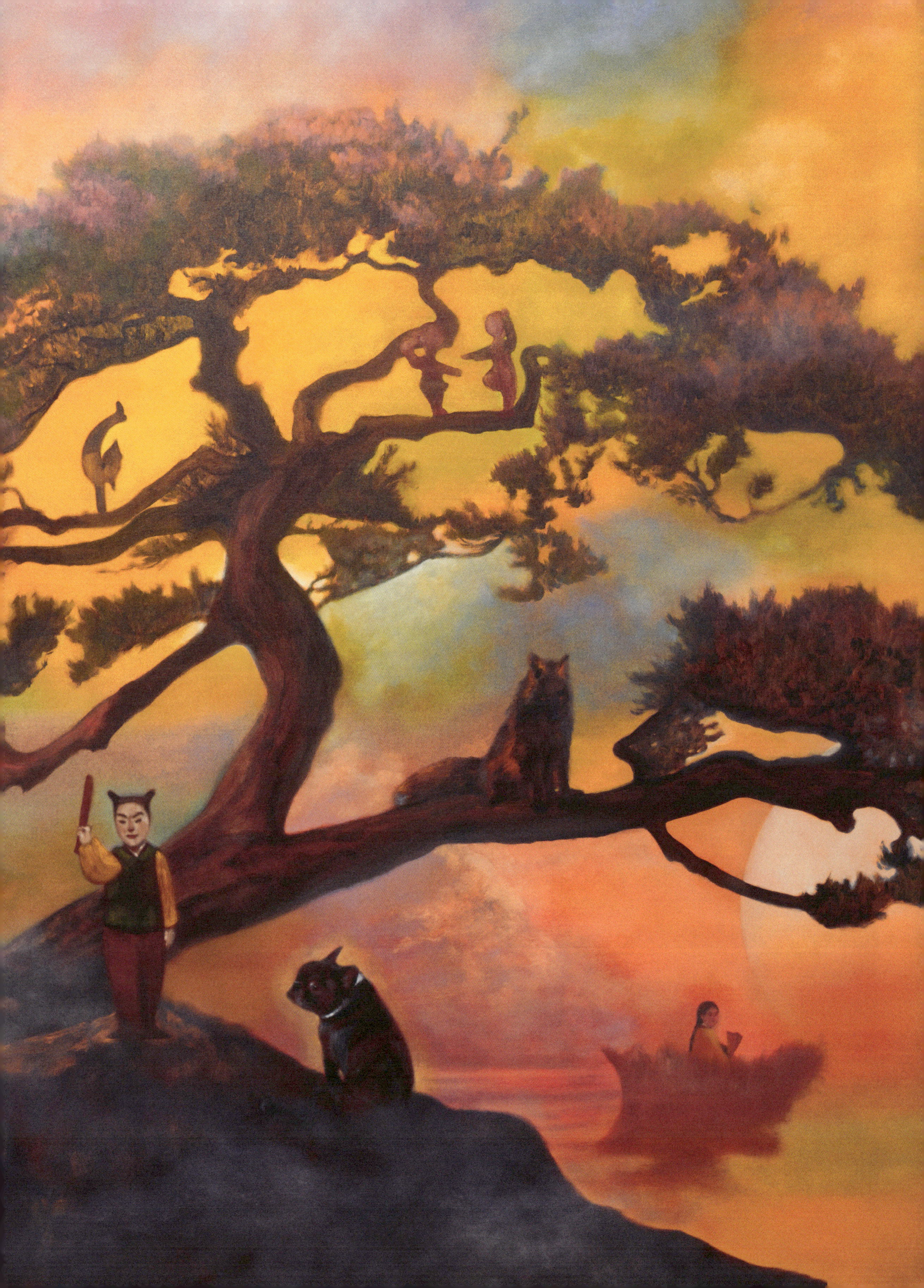

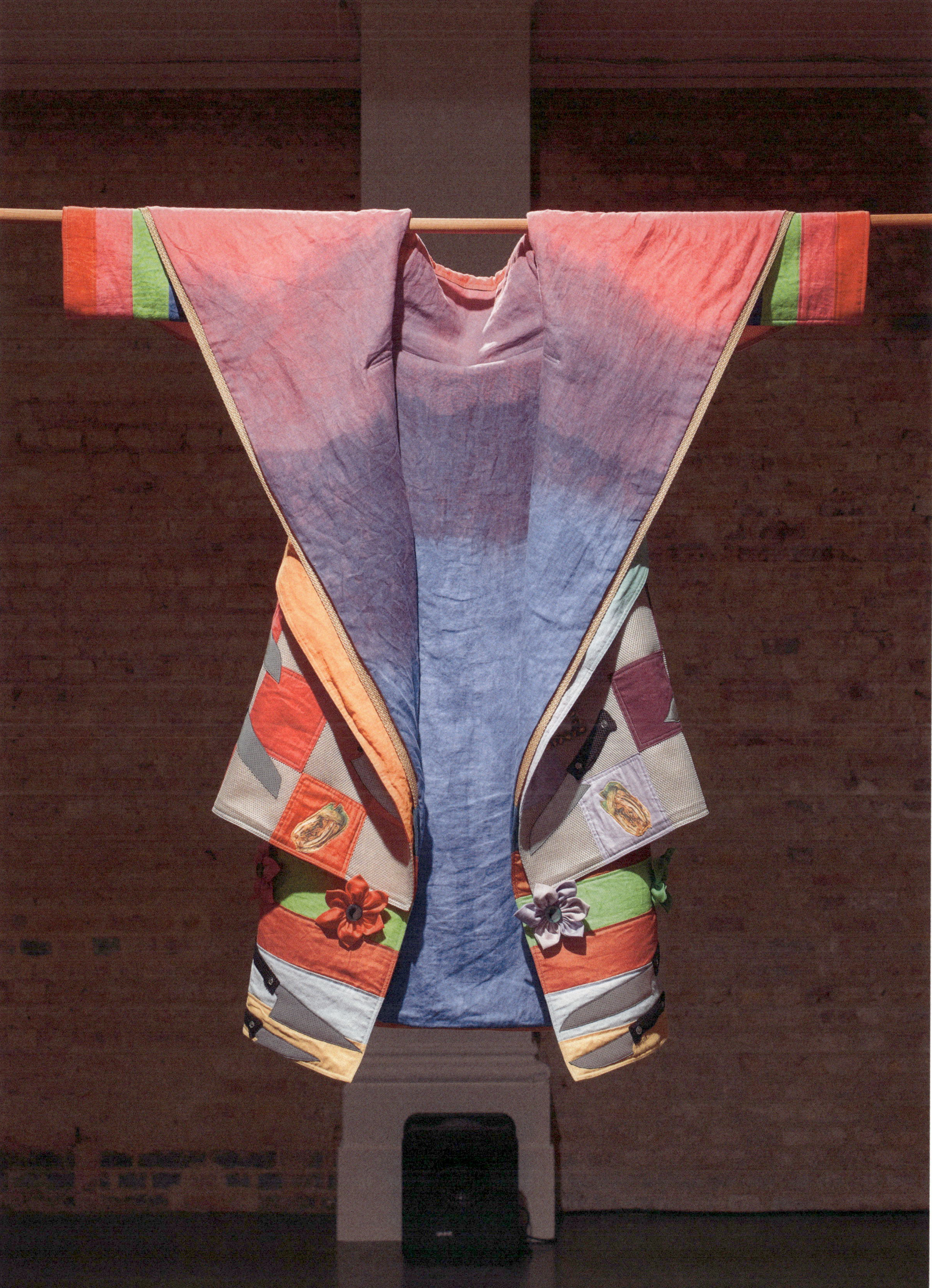

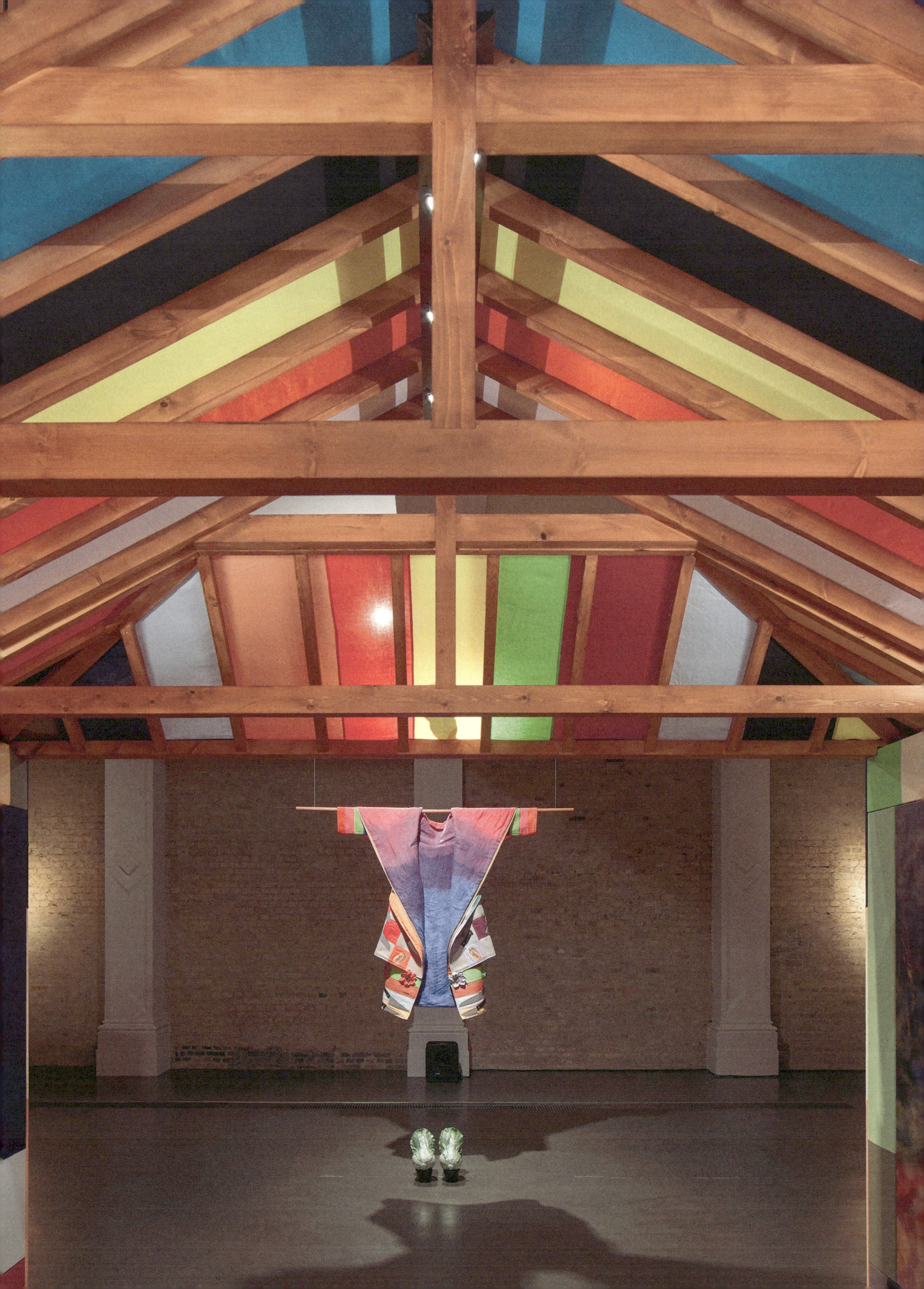

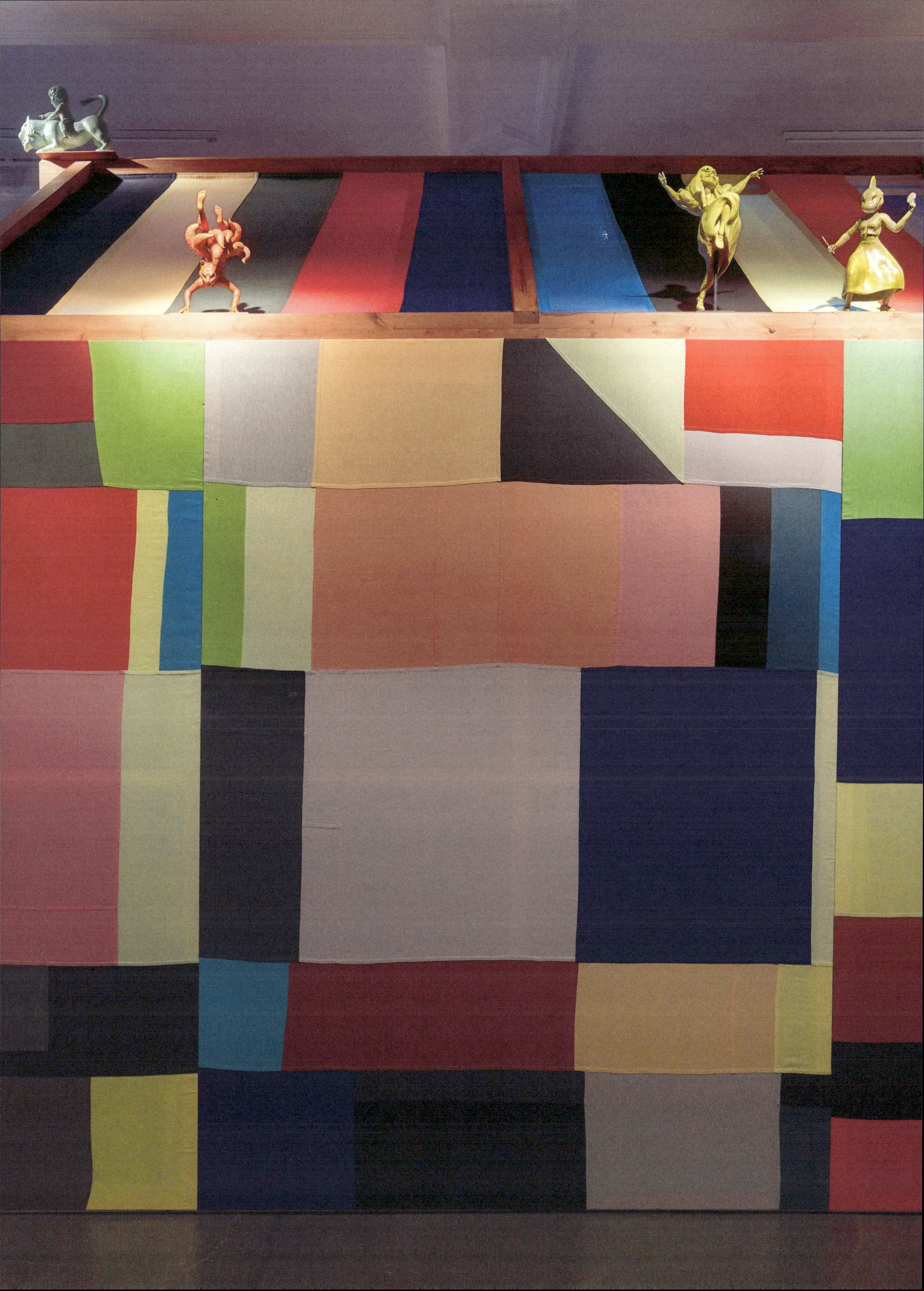

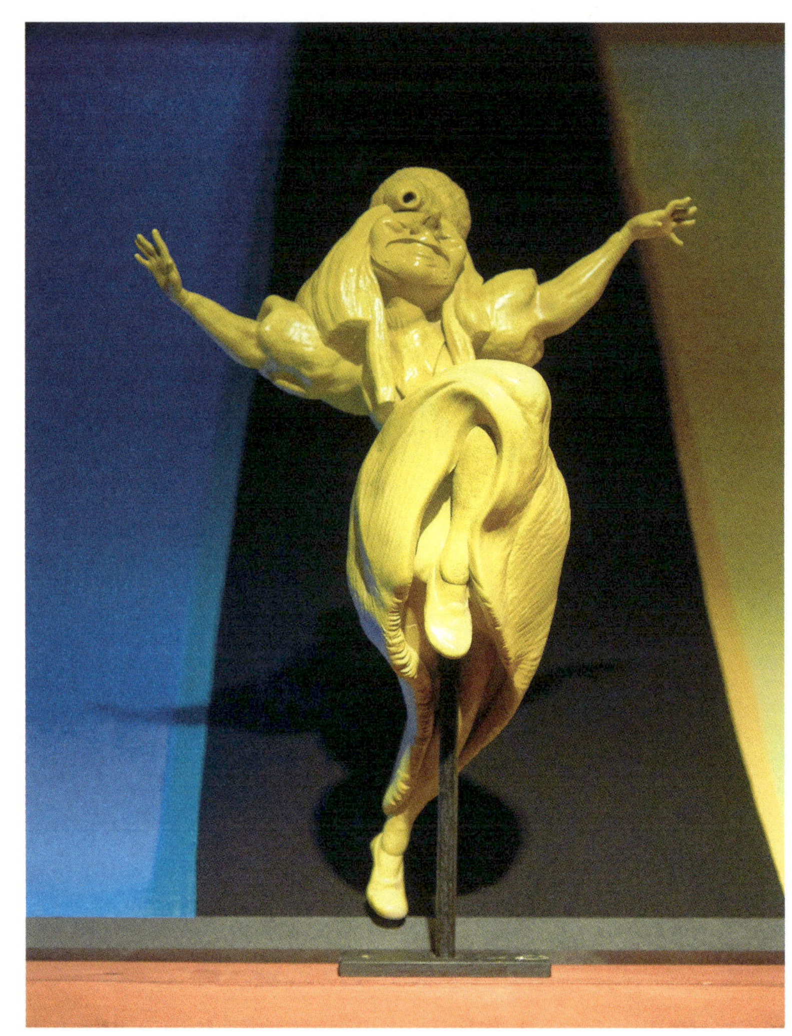

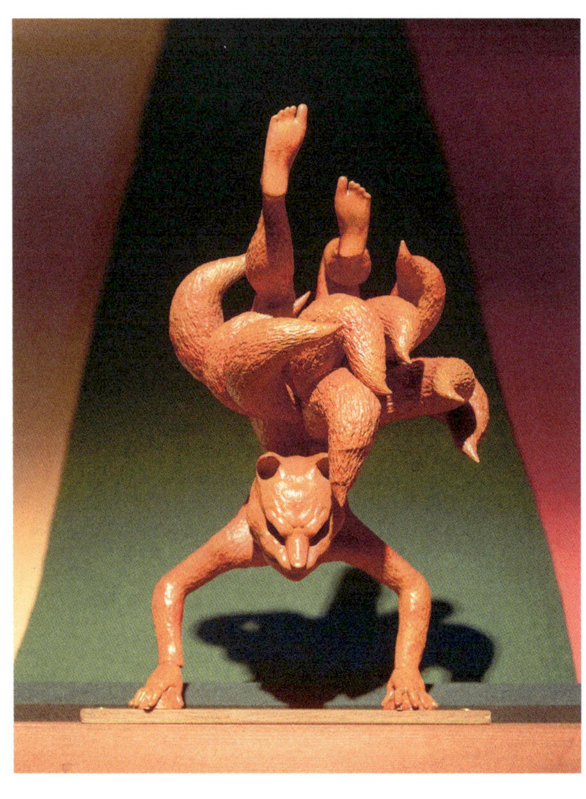

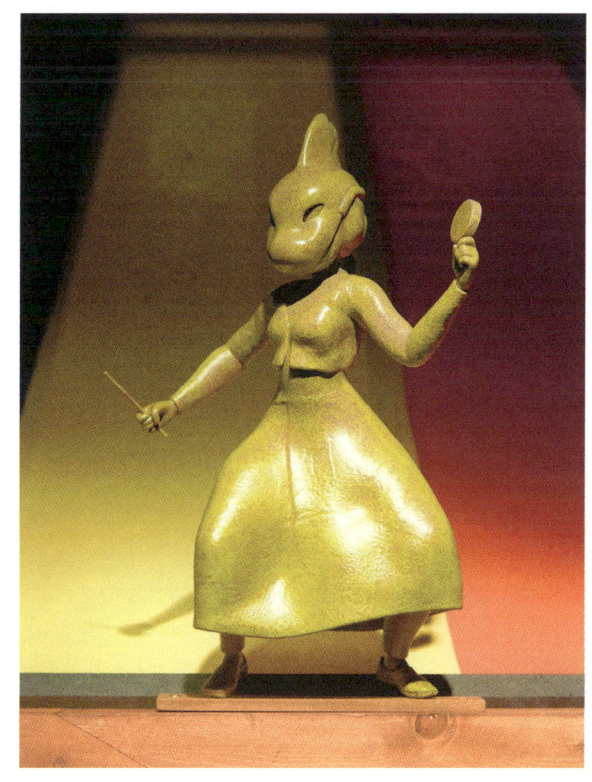

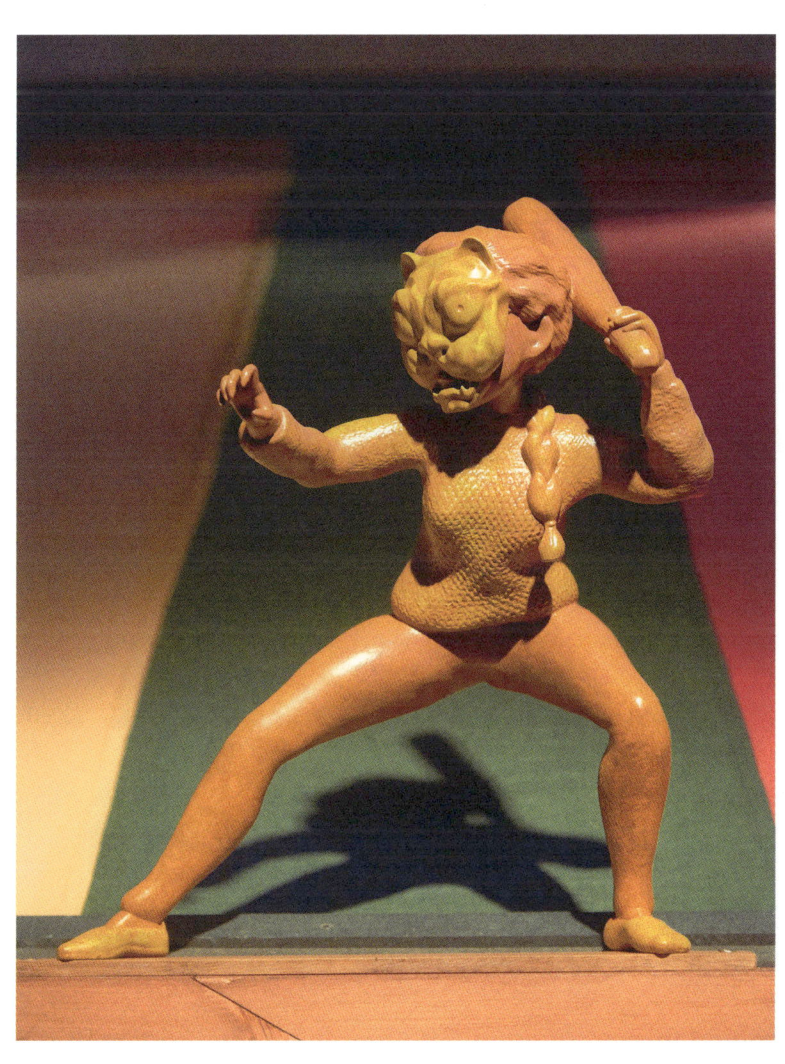

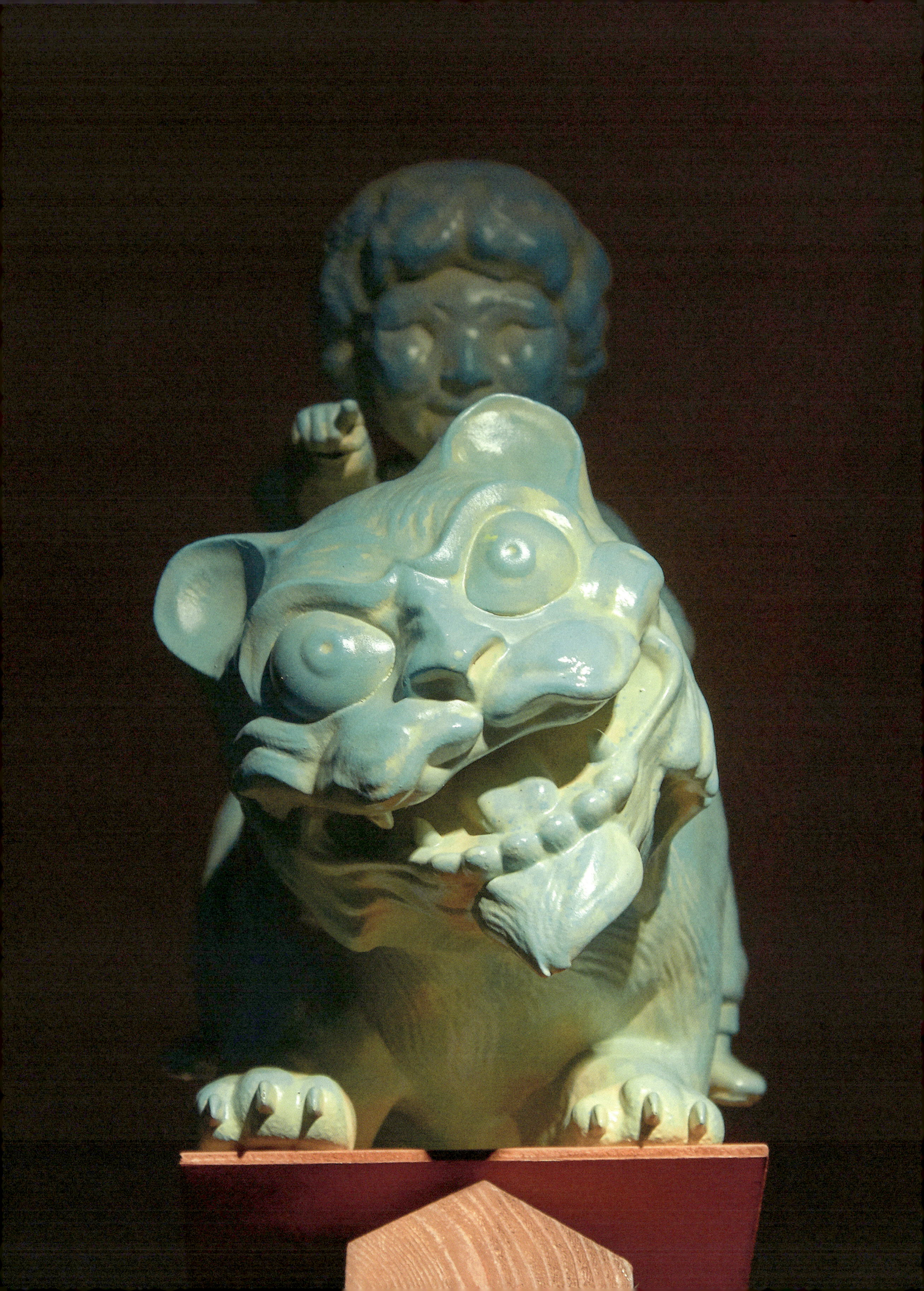

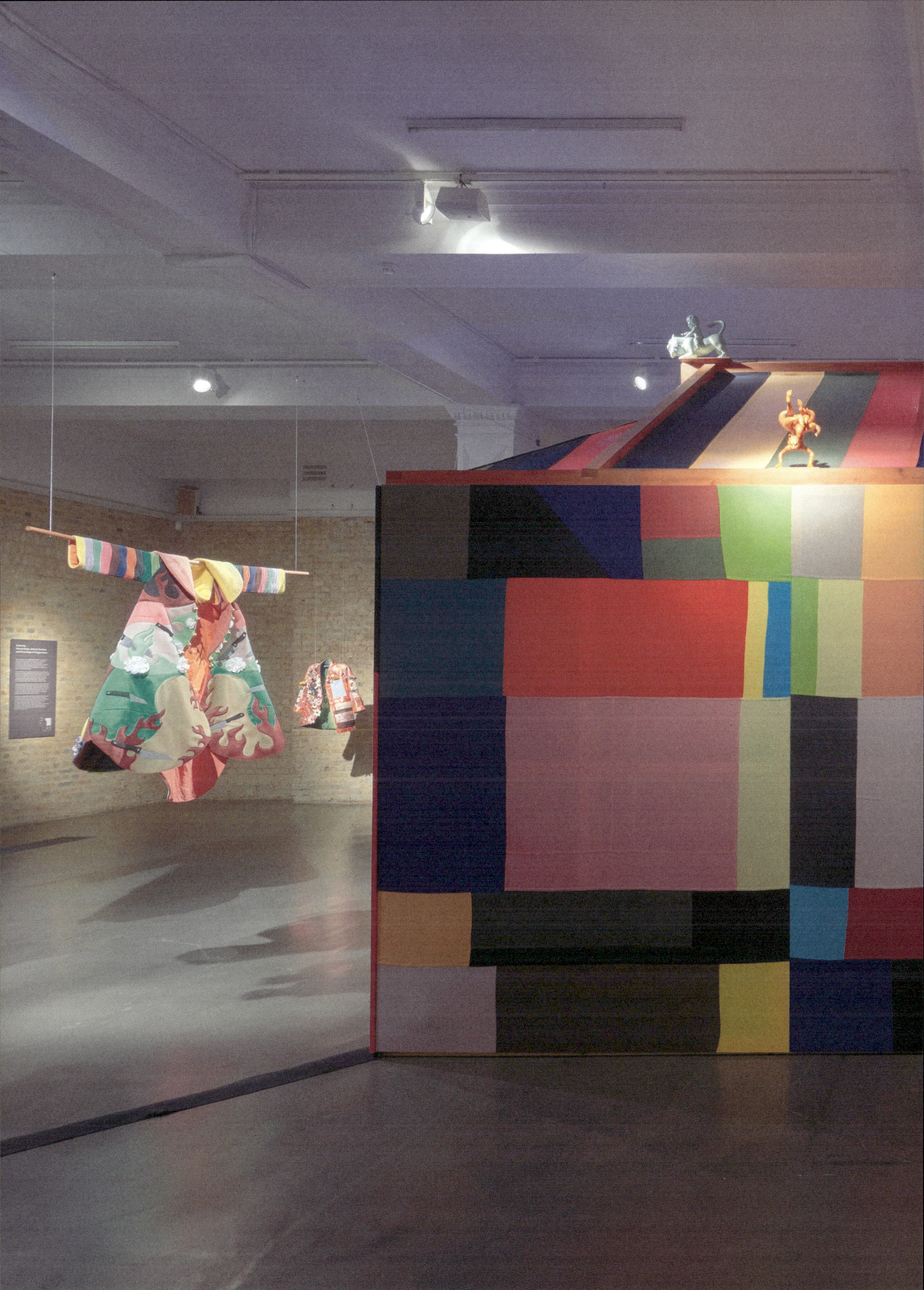

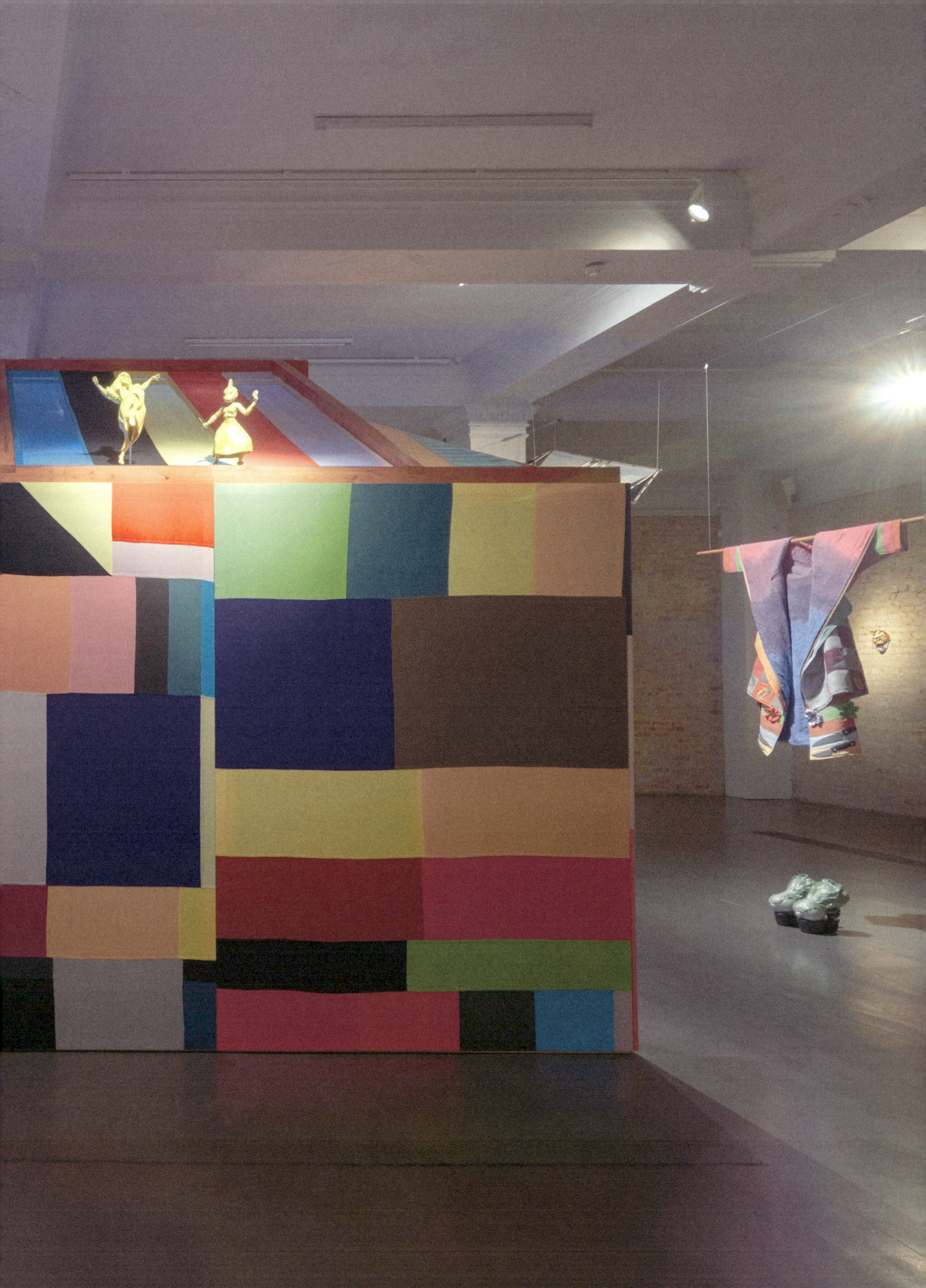

Zadie Xa: House Gods, Animal Guides and Five Ways 2 Forgiveness

by
Tarini Malik
and
Inês Costa

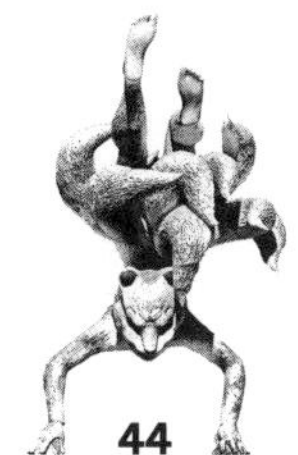

44

Born and raised in Vancouver, Canada and of Korean heritage, multidisciplinary artist Zadie Xa (b. 1983) investigates the systems of power that shape our sense of home and belonging. Her artistic practice draws on sources as wide and rich as pop culture, folklore, science fiction and global histories in order to articulate the multiplicity of the human experience both within postcolonial discourse and in relation to the natural world. Xa has established herself as one of the most innovative artists working today, deftly combining multiple materials and mediums in immersive and layered installations that comment on the socio-political state of our world through storytelling, play and costuming.

By drawing on her lived experiences and representing the many different facets of Korean culture – familial and spiritual – Xa deploys a continuous and experimental process of self-discovery and reflection in her work. Through the study of its history, both ancient and modern, she ultimately bridges the physical distance to Korea that is present in her own reality. Touchingly, she often pays homage in small ways to her personal heroes in her artworks; figures as wide ranging as writer Octavia Butler, rapper Cam'Ron, filmmaker Park Chan-Kyong and artist Lee Bul, to her close friends and family members, who have been particularly influential or inspiring to her at different points of her life. As such, Xa's art can in many ways be read as manifestations of a continual state of becoming.

The artist's benchmark exhibition at Whitechapel Gallery, entitled 'House Gods, Animal Guides and Five Ways 2 Forgiveness', is a culmination of these motivations and points of research. Featuring a new body of sculptures, textiles and paintings that are positioned in and around a large-scale fabric installation that resembles a house, Xa's exhibition also includes bespoke, choreographed lighting and audio elements that guide visitors through the gallery space.

On invitation, Xa was first inspired by East London's local legends of apparitions and spectres, as well as the rebuilding of the city post-war. In imagining the Whitechapel Gallery's historic architecture as a home for the ghosts of artworks, artists and visitors, her desire for this commission was to immerse the viewer in 'another realm'. By conceiving of her exhibition as an 'intervention' in the space that draws upon presentational aspects of funerary rites and ancestral shrines, specifically within the Korean tradition, Xa explores the notion of liminality and how it may be possible to connect the world of the living with that of the dead. This is key within the artist's own journey and her study of how the diaspora are disjointed from their cultural communities. Here, she questions if a sense of belonging, reconciliation and peace can be attained by acknowledging those that came before.

Upon entering the exhibition, one is first confronted with a suspended cloak (*Princess Bari*, 2022) made of hand-dyed linen and photo-printed cotton, with embellishments in mother of pearl and copper. Representing Princess Bari or *Bari Gongju* (translating as 'throwaway' or 'abandoned princess'), the deity recurs in Xa's practice over the years as a key figure from Korean folk religion or shamanism. According to these oral traditions, Princess Bari is believed to guide the souls from the world of living into the underworld. Her ability to cross between different realms is representative of Xa's own navigation of her diasporic and hybrid identity, and a desire to connect with ancestors that she did not have the opportunity to meet.

Widely practiced throughout the Korean peninsula since prehistoric times, shamanism is defined by faith in multiple gods or deities and animism: the belief that creatures from the natural world possess a distinct spiritual essence and the worship of ancestors. The role of the shaman is essentially to act as mediator between life and death. The artist's representation of Korean shamanism is motivated by its history as a strongly women-centred spiritual practice, which stands in contrast to the patriarchal leanings of Confucianism, as well as the act of paying deference to 'household deities': spirits that protect the domestic space in order to ensure prosperity and health.

House (2022) is inspired by a traditional Korean home known as a *hanok* made with exposed wooden beams and a triangular roof. Here, its walls are wrapped in hand-dyed linen, alluding to *jogakbo*: a style of patchwork used to create domestic wrapping cloths (known as *bojagi*) from scraps of fabrics. During the Joseon dynasty (which ruled Korea from 1392 to 1887) and within Korean folk religion, *bojagi* were largely made by women who would wrap objects of value with the hope of increasing good fortune. In a nod to these traditions, Xa wraps the frames of the house to create a space of sanctuary and care. Placed on the ceiling beam is a *danji*: an earthenware jar filled with rice and small offerings such as tobacco, alcohol and handwritten notes, that enshrines a household deity to protect the home.

Lining the roof of the house are seven hand-painted figurines called *kkoktu*. In Korean funerary rituals, these objects accompany the deceased into the afterlife, protecting and caring for them. Each figure has a different role indicated by its name, such as *The Dancer* (2022), *The Warrior* (2022) or *The Acrobat* (2022), and is drawn from both mythology as well as close friends and performers who collaborated with Xa on previous projects. Within Korean shamanism, it is also believed that deities and spirits reside in roof of a home.

Many works in Xa's exhibition, including the masks, marionettes, kites and paintings, feature different animal species. In fables from around the world, animals are often protagonists to help instruct society, as well as to speak of power structures and moral quandaries. Over a number of years, Xa has returned to the figure of the animal in order to explore how different species can speak to our behaviours and of society more widely. The artist describes animals as 'avatars': embodiments of ecological, political and cultural shifts within the world.

Flanking *Princess Bari* are two marionettes suspended from the gallery's ceiling that are *haetae*: horned, hybrid creatures that resemble both lions and goats. In East Asian mythology, they are seen as protectors that help society distinguish between right and wrong and are often represented in sculptures that sit at the threshold of important state or religious buildings. In a nod to these traditions, Xa's *haetae* are named after her beloved pet dogs *Chicho* (2022) and *Fizzgigmo* (2022). Chicho, who is deceased, sits higher than the living Fizzgigmo, with a longer horn that represents his age as well as the wisdom and prowess he has ascertained in the spirit world.

In Xa's epic eight-panel canvas (which shares its name with the exhibition's title, *House Gods, Animals Guides and Five Ways 2 Forgiveness*, 2022), there are reoccurring motifs of tigers, foxes and seagulls painted into a scenic landscape that shifts from sunrise to sunset and eventually twilight. These animals speak to Xa's continued exploration of the 'trickster' archetype: a disruptive outsider whose presence both provokes and inspires change from dominant social and cultural orders.

In Korean folk painting – of which Xa was inspired for this particular work – the figure of the tiger is both depicted as an apex predator, as well as having a foolishly arrogant disposition that satirically represented the upper classes within the Joseon dynasty's feudal society. That sense of duality is ever present within our reality where tigers are still deemed sacred in much of South and East Asian religion, yet are an endangered species as a result of human actions. The tiger is also represented in the two mask works, *Horangi (Orange tiger)* (2022) – modelled on a scan of the artist's own face – and *Halmoni (Grandmothers)* (2022) which depicts an older female tiger and pays deference to women elders within our society.

Suspended over the entrance to *House*, are two kites fabricated from hand-sewn linen stretched over wooden frames. Kite flying has a long-standing history in Korea and here they take form as a *Magpie* (2022) and *Seagull* (2022) in flight: two birds that are also heavily represented within oral histories and folklore.

The final part of the exhibition's title 'Five Ways 2 Forgiveness' is inspired by an eponymous anthology of short stories by the American author Ursula K. Le Guin (1929–2018). A rigorous critique of colonialism, Le Guin's writing combines speculative fiction, science fiction and parable. These are languages that Xa also employs in her work to disrupt and expand our perception of the world around us. By drawing on folktales, mythology and spiritual and religious rituals, Xa elevates belief systems and ideologies that have often been marginalised during the rapid industrialisation of the nineteenth and twentieth centuries, as well as by legacies of colonialism.

'Five Ways 2 Forgiveness' also references the belief that by paying respects to one's familial ancestors, past wrongdoings could be forgiven. The pursuit of forgiveness is critical to Xa's own process of exploring how diasporic communities can become isolated or alienated, and how reconciliation may be sought by acknowledging those who came before us.

In the early stages of developing her site-specific exhibition at the Whitechapel Gallery, Xa noted how, to her, the gallery's dense brick-lined walls and uniformed sequence of tall white columns resembled the quiet grandeur of a neoclassical mausoleum or sarcophagus. For her exhibition, she was then inspired to create a journey to the underworld in order for visitors to feel as though they might transition into a different way of being or reality as they move through the space.

Xa positions her sculptural installation, *House*, centrally and to a specific scale in order to procure wide corridors either side of its walls. For the artist, the function of the corridor as a liminal passageway or as an interlude between one space to another is especially poignant. Through sequenced and shifting lighting that evokes the transition from day to night, and a multichannel audio system that emits sounds from nature, percussion and voiceover, Xa traces a ghostly presence, pointing to the passing of time and into another state of consciousness. Above the door exiting the gallery, Xa has pinned three paper talismans with Korean script that bestow visitors with wishes of good health, prosperity and respect for their ancestors.

dreamhouse dollhouse

(agoraphobia interlude)

by
Wong Binghao

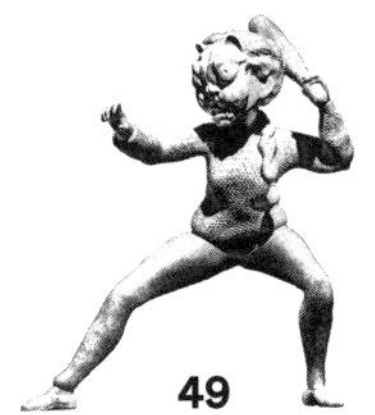

49

By the standards of my own constitutional auditory barometer, I used to, and still do, have really noisy neighbours. It remains a constant source of consternation how those living with or adjacent to you can stand to be so inconsiderate. Is it a physiological (are they not as sound-sensitive?) or a social maladjustment (do they just not care?). Conceding that there is no polite answer to this rhetorical question, I have since set my mind to dispelling my devotion to the principle of absolute tranquility. Any more harshness or discipline in that kind of situation, I've concluded, would only put me even more out of place. The acoustic environment of Zadie Xa's enveloping, four-metre-tall house-installation, amenably proximal to Whitechapel Gallery's street-level visitors, is decidedly more calming. The sonic piece that Xa developed for the artwork – one each for the interior and exterior of the house structure – also serves as its temporal marker, demarcating, on a broader scale, the exhibition's 'journey' from sunrise to sunset, consciousness to rest, life to death.[1]

The 'atmospheric' sounds of nature and animal life that permeate the gallery diffuse experientially with 'ghostly' and 'poetic' whispers, evocative of one of Xa's house gods as they paradoxically render the desired unyielding foundation of a house abstract, transitional.[2] Also located within the house structure, Xa's renderings of *kkoktu* (human and mystical funerary figures meant to 'accompany' the dead on their journey to the underworld), underscore that her house is an impermanent, ritualistic context. Not to mention the primacy of Korean shamanic deity Princess Bari, chaperone of souls from the world of the living to that of the dead, in Xa's installation. In similar ways, ethnomusicologist Barley Norton has observed that in *Đạo Mẫu,* or the veneration of Mother Goddesses, a popular Buddhist religion characterised by gender-traversing spirit possession that is practised in Vietnam and its diasporas, 'songscapes' generated by a band are essential to facilitate a social and 'sonic environment for possession.'[3] Sound, in Xa's domicile artwork, ushers in an uncanny inhabitation of place, embodiment, and home. But, I would argue, the dwelling she has constructed is recuperative precisely because of its transience, which heightens the poignancy of the large-scale, geometric *bojagi* (traditionally a humble fabric used to wrap small items of importance, from birth certificates to food containers) that cloaks her towering house structure, ensconcing it like a protected parcel. It is as if the artist is trying to ground her vagabond house, trying to make it stay longer in this realm, to grasp its belovedness.

The simplest way out of my domestic neurosis was also spatial, literal: get out of the house. Go somewhere else, anywhere, to work, relax, space out. Sounds easy enough. In that house that wasn't my home, I really did want to get out, to manoeuvre impossibly and phase through the walls, which felt thicker and more impenetrable as the days passed. I just couldn't and didn't. Most days I voluntarily trapped myself in that little cell of a room, reluctant to leave because I was convinced that, regardless of fanfare or fatality, whatever was out there was uglier, scarier, and more intense than being in here. I won't (can't) put all those horrible experiences, which are mostly variables, to paper because I'm extremely superstitious and believe in the performative force of words, so doing that would somehow feel like I'm memorialising bad luck, or worse, re-enacting it, giving it second life. Verbalising something, even thinking it, makes it feel more real to me, let alone putting it to paper, textbooking its legacy. That probably explains why I like writing about impossibilities, scenarios that feel somehow mathematically dislodged from our

1
Zoom conversation with the artist, July 2022.

2
Zoom conversation with the artist, July 2022.

3
Barley Norton, 'Vietnamese Mediumship Rituals: The Musical Construction of the Spirits', *The World of Music,* vol. 42, no. 2 (2000) 76–77.

shared grid of actuality, like lab experiments gone awry. Better to study something circuitously, inconspicuously, endlessly, though no less intently – an art object, for instance – than to pierce the idea of it. 'No writer hopes for ideas to take complete shape', writer Durga Chew-Bose seems to confide in her reader, 'approximation is the mark [...] writing that clinches lacks incandescence [...] a need for completeness can [...] squander cadence'.[4] Though I'm rarely happy in non-places, this particular kind of suspension feels safe and hermetic, like a bubble of cotton flowers.

Drawing on art historian Briony Fer's exegesis of the 'desire for self-effacement' in Eva Hesse's mid- to late-1960s artworks, what might be 'gained' from this work of intentional 'detachment', this insouciant unfathomability, is possibly that 'the very presence of the [art] object heightens [...] the sense of losing a portion of oneself', a kind of precarity that we shouldn't want to hurriedly emplace or settle.[5] To conjure our parallel circumstance: while *Đạo Mẫu* lends itself to an effusive, 'performative mediumship'[6] that deploys gendered theatricality to successfully consummate spirit possession, it is indicative that mediums describe their role in this ritual as one of servitude, not stardom, perceiving themselves as humble 'seats' for spirits to 'sit' on,[7] or else meatless 'skeletons' and 'empty bodies' for the souls of goddesses to enter.[8] This ethereal interregnum is, to my mind, less a space of repletion or redemption than an epicene personification of fear: not so much of failing to attain some kind of omniscient correctness or awareness, but of not-trying before the body's demise, a destinyless disappearance.[9]

Xa's work elicits a similar trepidation, productive because, as spectators, we are immersed in and witness processes – of time, houses and homes, family histories, grief, bodies – passing-through. Xa's practice is mediation made manifest. Her artworks, especially when performatively instantiated, strike us only in the most tauntingly swift of temporal intervals. In their collaborative ethnography of the Chinese-Italian fashion firms in Prato, Italy, Lisa Rofel and Sylvia J. Yanagisako observed 'specific forms of social interdependence' and negotiations of value between the Italians' perceived intrinsic knowledge of fashion and style on the one hand, and the Chinese sense of entrepreneurship and cosmopolitanism on the other, an opposition that generated a lingering tension that spoke to the 'ongoing contingencies and instabilities of transnational supply chain capitalism'.[10] Of this 'unstable dynamic' and uneasy partnership, Rofel and Yanagisako noticed a mutual 'anxiety' and 'frustration' stemming from a prideful competition and need for recognition.[11] They are trying, perhaps a little too hard, to make it work, but it would be nightmarish not to even make the attempt at fulfilment. Painter of giant cabbages, conch shells, tigers, decorated orcas, foxes and sometimes altogether extraterrestrial beings and landscapes, like those in the impressive, sequential mural painting of earthly and temporal passages installed in her fabricated quarters at the Whitechapel, Xa meticulously stages and cushions the attempt for us.

4
Durga Chew-Bose, *Too Much and Not the Mood* (New York: Farrar, Strauss and Giroux, 2017) 23.

5
Briony Fer, 'Objects Beyond Objecthood', *Oxford Art Journal*, vol. 22, no. 2 (1999) 32–36.

6
Janet Hoskins, 'Trance Dancers or Interlocutors of the Immortals?: Gender and Vietnamese Mediums in Contrasting Traditions', paper presented at *Reassessing Ritual in Southeast Asian Studies*, Kyoto, Japan, (February 2013) 3.

7
Nguyen Thi Hien, '"Seats for Spirits to Sit upon": Becoming a Spirit Medium in Contemporary Vietnam', *Journal of Southeast Asian Studies*, vol. 38, no. 3 (October 2007) 550.

8
Ngo Duc Thinh, 'The Mother Goddess Religion: Its History, Pantheon, and Practices', in *Possessed by the Spirits: Mediumship in Contemporary Vietnamese Communities*, ed. Karen Fjelstad & Nguyen Thi Hien (Ithica: Cornell Southeast Asia Program, 2006) 26–27.

9
Kirsten W. Endres, 'Fate, Memory, and the Postcolonial Construction of the Self: The Life-Narrative of a Vietnamese Spirit Medium', *Journal of Vietnamese Studies*, vol. 3, no. 2 (2008) 53. 'Destined person[s]' must answer the spirit's calls, for if they do not, they usually suffer 'physical and mental illness and misfortune', believed to be inflicted by angry, dissatisfied spirits.

10
Lisa Rofel and Sylvia J. Yanagisako, *Fabricating Transnational Capitalism: A Collaborative Ethnography of Italian-Chinese Global Fashion* (Durham: Duke University Press, 2019) 45, 106.

11
Ibid 40–41.

but tell it slant:

Zadie Xa's more-than-human time[1]

by
Lucia Pietroiusti

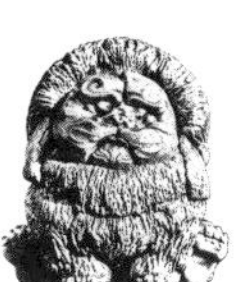

WITH
W
woman walks wasps
with whales
— Alexis Pauline Gumbs [2]

We had been working together for several years by then, but
in early 2020, scarcely two weeks before the COVID-19 pandemic
first shut down the UK, Zadie Xa and I joined paths in matriarchy
and orcas (or perhaps it is more accurate to say that I met her there,
where she was). At the time, we recorded a brief conversation on
her work, *Ancestral undulations and the transmission of knowing*
(2020), which delved into Xa's interest in a particular species of
killer whale from the Pacific Northwest. Specifically, Xa, who never
met her maternal grandmother, was fascinated by 'Granny', also
known as J2, who died between the ages of 80 and 105 and who by
that point had looked after five generations of descendants in her
long life. The matrilineal family and social structure of killer whales,
Xa told me, is organised in such a way that the elder female orca is
responsible for passing on knowledge to the young that is essential
for their survival. Crucially, this occurs for decades after the
elder passes through menopause. Learning from orcas, Xa reflected,
has political endurance: it is an incisive and more-than-human
reminder of the value of elder and ancestral knowledge, and of
the feminine, beyond and set apart from the ideology of reproductive
value, the stigmatised 'uselessness' of a non-reproducing,
female-identified body.

In much of Zadie Xa's works, as indeed is the case in her exhibition
at Whitechapel Gallery, 'House Gods, Animal Guides and Five Ways
2 Forgiveness', the artist's attention and attunement to the more-
than-human world works on the imaginary on multiple levels. On the
one hand, the magpies, seagulls, orcas, tigers and foxes of Xa's
painterly and multimedia bestiaria invite their human interlocutors to
take seriously the lived experiences and ecological entanglements
of the animals *as themselves*: these are tigers, seagulls, orcas, foxes
and magpies, the living, breathing ones – disrupted beings of this
planet, some endangered, some exhausted, some thriving in post-
anthropogenic landscapes, others mourned. From this angle, Xa
calls for a work of cross-species bridge-building and empathy. Her
work aims for us to fall in love with the more-than-human species
she represents: not because she has depicted them, but because
she has done so with attention, with kinship – because they tell their
own stories.

On the other hand, while they are *as themselves*, these more-than-
human companions are purposefully *never only themselves*: a seagull
and magpie, as if fluttering by the corner of our eye, shapeshift
into the artist and her long-time collaborator, Benito Mayor Vallejo.
Granny may be a lost grandmother (in the artist's own life story),
and also simultaneously, she may be a stand-in for the very notion
of the ancestral, and/or its erasure, through the meticulous and
slow-violent project of empire. A fox is a trickster figure – friend, foe,
flawed human, and reminder of the transience of life – everything
all at once.

Xa has long been fascinated by the oracular, writerly work of poet
Alexis Pauline Gumbs, who, in *Undrowned: Black Feminist Lessons
from Marine Mammals* (2021), weaves a manual for emancipatory

1
With thanks to
Taylor J LeMelle for first
introducing us.

2
Alexis Pauline Gumbs,
'The Rhythm of Gray Whales
Praying for Audre Lorde
and May Ayim' in *Flows – Bodies of
Water – A Reader*, ed. Filipa Ramos
(Dijon: Les Presses du Réel, 2021)
69. In this essay
– a tribute to the two poets, Gumbs
composes from words found in
Audre Lorde's 1984 poem, 'Berlin
is Hard on Colored Girls'.

justice and reparative social-movement work out of cetacean rhythms, life experiences, habitats and songs. At a time where ecological and social justice practices, which have often existed in relative friction with one another, may be beginning to recognise the complex and interlinked nature of the crises that befall the present moment, as well as their unequally distributed causes and effects, Gumbs and Xa share part of a journey. The poet and the artist come together in their search for ways in which a kinship-based and self-present attention to more-than-human beings offers lessons, oracles, 'field guides' to human ways of thinking about human history. If taken seriously, the planet's deep history; its repetitive cycles, unbroken rhythms, troubles and renewals, all offer up paths for imagining a kind of time (past, present and future) that is different from ones rooted in cynicism and neo-Darwinian nihilism.

'Nature' (a term I use reluctantly), in the sense of a human imaginary of something separate and 'out there', is a human construction – more an ideology of what is or should be. Like technology, like gods, we shape nature in our own image, time and time again. In this sense, nature is fundamentally what we make of it. Throughout modern history, any pre-eminent general theory of how more-than-human life organises itself has mapped fairly accurately onto the dominant economic or political theory of its time. These are myths. We live and breathe the myths we create, and every day we renew those myths, re-create that 'nature', that planet, in the shape in which we believe it to be. Could this, in turn, also begin to uncover the transformative potential inherent in the work of those who redraw, re-read, and recuperate myths that point towards a 'somewhere else'? From artistic practices to ritual, from poetry through to recent scientific research in symbiotic life or plant intelligence, all are new and different re-tellings of a story, one that, without them, is situated, incomplete, biased and ultimately impoverished. These are also questions at the very heart of novelist Amitav Ghosh's recent publication, *The Nutmeg's Curse: Parables for a Planet in Crisis* (2021), in which his analysis of settler-colonial extraction and extermination in the Americas fundamentally begins as a cultural project: before lives, livelihoods and landscapes can be decimated, they must be rendered inert, they must become pure matter. Personhood and animacy must be exterminated in the mind before people and planet can be cut up into pieces. This is what has made, and continues to be capable of making, myth and folktales so terribly seditious, potentially. It is what makes Zadie Xa's work so engaged, even in its speculative and prismatic fabulations. As Ghosh puts it, 'if [...] nonhuman voices are to be restored to their proper place, then it must be, in the first instance, through the medium of stories.'[3]

Zadie Xa and I share a secret passion for superhero movies. The fact may strike the reader as unlikely: Xa's decolonial commitment is unwavering – her inner and artistic work around ideas of home and belonging is as profound as it is acute – and there is little more fascistic (or for that matter, anthropocentric) than the glorification of a superhuman hero standing between order and chaos. But archetypes run strong amidst superheroes, and we could – if we loosened the weave just a tiny bit more – reimagine these figures in the way we relate to the gods: plural. In other words, asking not so much what kind of version of hegemonic capitalism do they glorify, but rather, what could they awaken (some in horror, some in potential) within us watchers, readers and listeners, that belongs to deep time, to the timeless?

3
Amitav Ghosh,
The Nutmeg's Curse: Parables for a Planet in Crisis
(Chicago: University of Chicago Press, 2021) 204.

At this point, one may be keen to ask (and Zadie Xa certainly does),
what are the stories we tell ourselves about past and future and
how do they make sense of our being-in-the-world? And where do
they come from? Who has told them and what projects can they
subtend, or indeed what wounds could they heal? Often diffracted
through the prisms of myth, folktale, legend and speculative
fiction, Xa's environmental and social consciousness, across species
and beings, shines through in vivid palettes. In Whitechapel's
galleries, Xa's paintings and sculptures resonate with the ghostly
presences of paintings and sculptures that have shared the
same space but at another time, as birds coexist in a landscape
by singing at different frequencies. If we step into the artist's
deep-time and simultaneously timeless paradigm, those works
are still here, co-present, in dialogue. Xa's overlooked goddesses
and marginalised shamanic practitioners – endangered lives,
human and more-than-human, from this dimension and beyond it –
all are honoured and find agency in her installations: they greet us,
they watch over us. But also: they watch us, as we them. They remind
us that all life finds its meaning in death and transformation as it
does in self-determination and affect; that all life is relational and
bound to practices of attention and mutual responsibility. That time
may sometimes appear as a line, but the time of myth and story is
ancestral, present and speculative, and all at once, because myths
are guides, not events. They are invitations.

From Sumerian poetry through to Greek goddesses, in the interstitial
spaces between the lines of creation myths the world over – we
intuit agricultural practices, social structures, ways of making sense
of the weather. So many stories, in one way or another, are about
the weather, after all, or about death and ancestors – that is to say,
about life in its perennial reconfiguration. And besides, aren't
those (the weather, death) also already one and the same – haven't
we been mineral, and so rain, and so mountain, at some point or
another? Across Xa's canvases, colours and sounds journey, with
the eye and the ear, from dawn to dusk. Again: outside of time,
or in eternal time, isn't it always dawn to dusk and then dawn again?

Kindred Spirits

by
Ana Teixeira Pinto

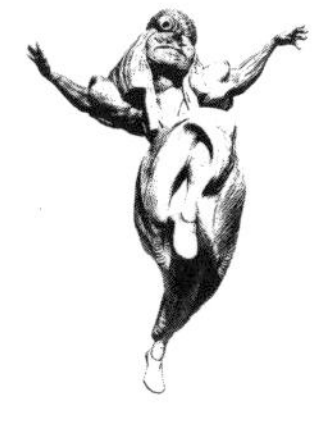

Though, at present the concept of *media* is almost wholly equated with technology, throughout the modern period, it extended beyond the technological field, to include aesthetic and spiritual registers. As T.J. Clark noted, the very notion of mediation already entails some mixture of sensory, perceptual and semiotic elements: what the word 'media' refers to, in its widest sense, is a coded mode of materiality, which could be generalised to include all 'domains of cultural exchange.'[1] Another prominent example can be found in Marshall McLuhan's notion of media, which includes any material in unfixed form, or even formless material, such as electricity. The body, or more accurately the nervous system, is the locus of technological interaction, the site upon which all media intersect. By emphasising the notion of light as a medium – howbeit one without *any* content – McLuhan underscores its power to shape the forms of human expression, association and interaction – politically as well as spiritually.[2] Almost every human culture has a figure that fulfils a mediator-like role, someone who can travel, or act as a psychic conduit, between worlds. Often termed 'shamans'[3] by anthropologists, these figures became a cypher for the religious 'other' of Europe, during the period in which the West reconceptualised the entities, which are to be assigned the function of a medium, and the ways and means of mediation. Around the 1870s, a plethora of psychics claimed the ability to act as conduits or transmitters; much like a human radio frequency receiver, they could allegedly capture cosmic vibrations that were said to manifest in a fashion similar to electro-magnetic waves. At the time the field of physiology dealt with telepathy and telekinesis, and there was no clear distinction between the scientific domain of neurophysiology, the emergent field of electromagnetic technologies, and the para-scientific circles of esoteric beliefs and séance gatherings.[4]

Exploring the mediated nature of sociality and subjectivity, in Zadie Xa's 'House Gods, Animal Guides and Five Ways 2 Forgiveness', the concept of media is tied to liminal stages rather than to technology – though technology is not absent either, and drones are at times heard hovering in the background – that collapse the distinction between different worlds: spiritual, historical, social. The exhibition's centre piece is a cabin-like structure inspired by a traditional Korean home known as a *hanok* (designed in collaboration with artist Benito Mayor Vallejo). The house's wooden frames are shrouded in a traditional type of wrapping cloth meant to bring good luck, here perhaps to both the dead and the living. Inhabited by several deities, like the *kkoktu* (funerary figures that assist the dead in their journey to the afterlife and ease their confusion by guiding and entertaining them), or Princess Bari, also known as *Bari Gongju*, the deity that presides over the crossing and conducts their souls. Positioning themselves at, or on both sides of, the boundary or threshold between natural and supra-natural, outer- and under-worlds, Zadie Xa's manifold works – paintings, sculptures, textile works, suspended marionettes or masks – could be said to dramatise the circumstances under which the effects of liminality are made manifest as visual or audible form. The two moments, dusk and dawn, or neither night nor day, the exhibition soundtrack alludes to, also point to a liminal stage, while its haunting sounds conjure the feeling of a borderland, of somewhere neither land nor water, of something like a gateway to another world.

In ghost stories the house is typically the centre of hauntings, but Xa is not concerned with ghosts, not the chain rattling kind at least. For Xa a ghost is not simply a dead person, but to paraphrase Avery

1
David E. Wellbery. 1990. Foreword. In Friedrich Kittler, *Discourse Networks 1800/1900* (Stanford, CA: Stanford University Press, 1990) XIII.

2
Ibid.

3
This designation is a Western construct created for comparative purposes that cannot capture the diversity of these practices.

4
See Courtenay Grean Raia, 'From ether theory to ether theology: Oliver Lodge and the physics of immortality', *Journal of the History of the Behavioral Sciences*, vol. 43, no. 1 (Winter 2007) 18–43.

Gordon, a form by which something that was lost makes itself known or apparent to us, even if fleetingly or in a barely visible manner.[5] What was lost via the process we call modernisation was a lifeworld, a sense of belonging and of continuity, a sense of balance and justice – expressed by the Haechi, a figure that recurs in Xa's installations, a mythical animal that can tell right from wrong – but also a sense of becoming animal or becoming other.

Therianthropy, the ability to shapeshift into an animal form, or what Tom Gunning described as 'the mythical potential of moving between species' is, in folklore, a metaphor for either escape or entrapment. But we no longer speak of forms with the ability to change into new entities, of Ovidian metamorphosis or mythical mutability. In the modern era all economic and geopolitical flows, however mobile, are fixed within an imperial frame. In the Gothic novel, most saliently, shapeshifting is figured as a deformation or transmogrification, and all representations of monstrosity are organised by an evolutionary schema, and embellished with racialised inscriptions of difference, in order to strengthen colonial categories of Self and Other.

'All creation legends are true,' say the narrators of Zadie Xa's film *Child of Magohalmi* and the *Echoes of Creation* (2019). Unlike monotheism, the vernacular religions Zadie Xa mobilises did not have a theological system. They evolved organically from the institutional and material conditions of society as a 'system that is not just coextensive with culture but practically identical to it.'[6] By contrast, monotheistic religions 'owe their existence to an act of revelation'[7] and differentiate themselves from vernacular religions by 'denouncing them as paganism, idolatry and superstition.'[8] For monotheism:

> 'the truth to be proclaimed comes with an enemy to be fought. Only they know of heretics and pagans, false doctrine, sects, superstition, idolatry, magic, ignorance, unbelief, heresy, and whatever other terms have been coined to designate what they denounce, persecute and proscribe as manifestations of untruth.'[9]

Monotheism, in other words, is not coextensive with culture but antagonistic to it, and thus not only entails a different conceptualisation of the divine and of the relation to divinity, but also has political repercussions, in the sense that religion changes to become an autonomous system that can emancipate itself from the social to 'transcend all political and ethnic borders, and transplant itself into other cultures.'[10] This process has also been described as the eclipse of magical and animistic beliefs about nature, but one could be excused for thinking of it as precursor, and enabler of, the subsequent expansion of monoculture that came to replace the diverse economies of the pre-colonial world. Another figure beloved to Xa, the trickster, who 'only comes to life in the complex terrain of polytheism'[11] is also lost to it. The trickster is both a shapeshifter and a boundary crosser, here personified in the figure of the tiger, fox and seagull, which Xa describes as avatars, not in the sense of an icon representing the player in a video game but in the sense of a manifestation of a deity, a spirit in bodily form, or an incarnate divine teacher (re)emerging at the threshold between spirit worlds and our cyber-modulated social milieus.

5
See Avery Gordon, *Ghostly Matters: Haunting and the Sociological Imagination* (Minneapolis, MN: University of Minnesota Press, 1997).

6
Jan Assmann, *The Price of Monotheism* (Stanford, CA: Stanford University Press, 2009) 2.

7
Ibid.

8
Ibid 1.

9
Ibid 4.

10
Ibid 4.

11
Lewis Hyde, *Trickster Makes This World*: Mischief, Myth, and Art, (New York: Farrar, Strauss and Giroux, 2010) 9–10.

As literary theorist Sladja Blazan notes, the sighting of a ghost always exposes the entanglements of horror and history. It is also interesting to me that *geist* – as in the Hegelian *weltgeist* – would mistranslate into ghost. The ghost, to return to Avery Gordon, 'is just the sign, or the empirical evidence if you like, that tells you a haunting is taking place.'[12] One could perhaps read the latter part of the exhibition's title 'Five Ways 2 Forgiveness' – a pun on Ursula K. Le Guin's collection of short stories *Five Ways to Forgiveness* (1995), detailing histories of enslavement and successful revolts – as suggesting that history in the Hegelian sense is nothing but a heap of messy ground-level entanglements at sites of imperial extraction or expansion, but Xa does not linger in sunken places. As Avery Gordon put it, 'the way of the ghost is haunting, and haunting is a very particular way of knowing.'[13] Rather the artist looks for a language for representing the hauntings that mark the limit of European modernity, while pointing to a different kind of access to the density of experience, one that conjures more than one story at the time.

12
Avery Gordon,
Ghostly Matters: Haunting and the Sociological Imagination (Minneapolis, MN: University of Minnesota Press, 1997) 8.

13
Ibid.

Grandmother Mago

Grandmother Mago,
live performance,
58th Venice Biennale, Italy, 2019

Live performance as part of a programme devised by
Ralph Rugoff and Aaron Cezar,
co-produced by Venice Biennale and Delfina Foundation,
and commissioned by Arts Council England
with support from High Commission of Canada.

Devised with and performed by
Iris Chan, Jia-Yu Corit, Mary Feliciano,
Jihye Kim and Yumino Seki.
Masks by Benito Mayor Vallejo.

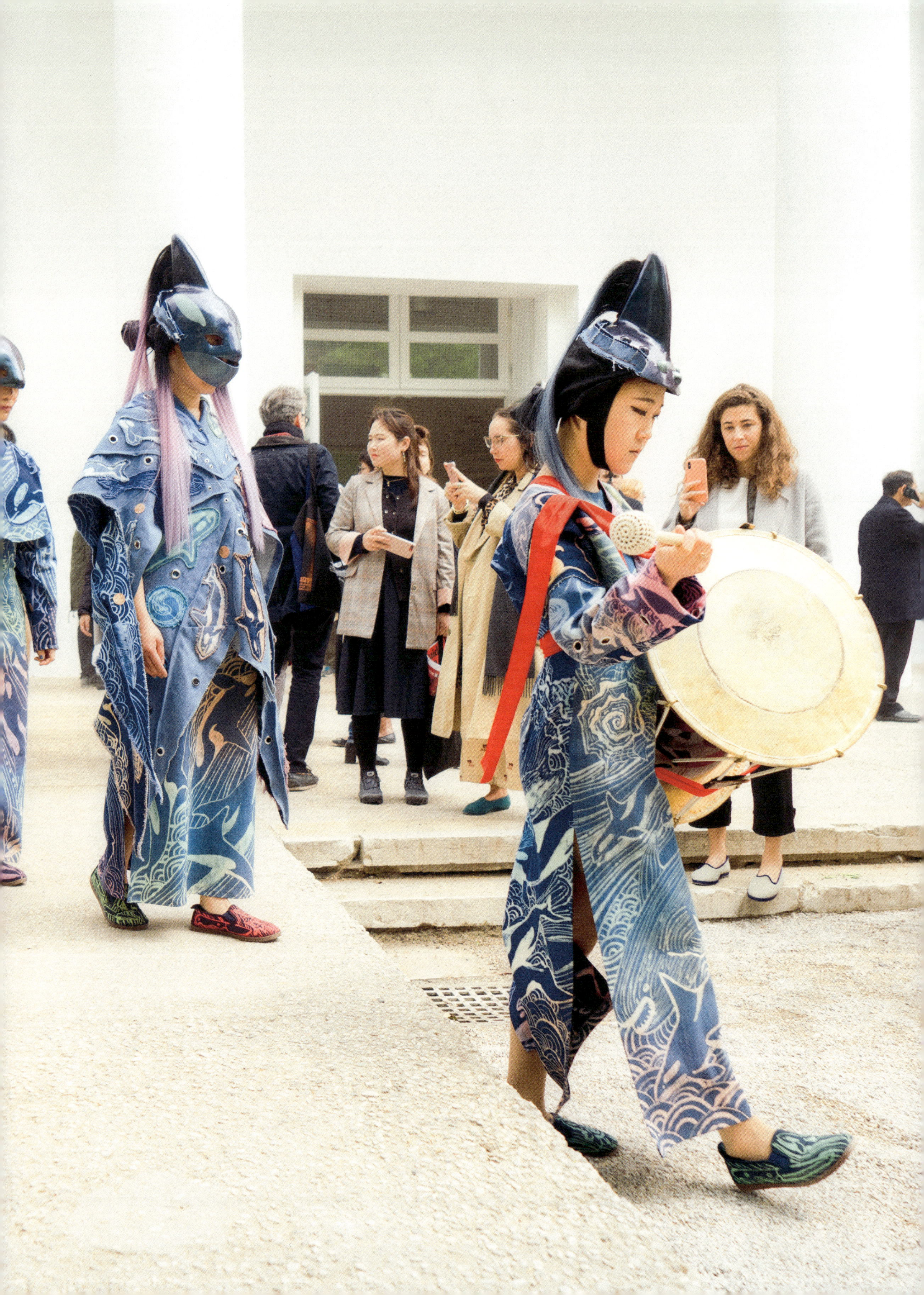

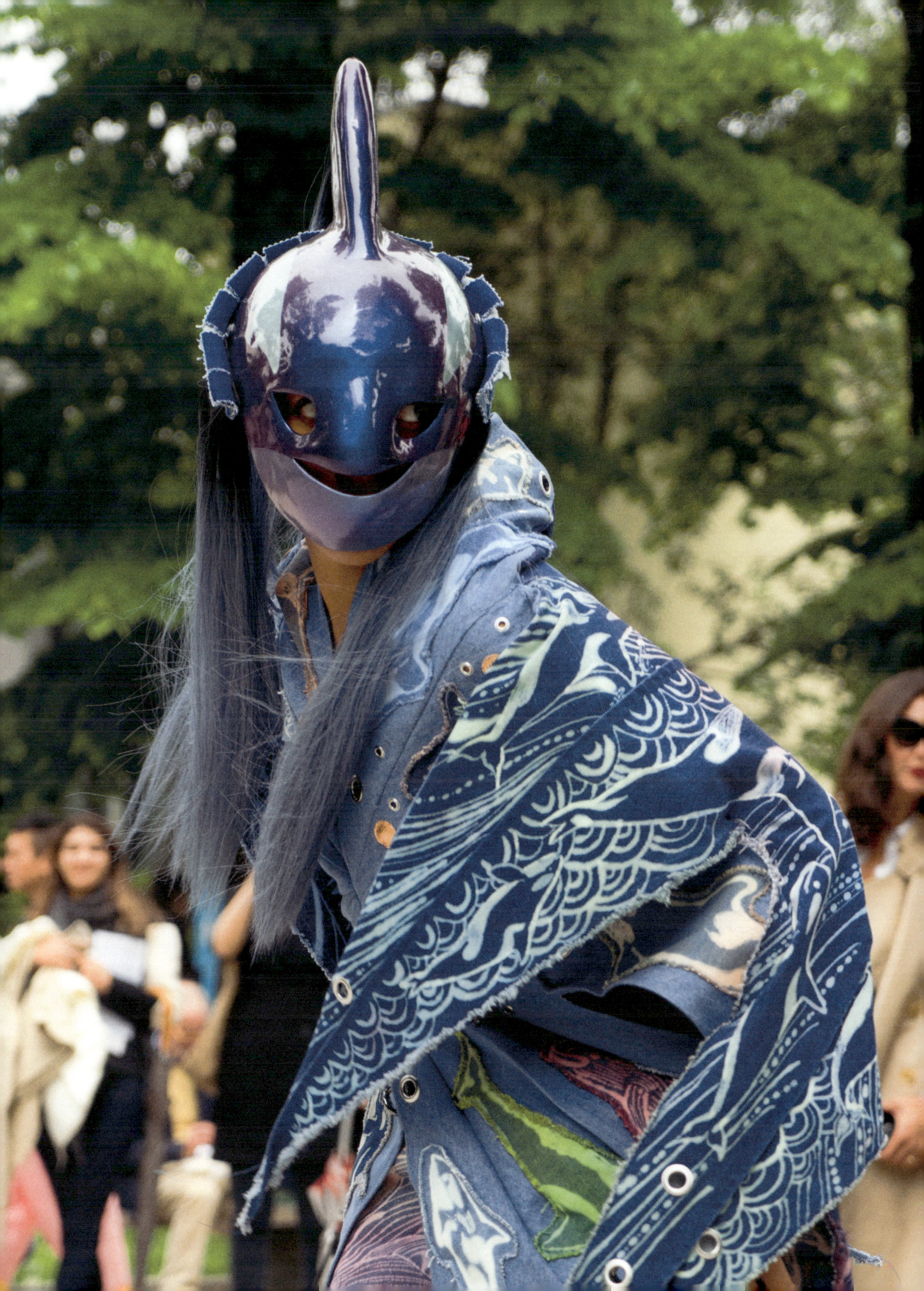

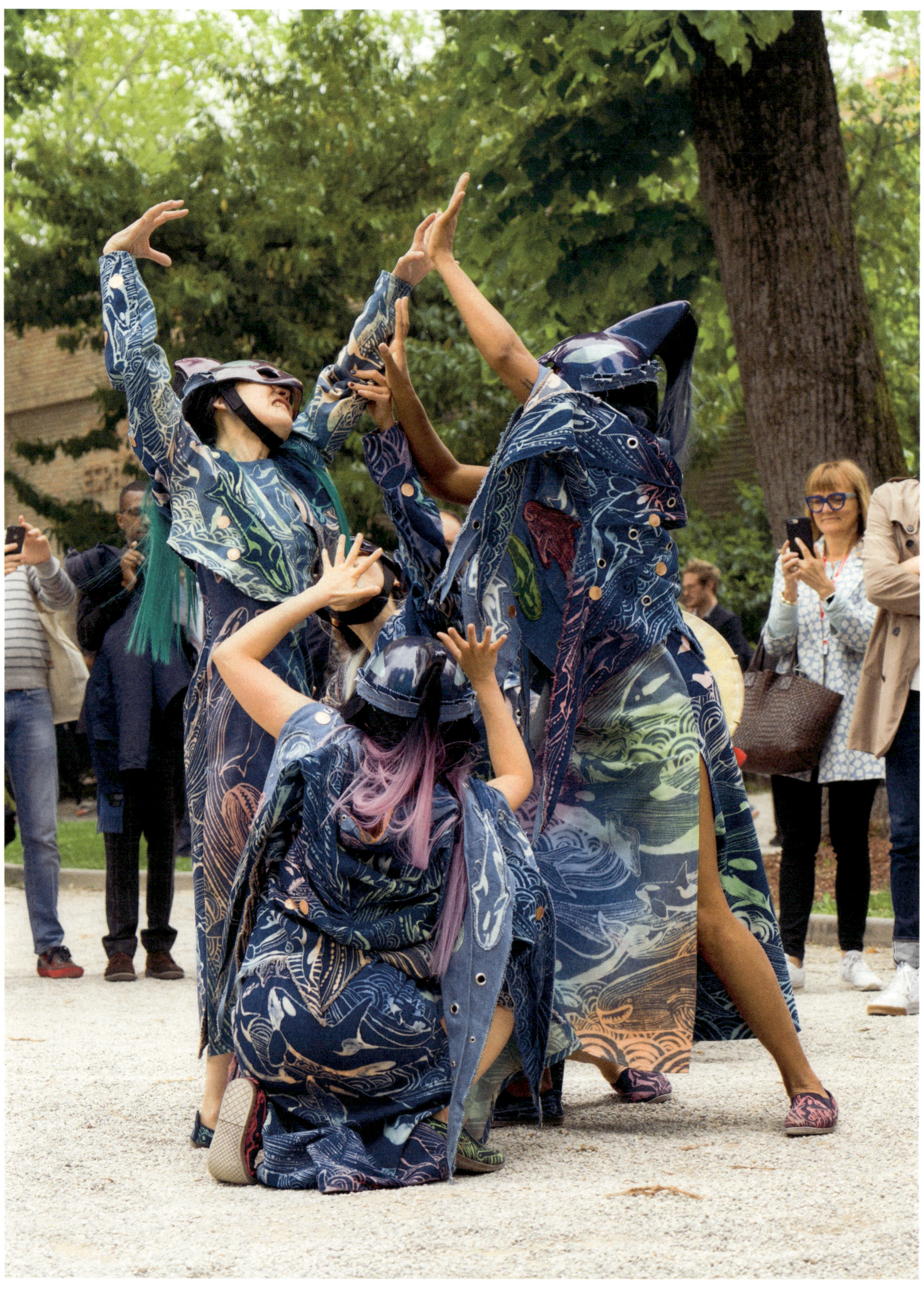

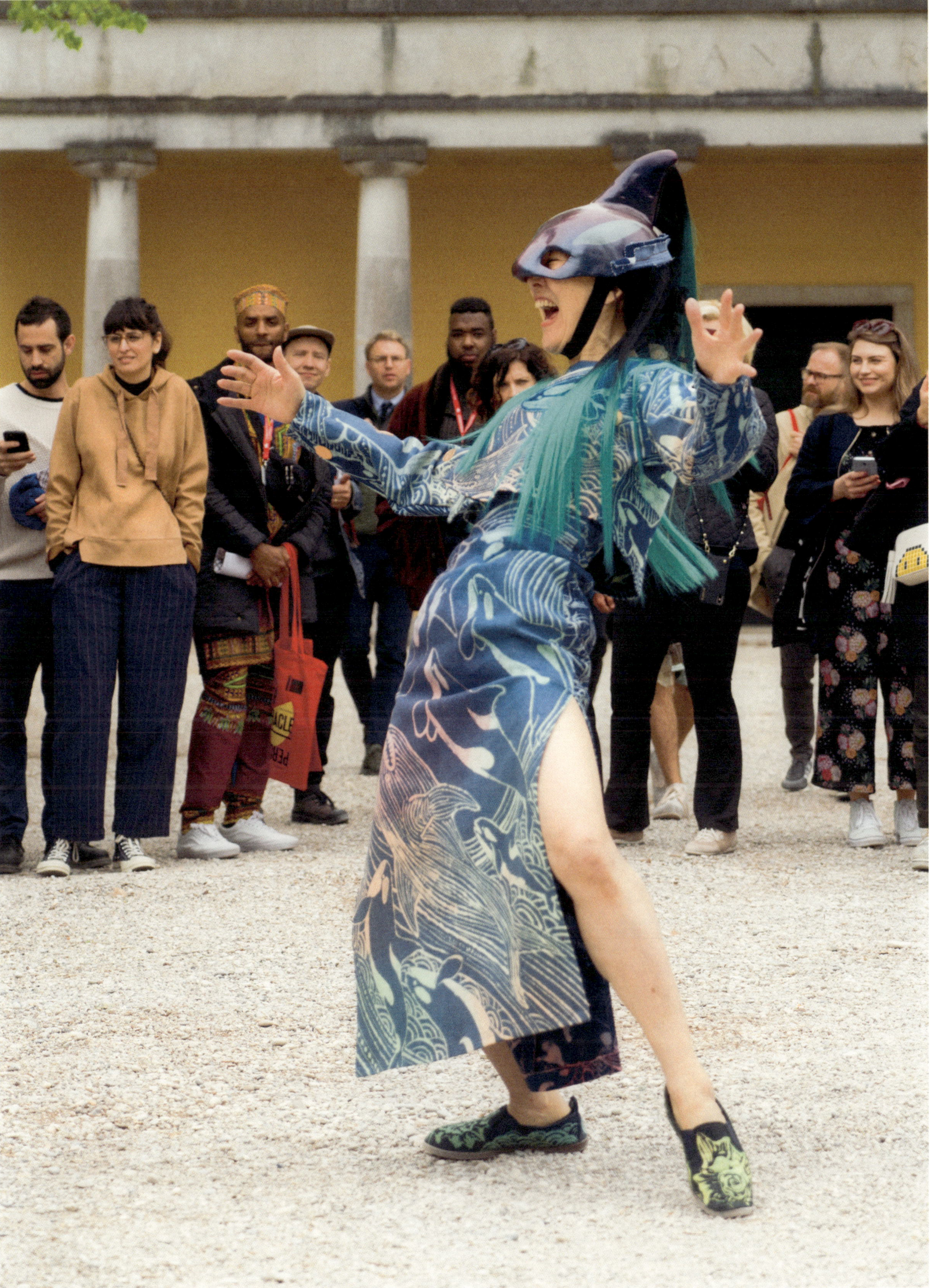

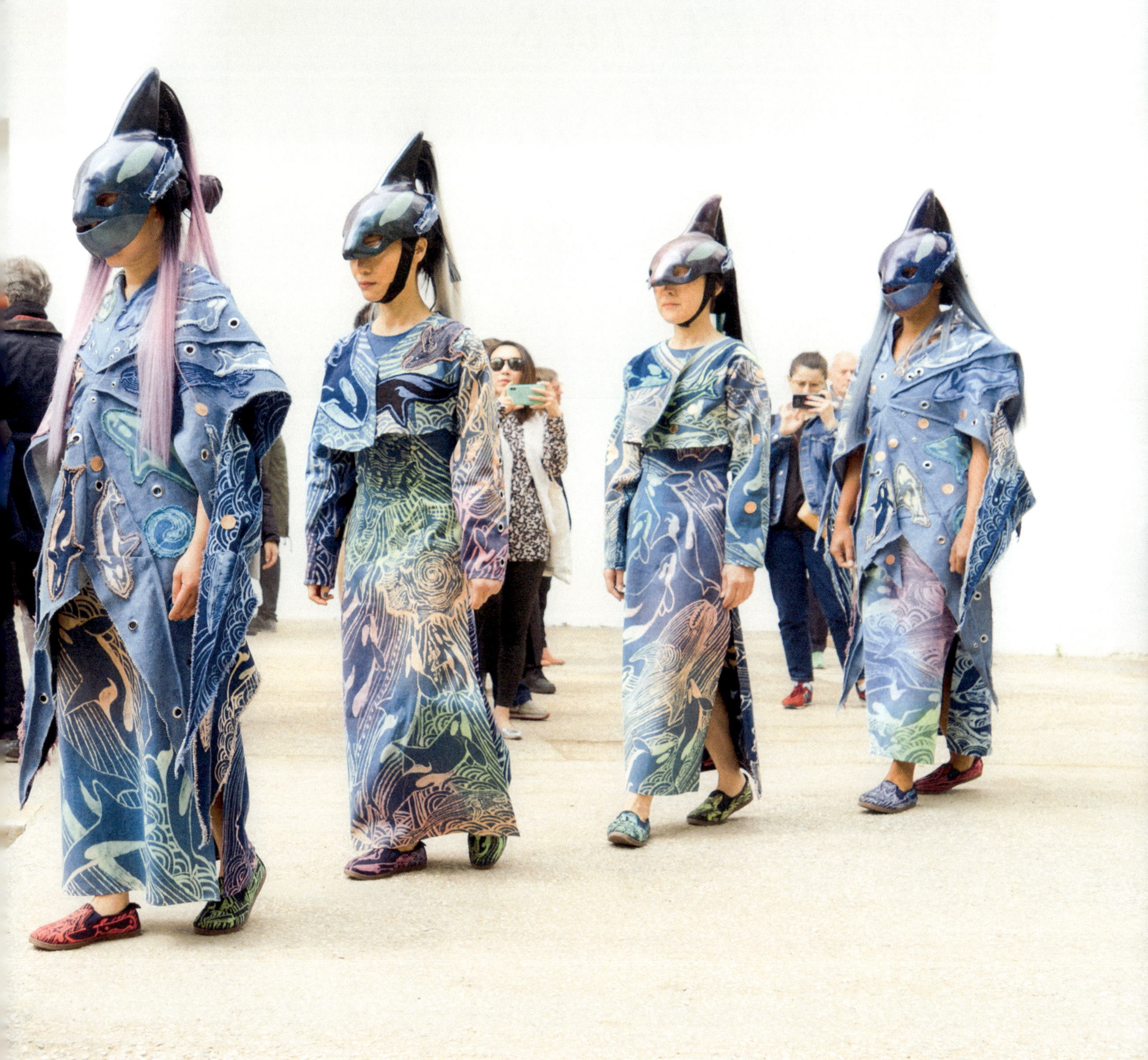

*Moon Poetics
4 Courageous
Earth Critters
and Dangerous
Day Dreamers*

Works included:

Orca, 2020
in collaboration with Benito Mayor Vallejo
Polymer resin, acrylic,
synthetic hair, fabric mixed media sculpture
59 × 27 × 45 cm

Orca, 2020
Denim, paint, dye, mixed fabrics
300 × 170 cm

*Moon Poetics 4 Courages Earth Critters and
Dangerous Day Dreamers,* 2021
in collaboration with Benito Mayor Vallejo
Oil on canvas
200 × 480 cm

Detail of *Cabbage,* 2020
Denim, paint, dye, mixed fabrics
145 × 170 cm

Cabbage, 2020
Denim, paint, dye, mixed fabrics
145 × 170 cm

Cabbage, 2020
in collaboration with Benito Mayor Vallejo
Mixed media sculpture
27 × 16 × 37 cm

Sotdae (Guardians of the Underworld), 2020
in collaboration with Benito Mayor Vallejo
Polymer resin, polystyrene,
mixed media, acrylic on wood
27 × 18 × 37 cm

Fox, 2020
Denim, paint, dye, mixed fabrics
210 × 170 cm

Fox, 2020
in collaboration with Benito Mayor Vallejo
Polymer resin, polystyrene, mixed media, acrylic
21.5 × 16 × 32 cm

Detail of *Conch,* 2020
Denim, paint, dye, mixed fabrics
155 × 170 cm

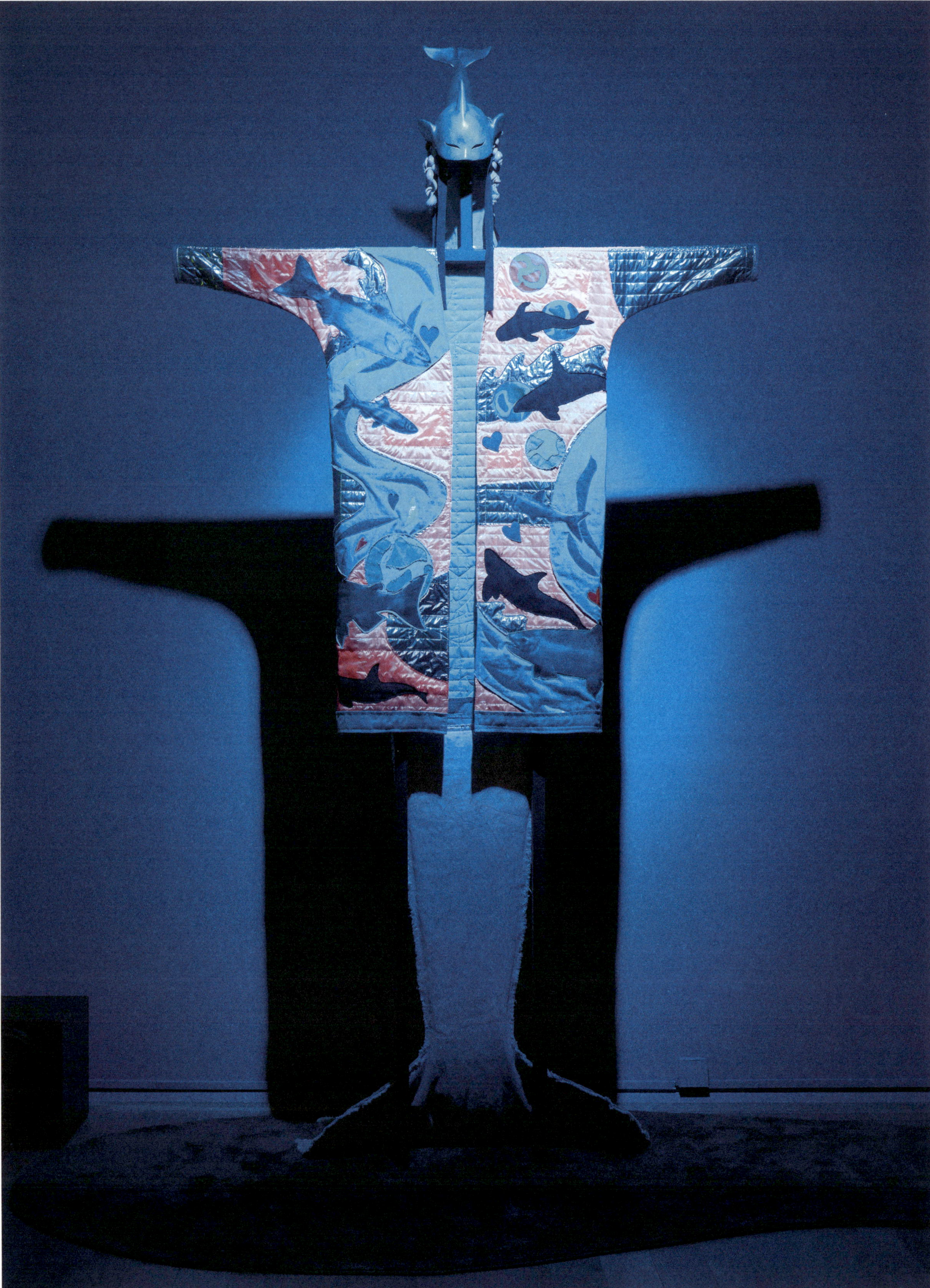

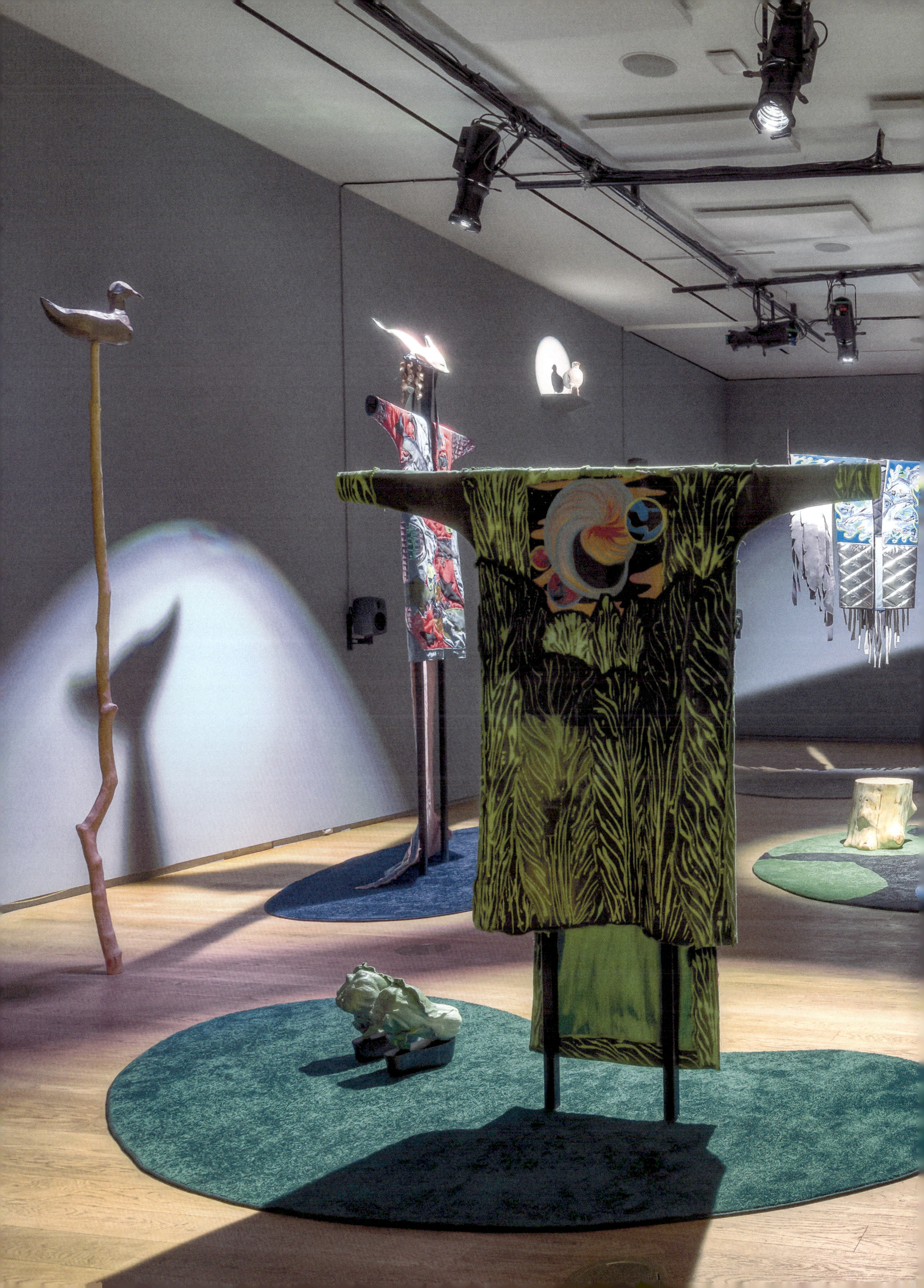

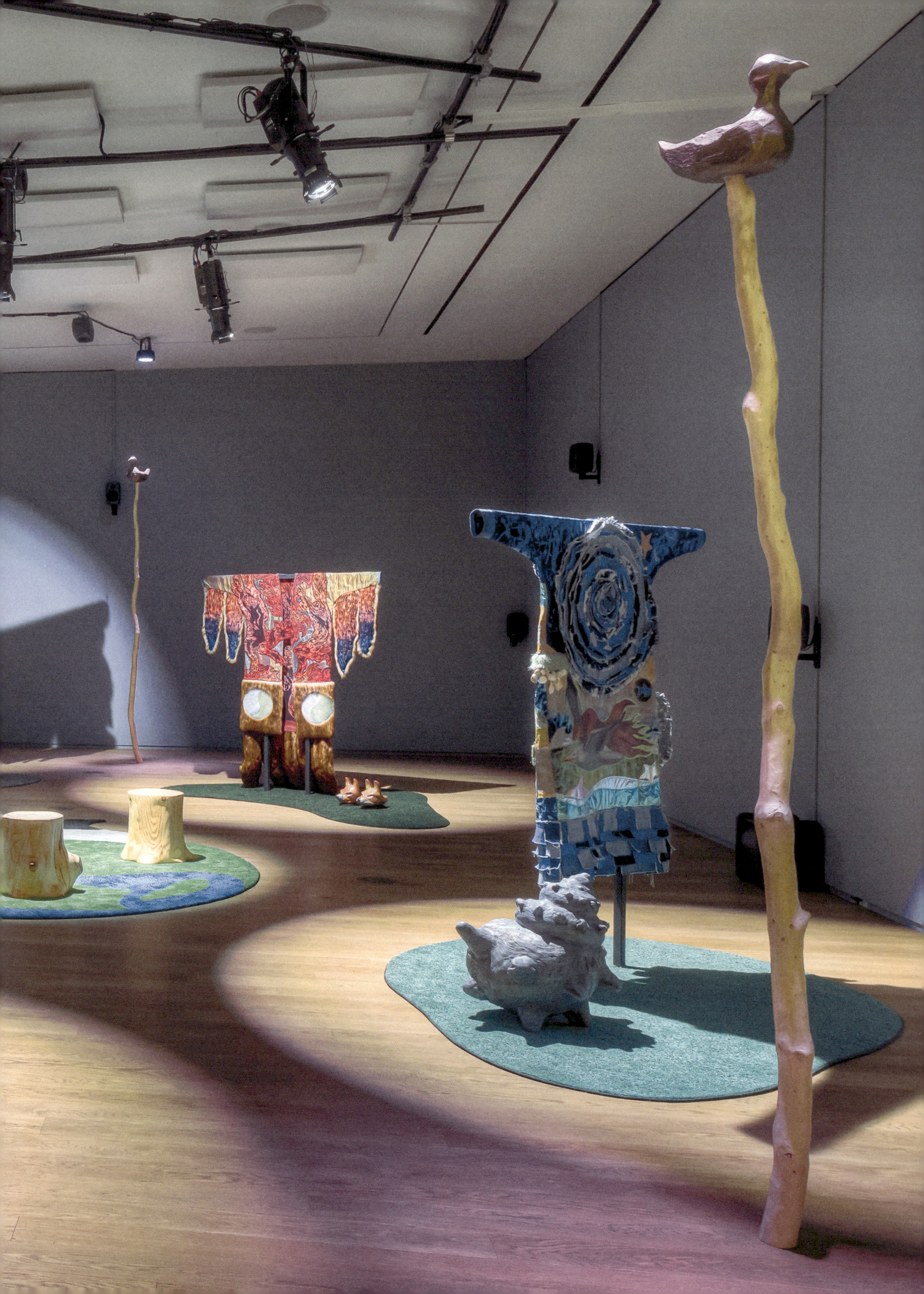

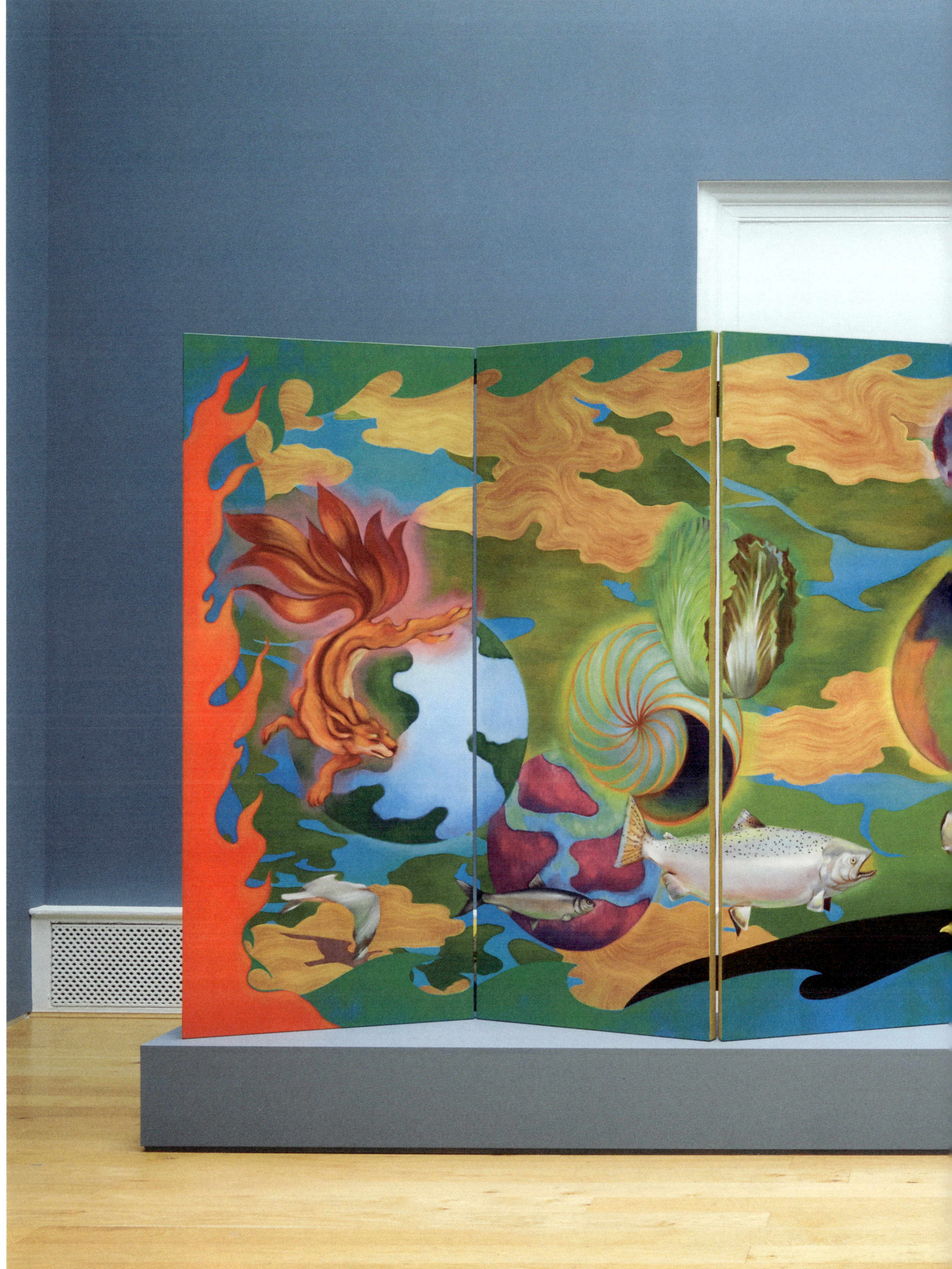

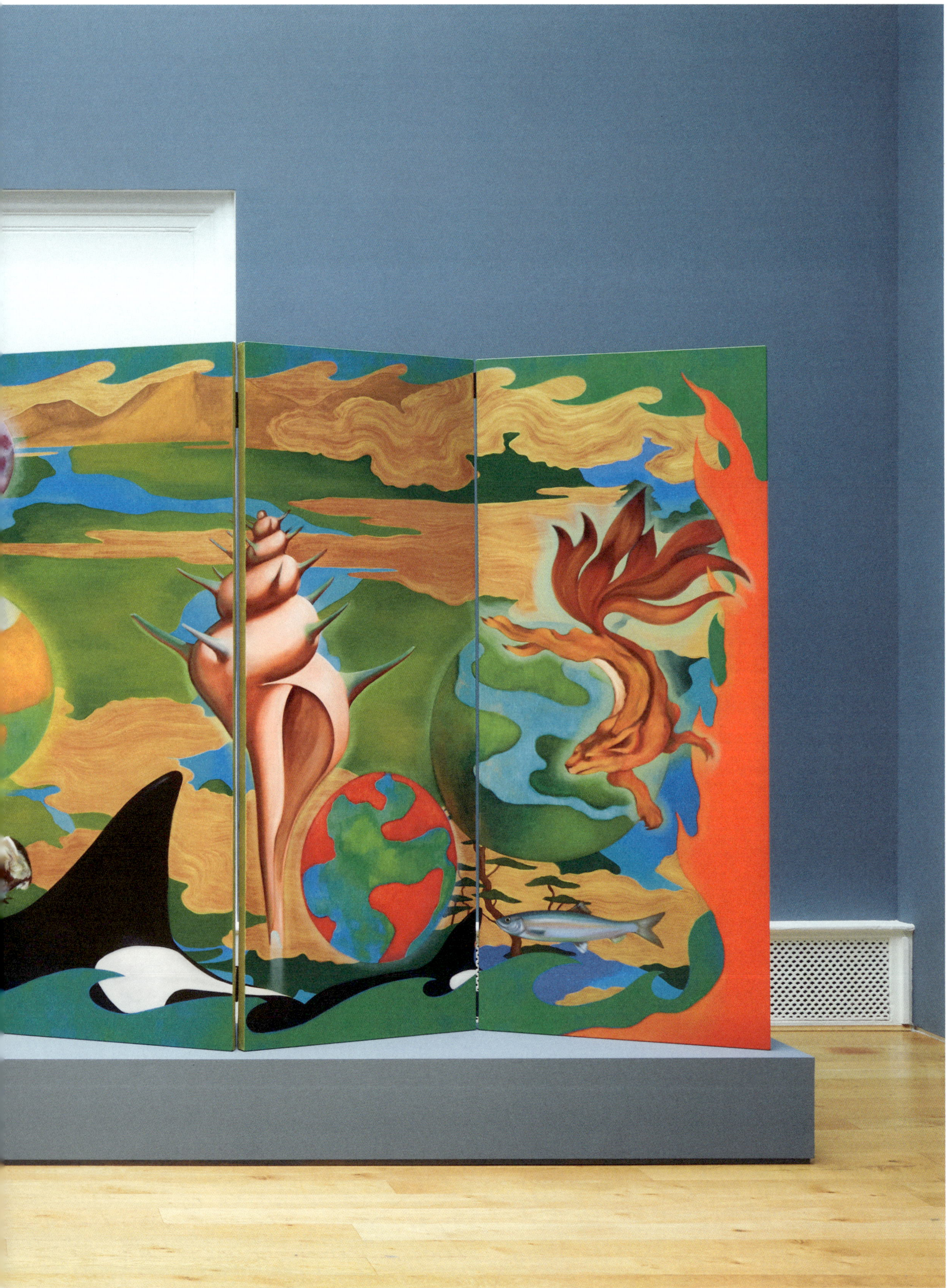

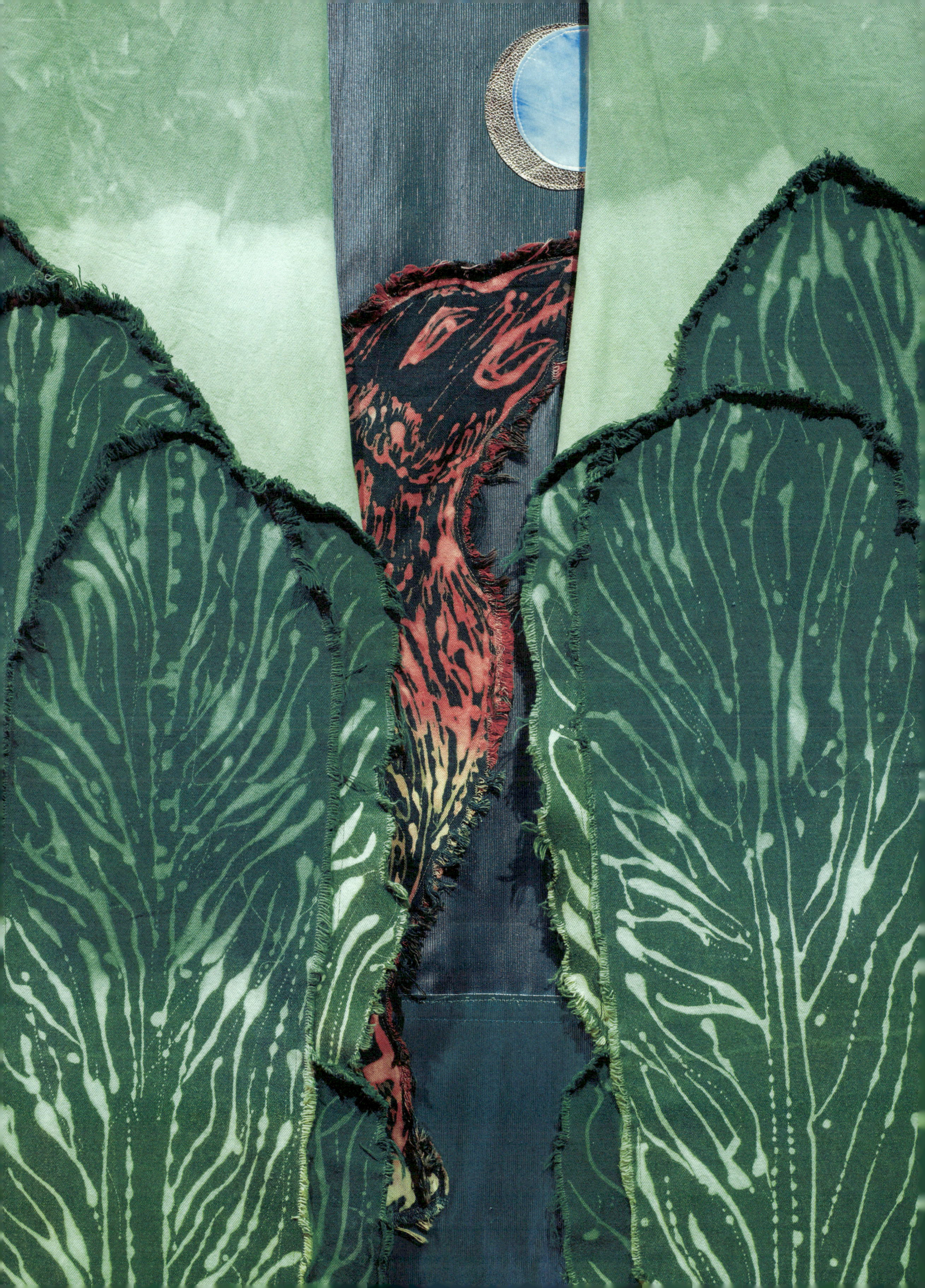

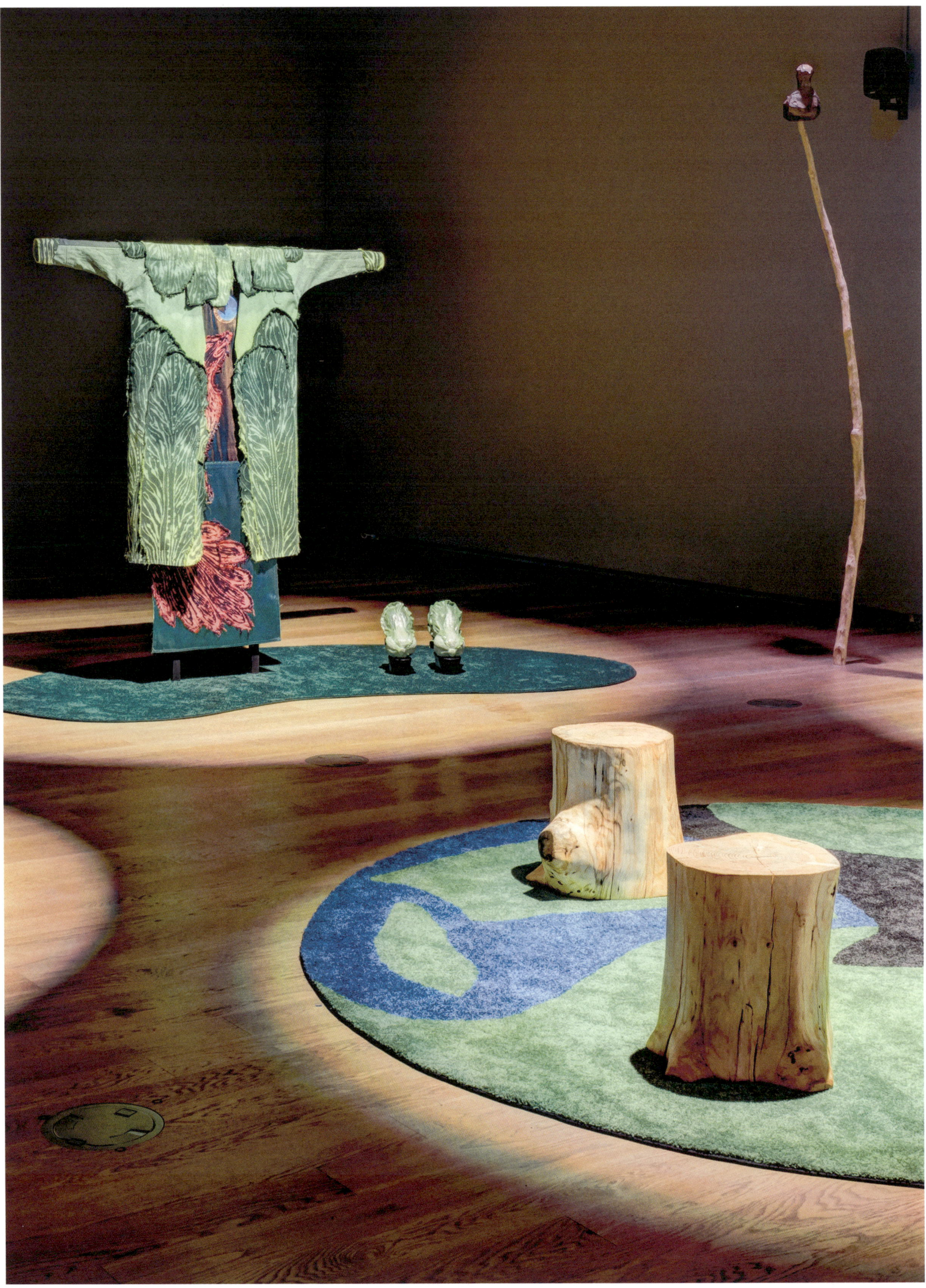

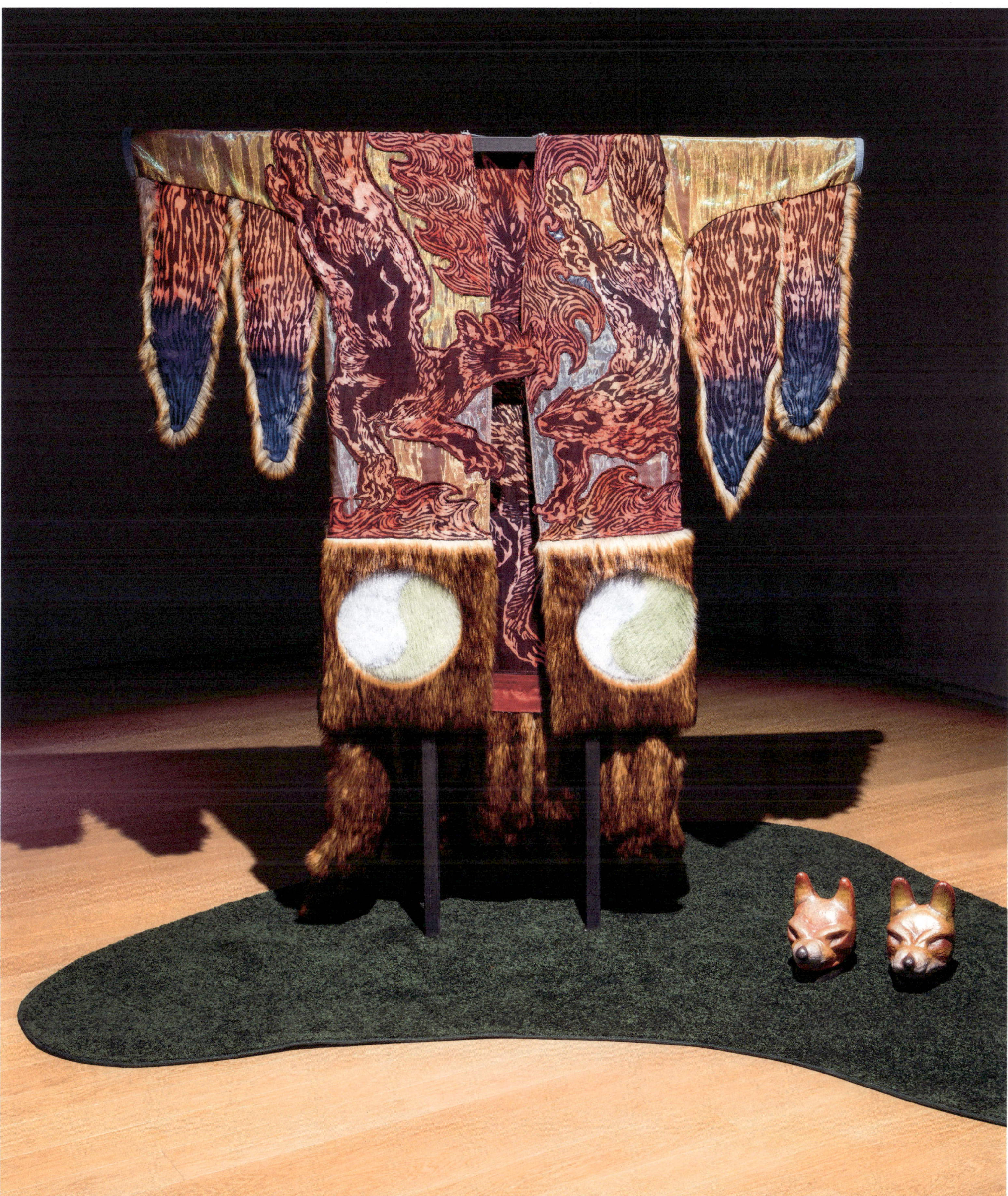

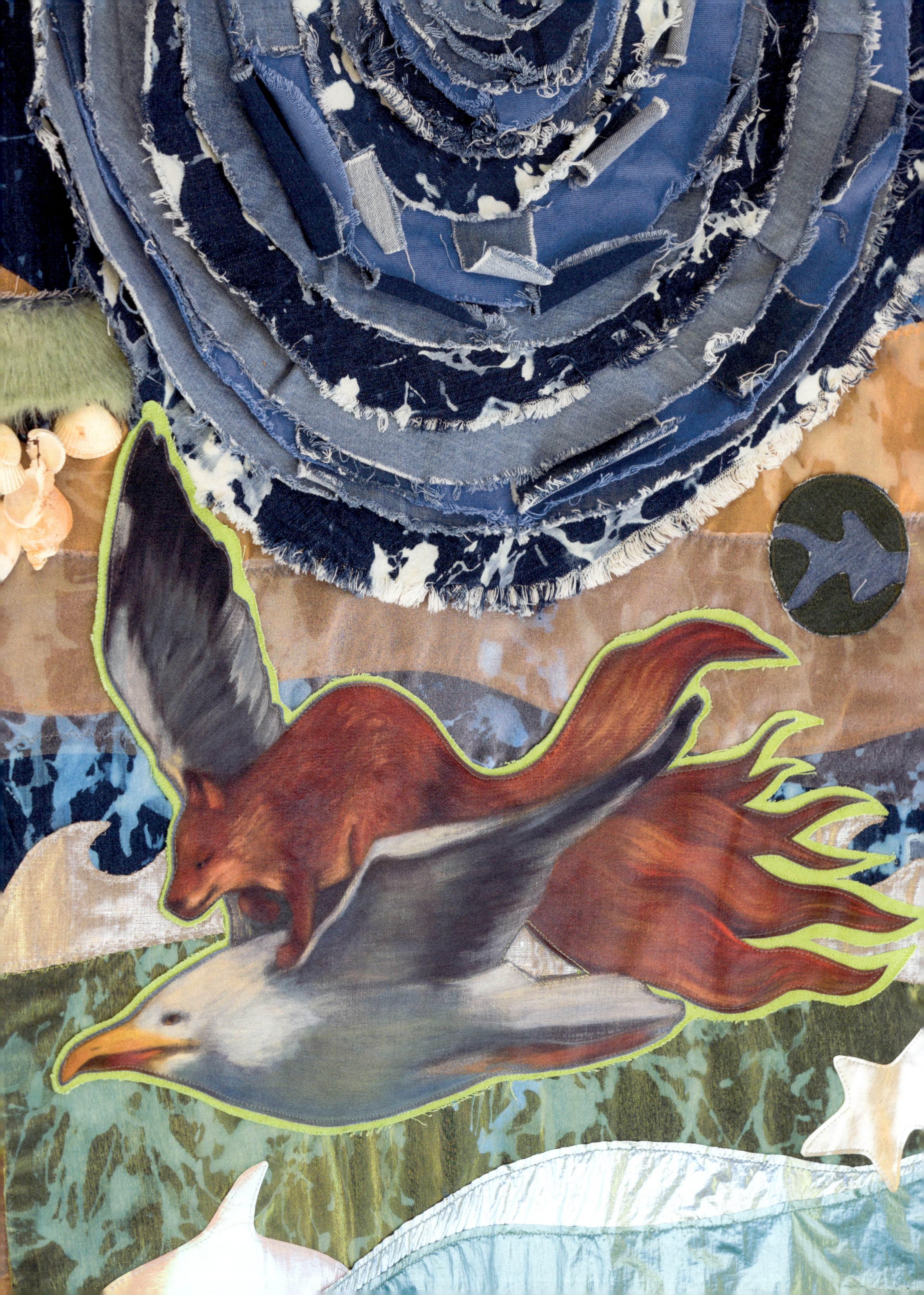

Dream Dangerous

Dream Dangerous, live performance,
Frieze Live: The Institute of Melodic Healing,
London, UK, 2020
in collaboration with Benito Mayor Vallejo

Performed by Jia-Yu Corti.
Make up by Ophelia Liu.

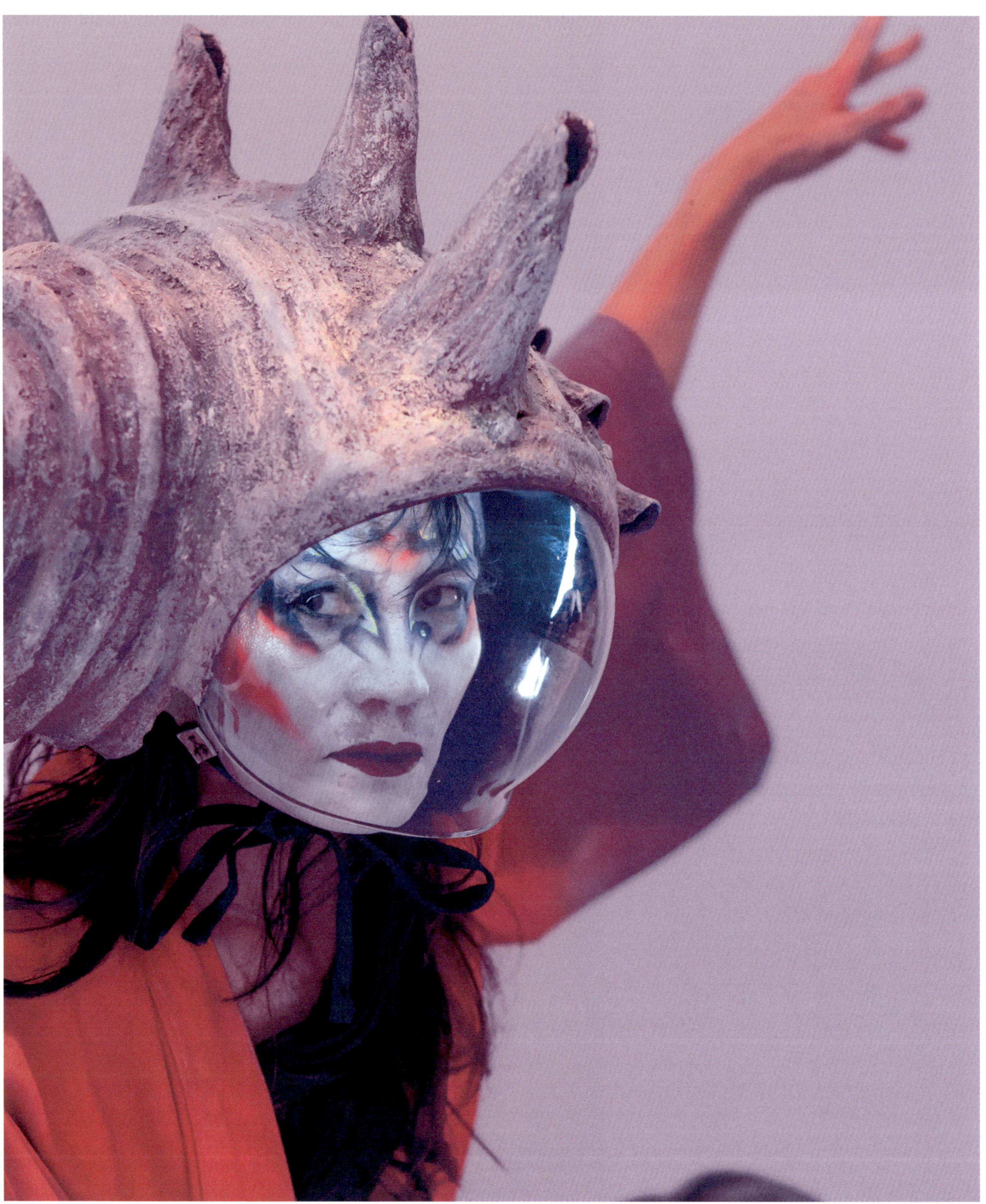

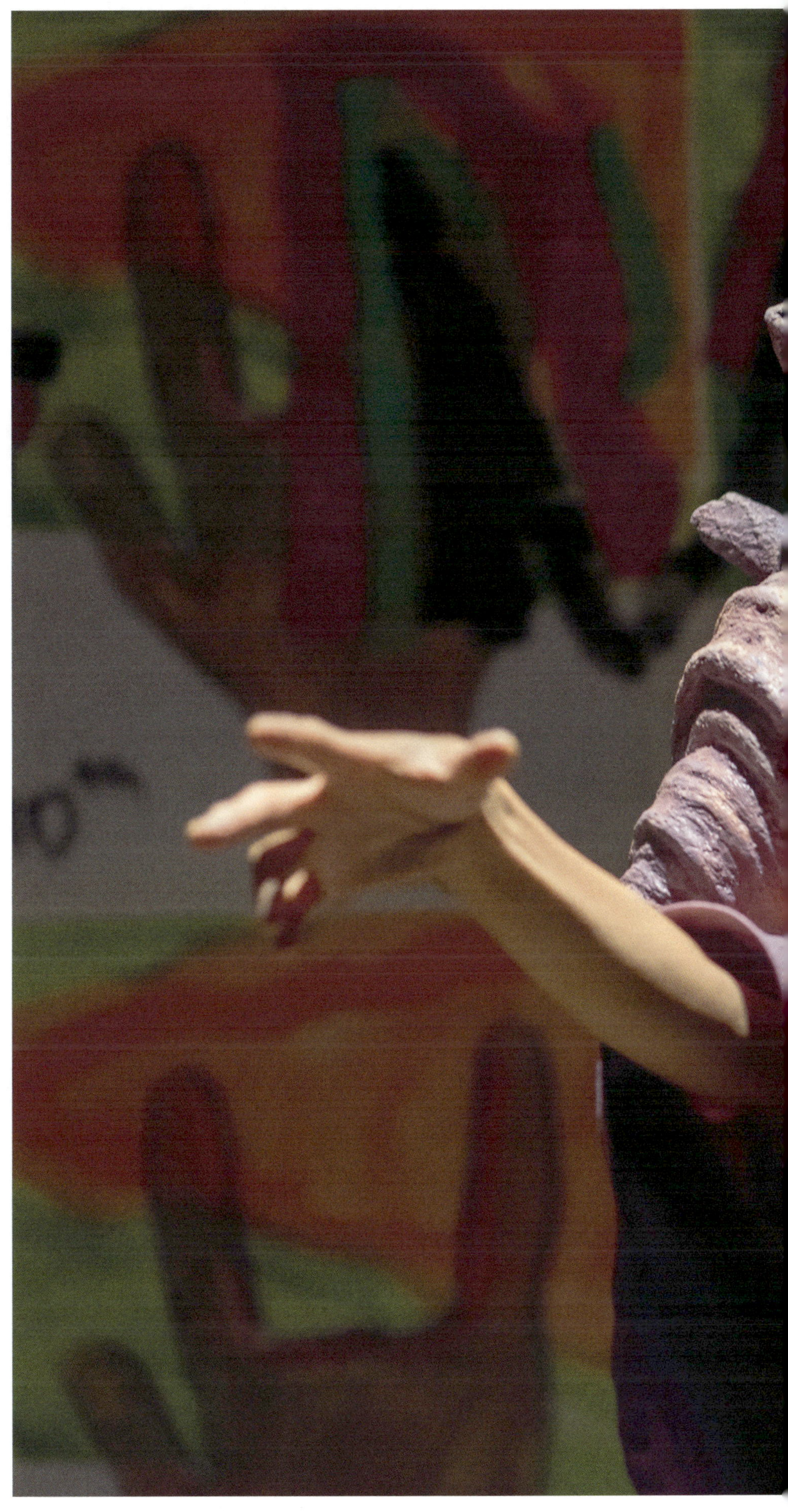

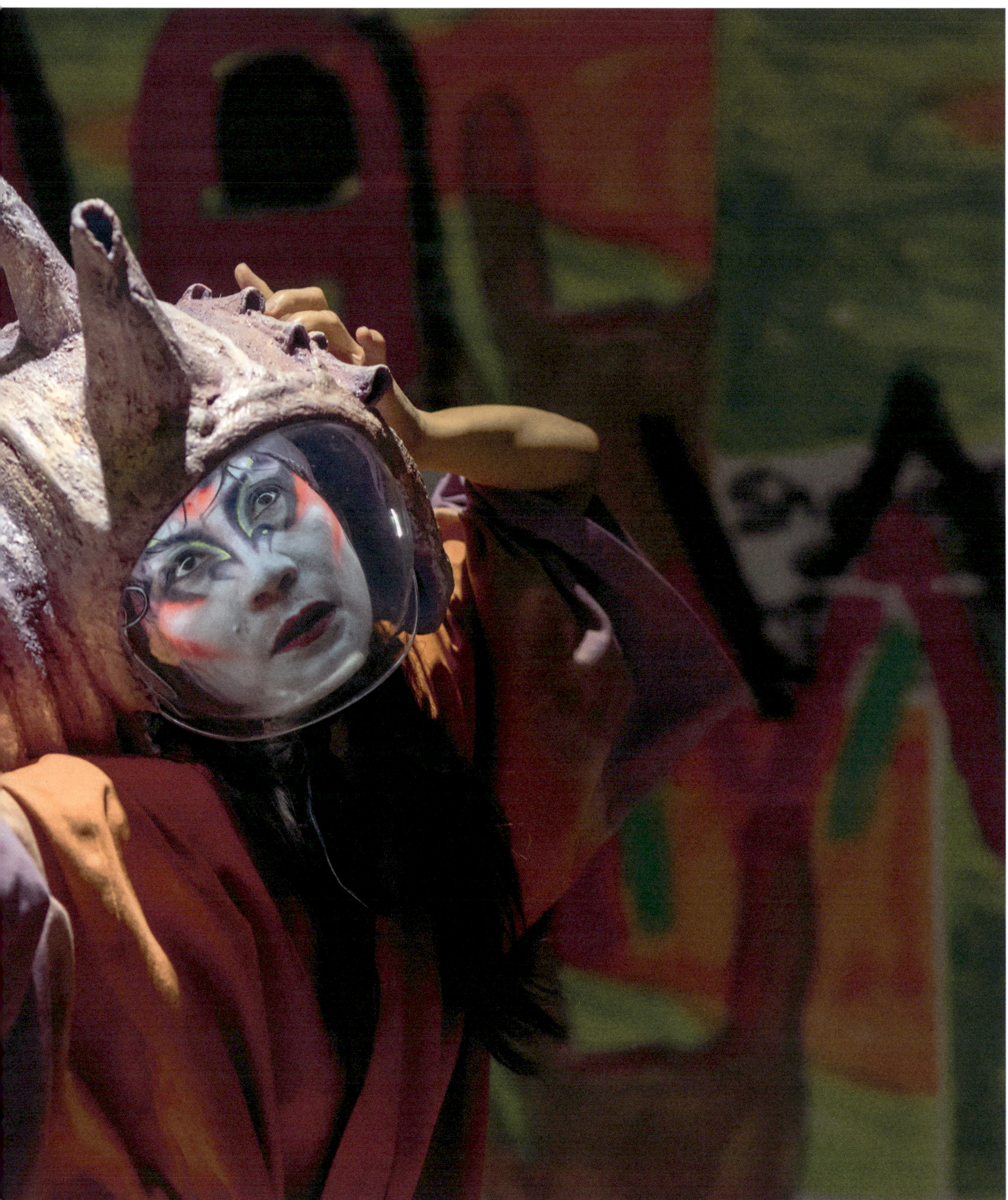

Scorpion

Scorpion, live performance,
The National Gallery, London, UK, 2021
in collaboration with Benito Mayor Vallejo

Costumes produced and designed by
Manuel Vadillo with Zadie Xa.
Special acknowledgement to Goom Heo, Paloma Proudfoot,
Monica Caudri and Money Wang.
Performed and choreographed by Jia-Yu Corti and Yumino Seki.
Original score by Sophie Mallett with jangguu
and woodblock excerpts by Jihye Kim.
Make up by Ophelia Liu, wigs by Wigchapel and
wig dressing by Abigail Sansome.

Works included:

Scorpion, 2022
in collaboration with Benito Mayor Vallejo
Oil on linen
220 × 900 cm

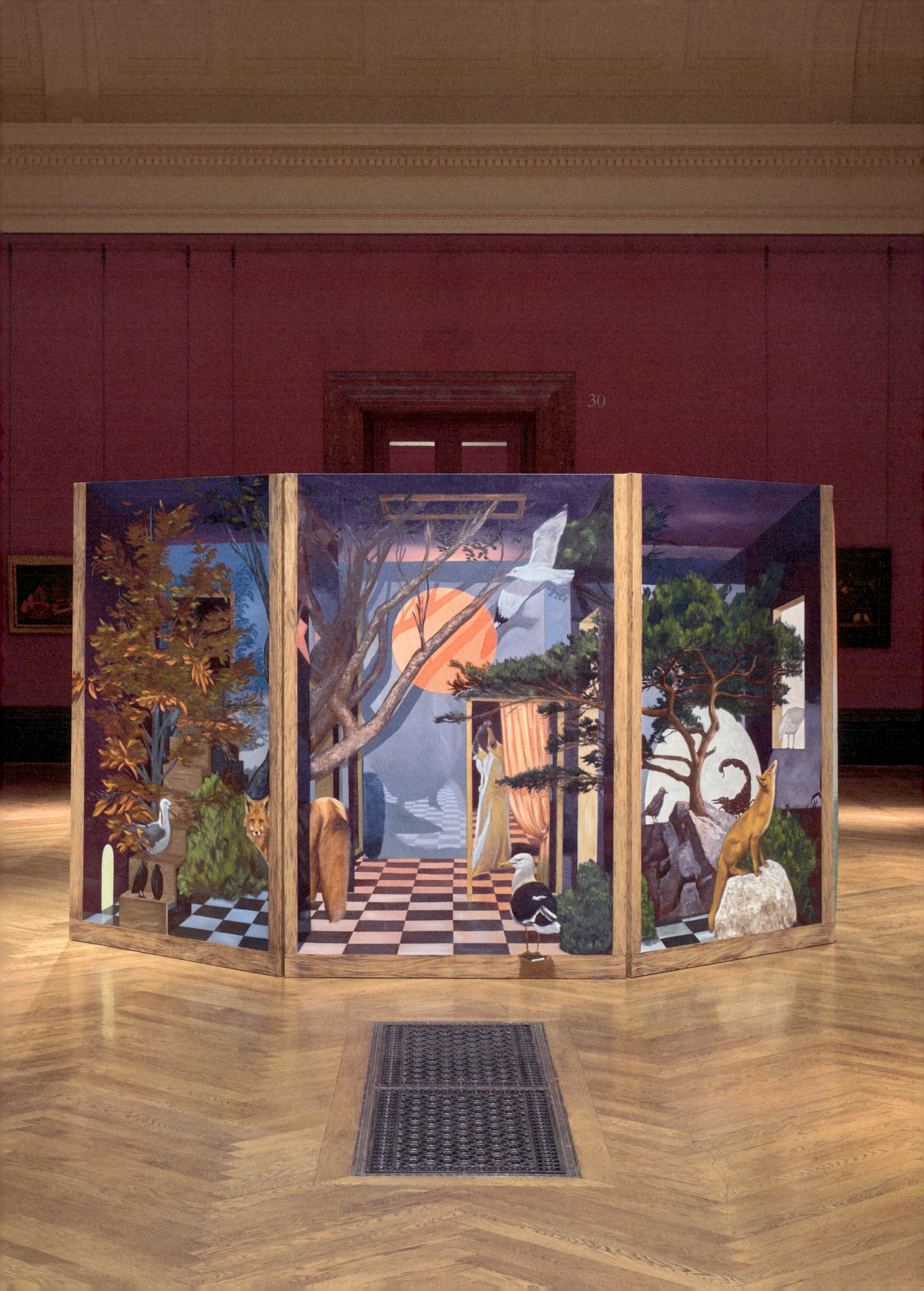

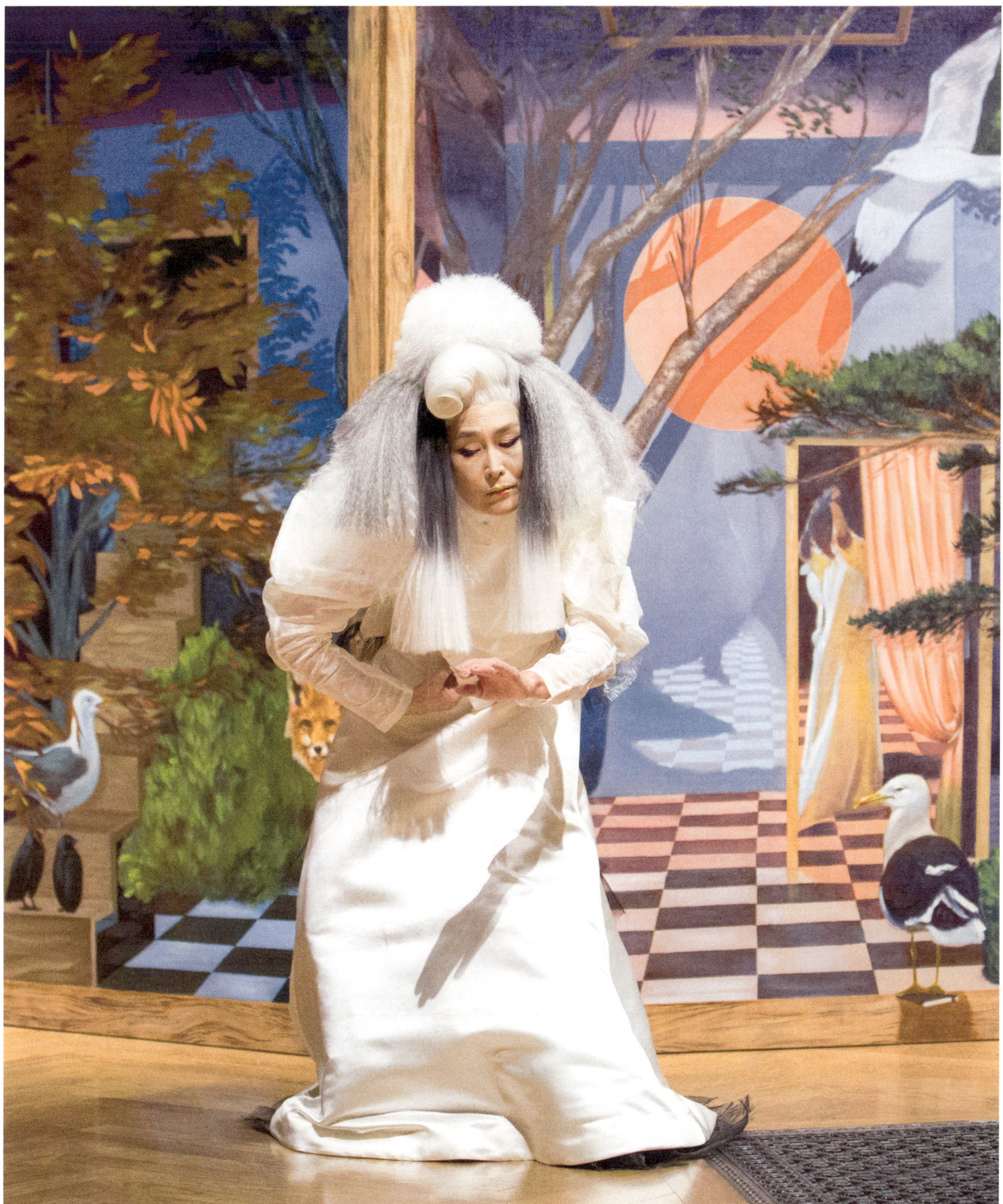

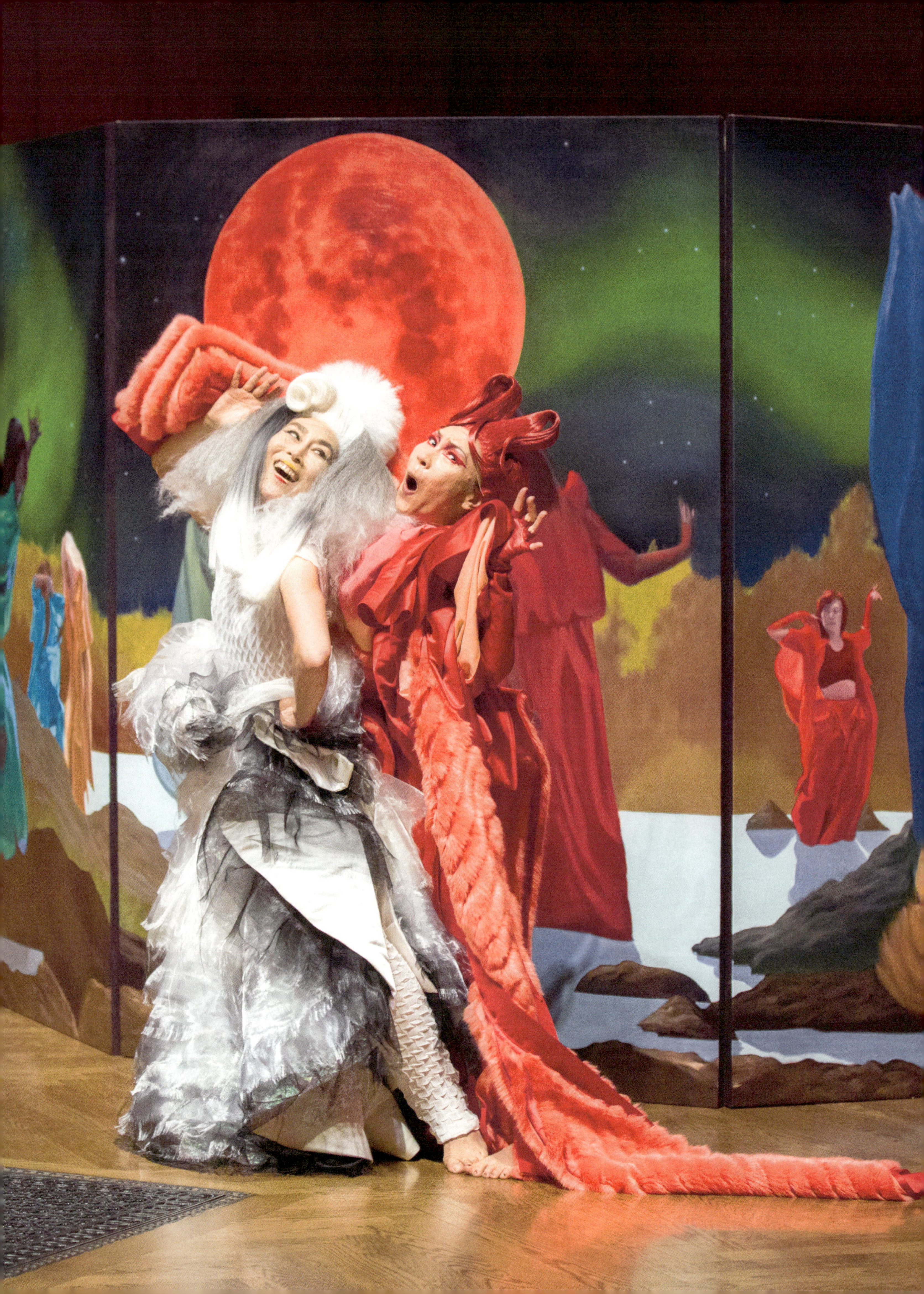

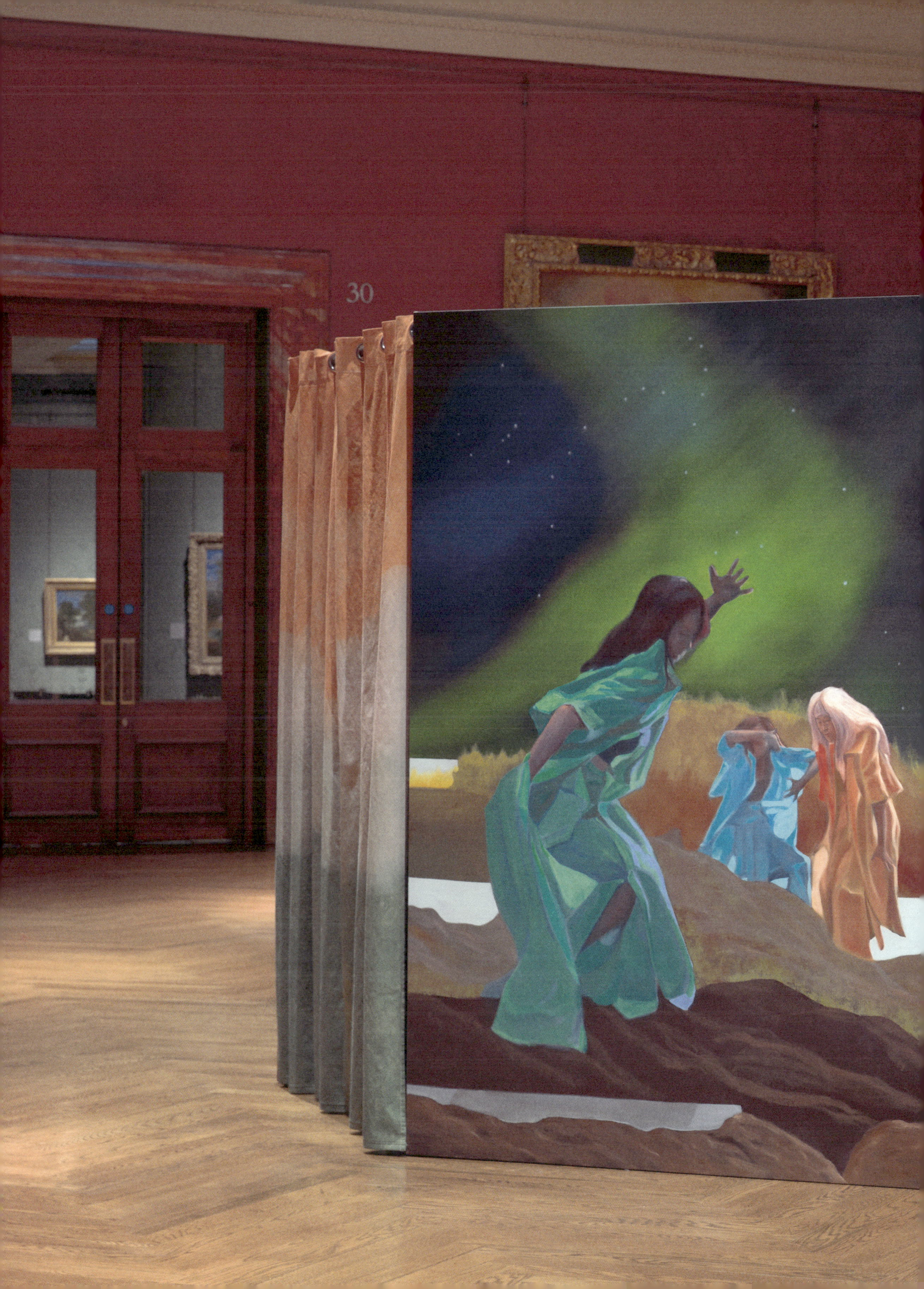

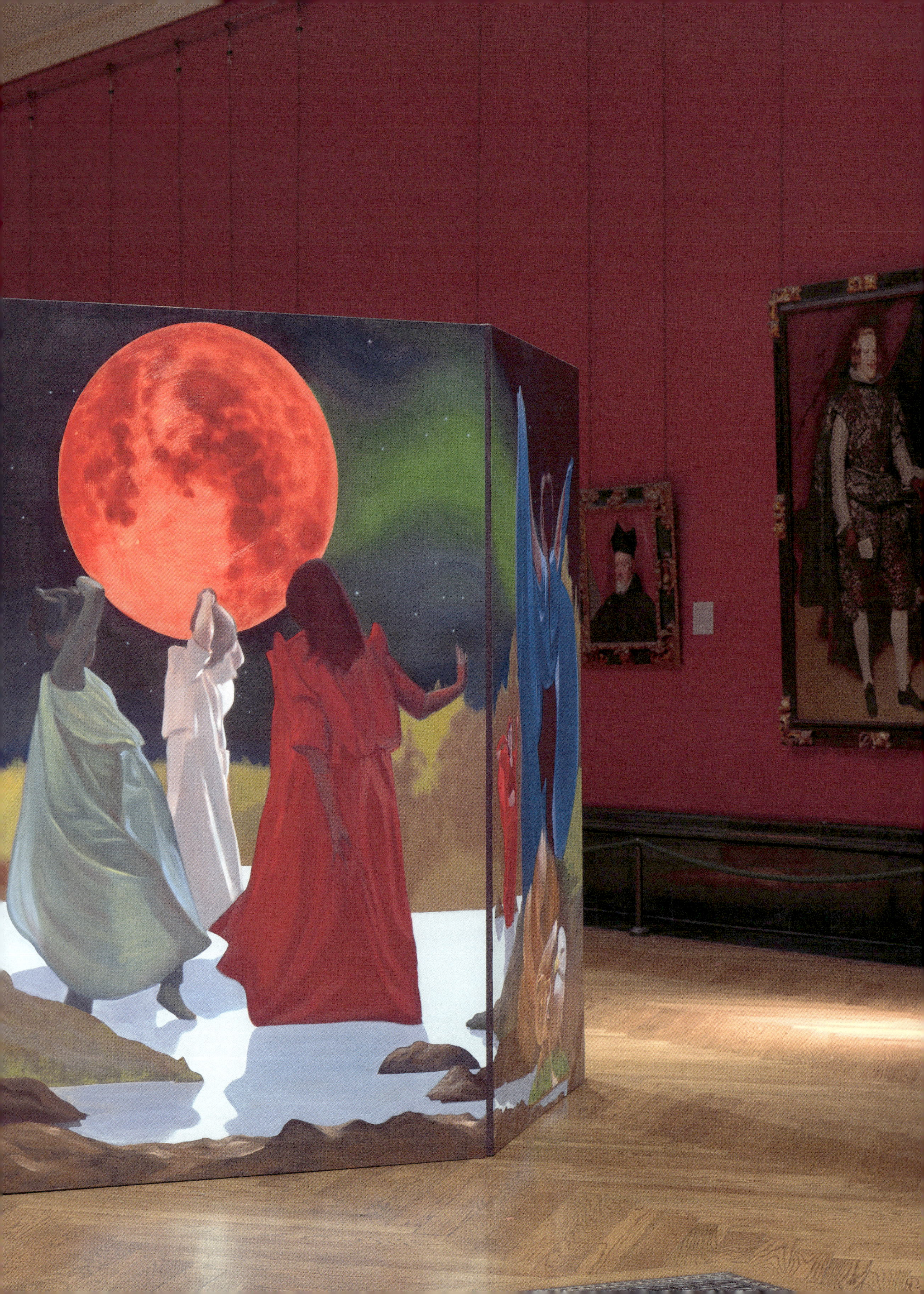

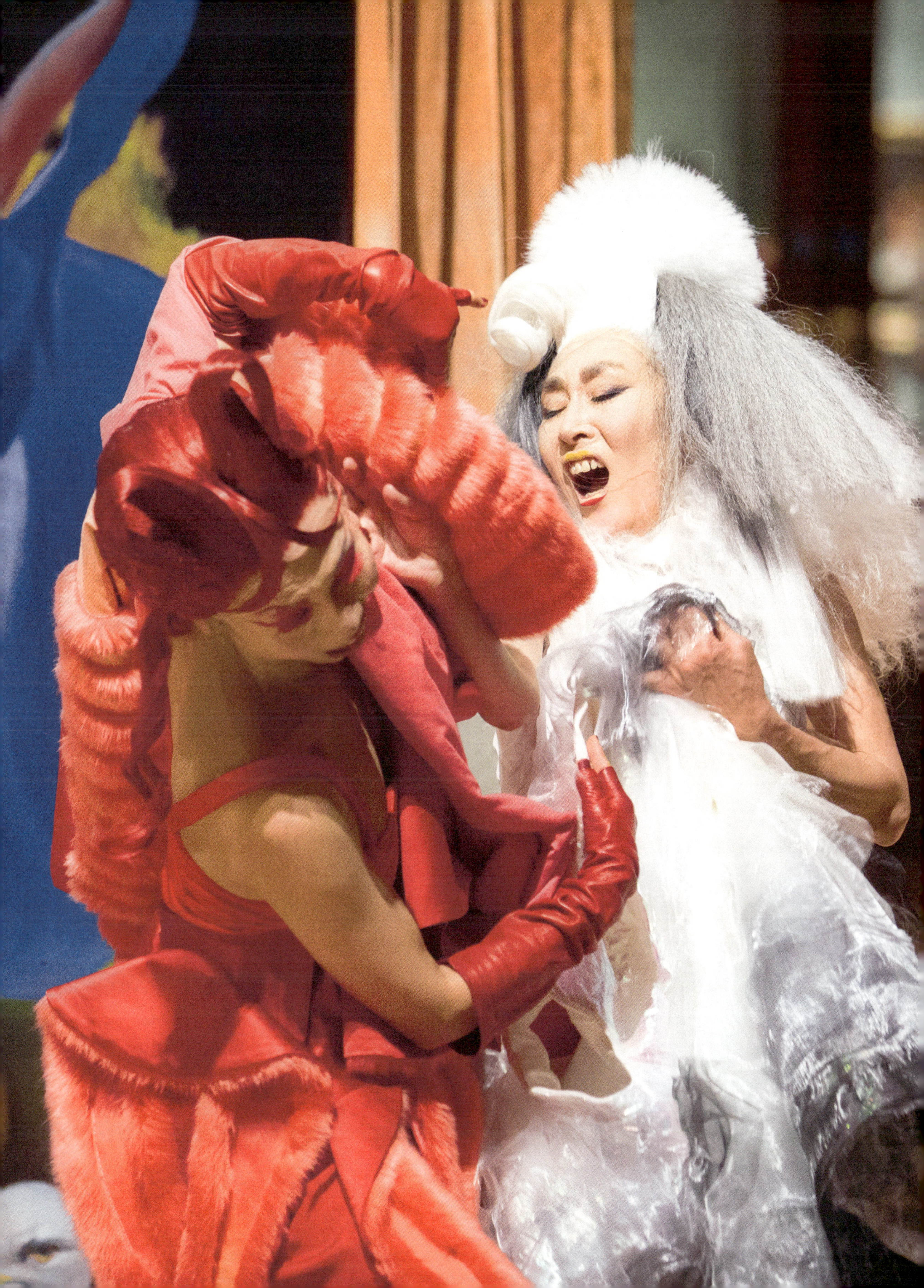

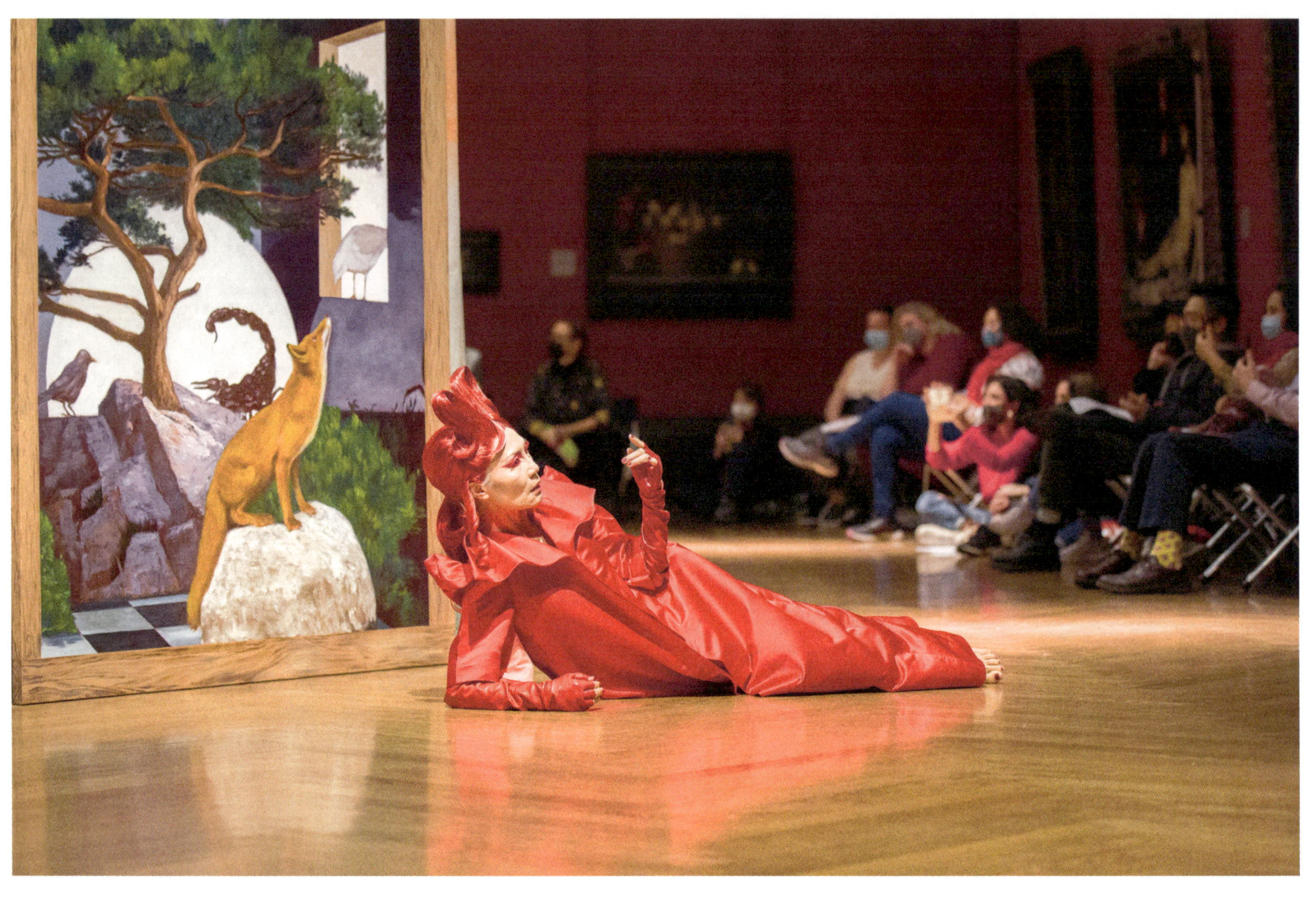

Long ago when tigers smoked

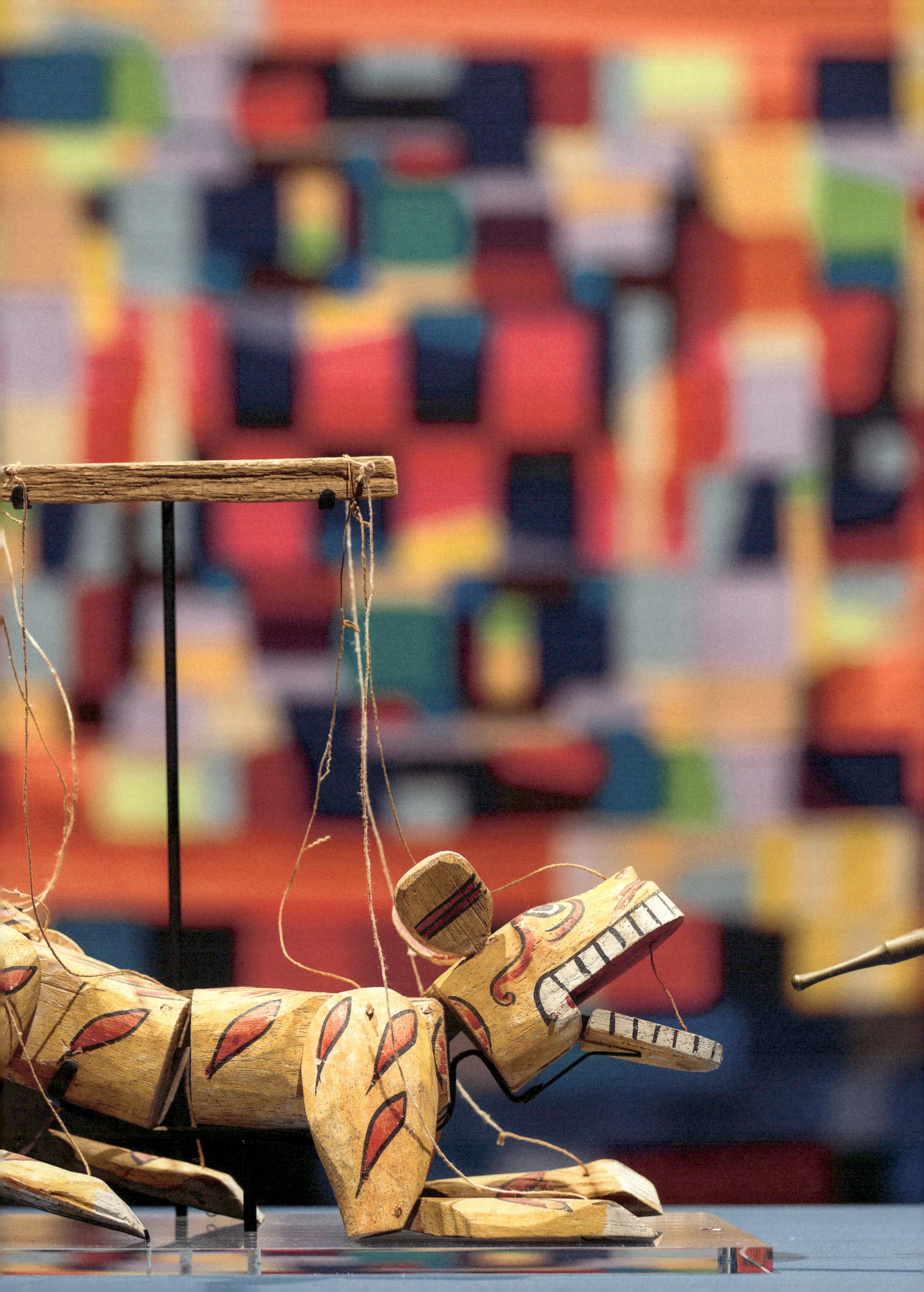

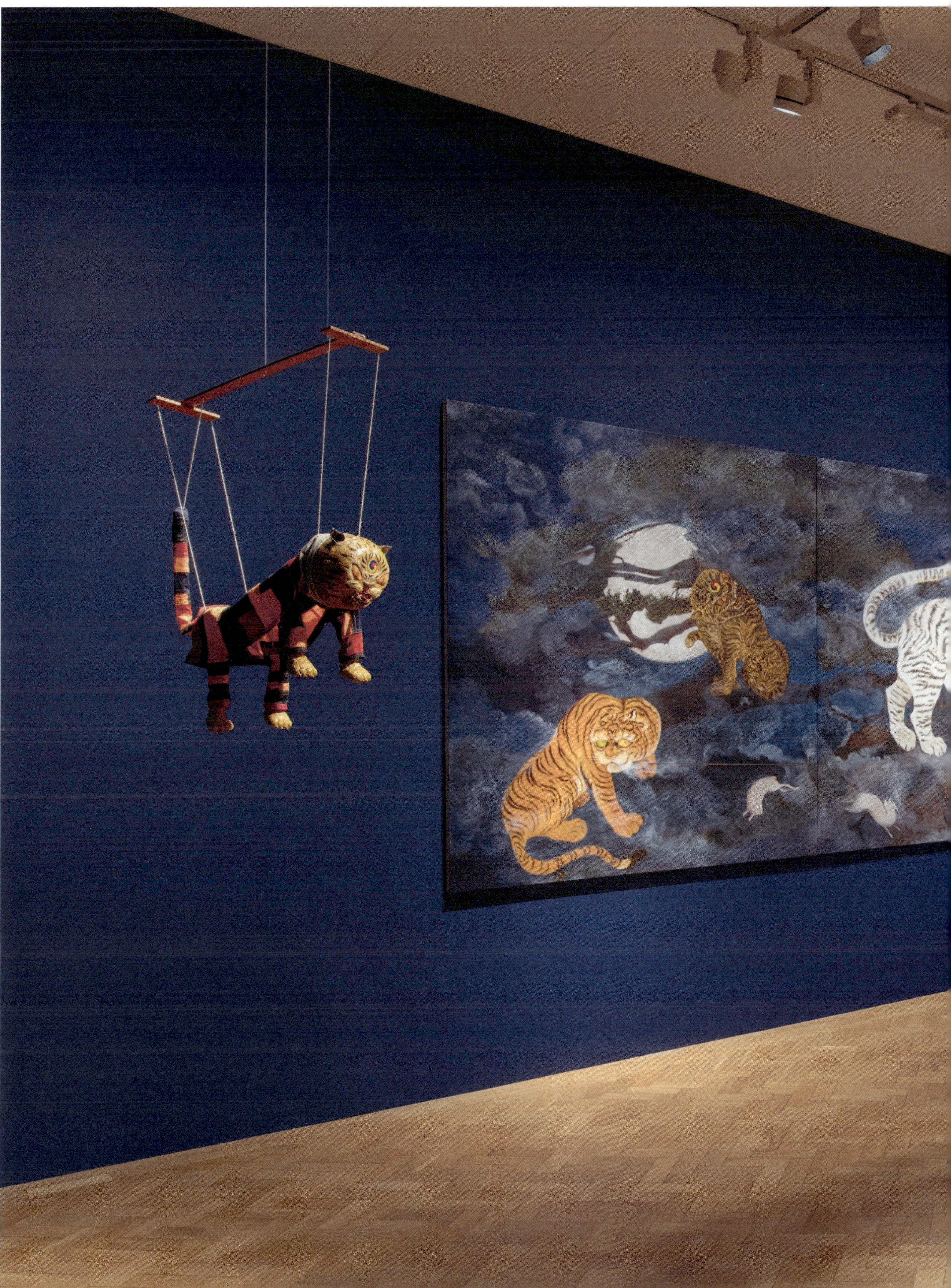

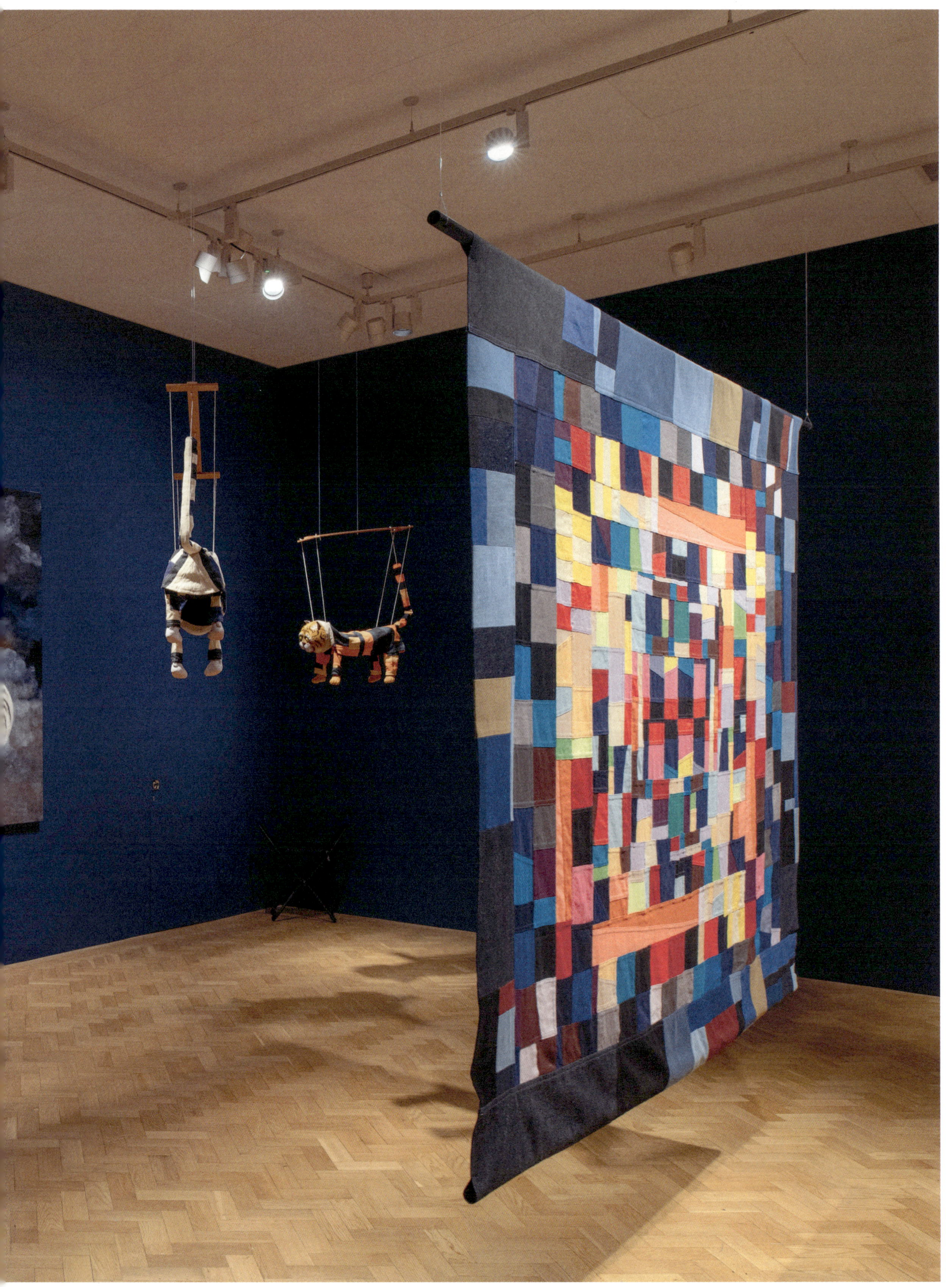

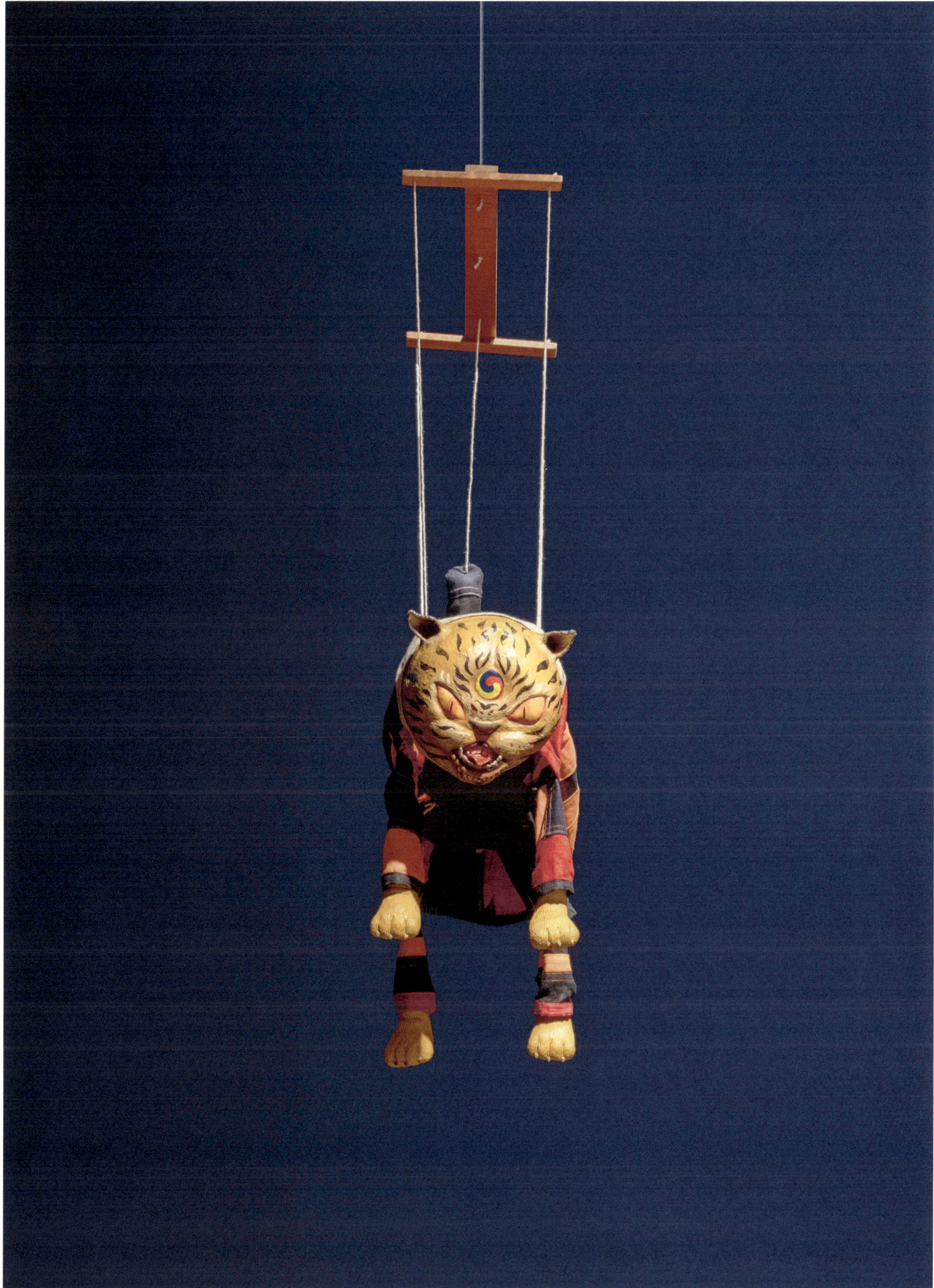

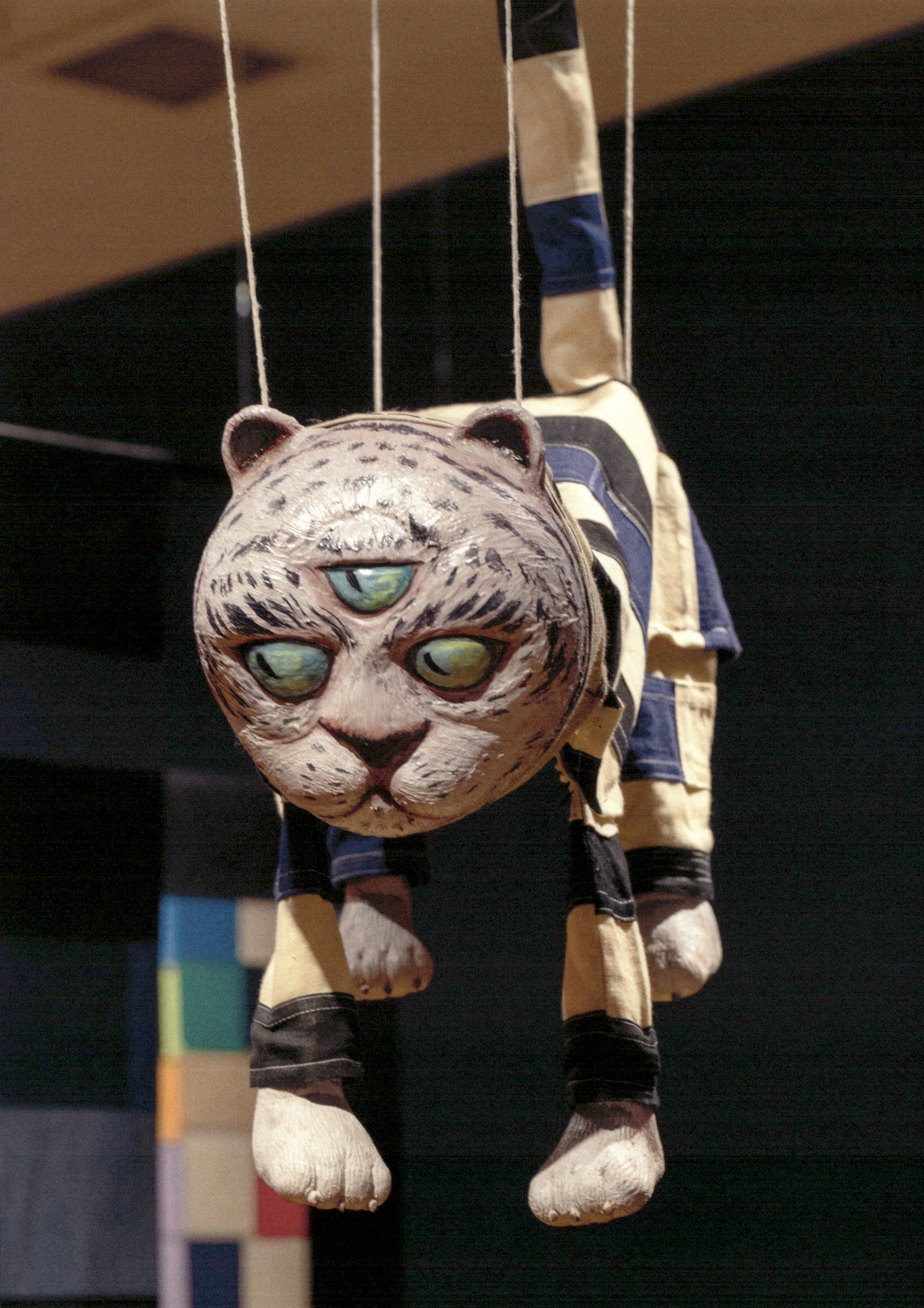

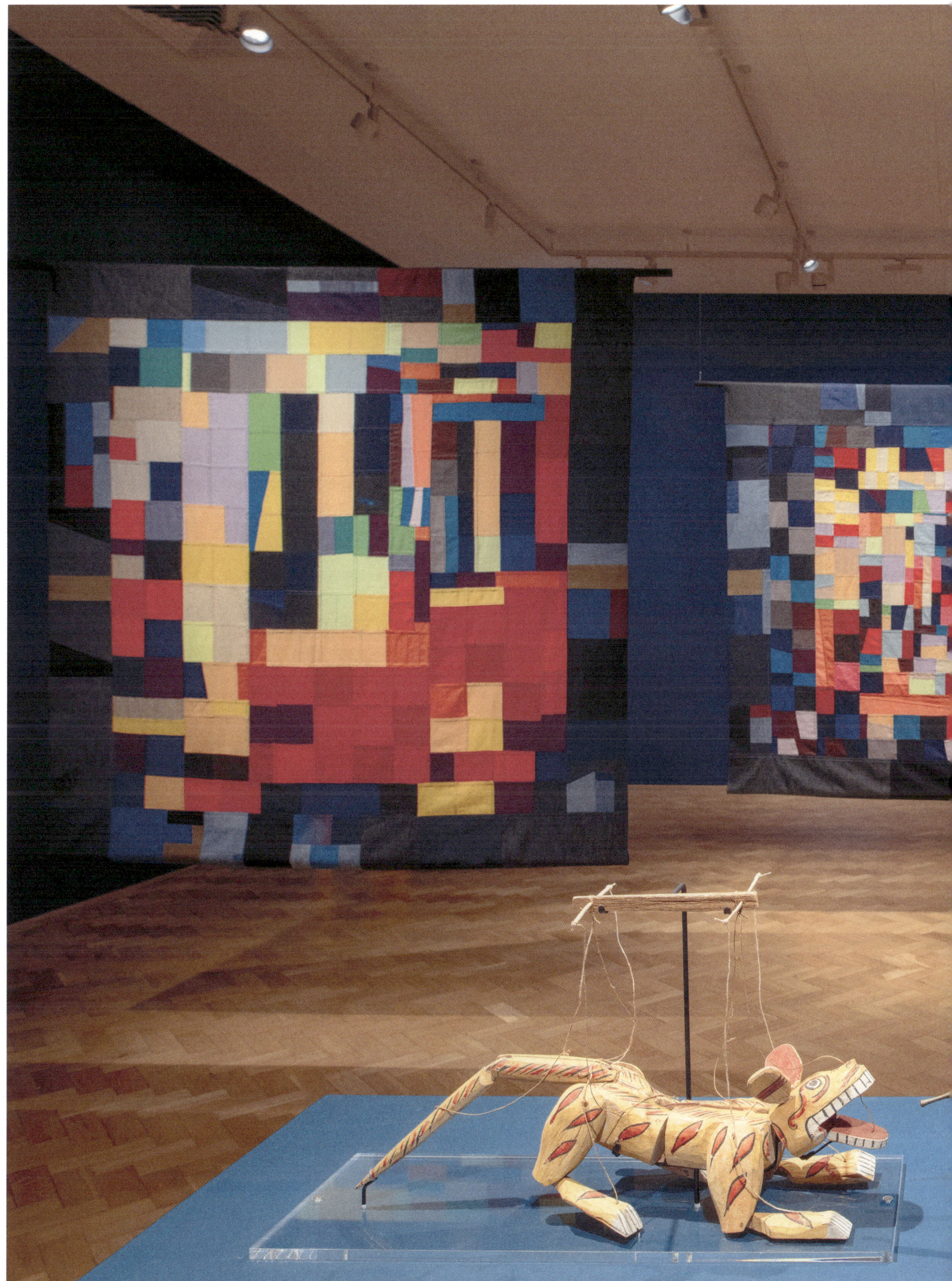

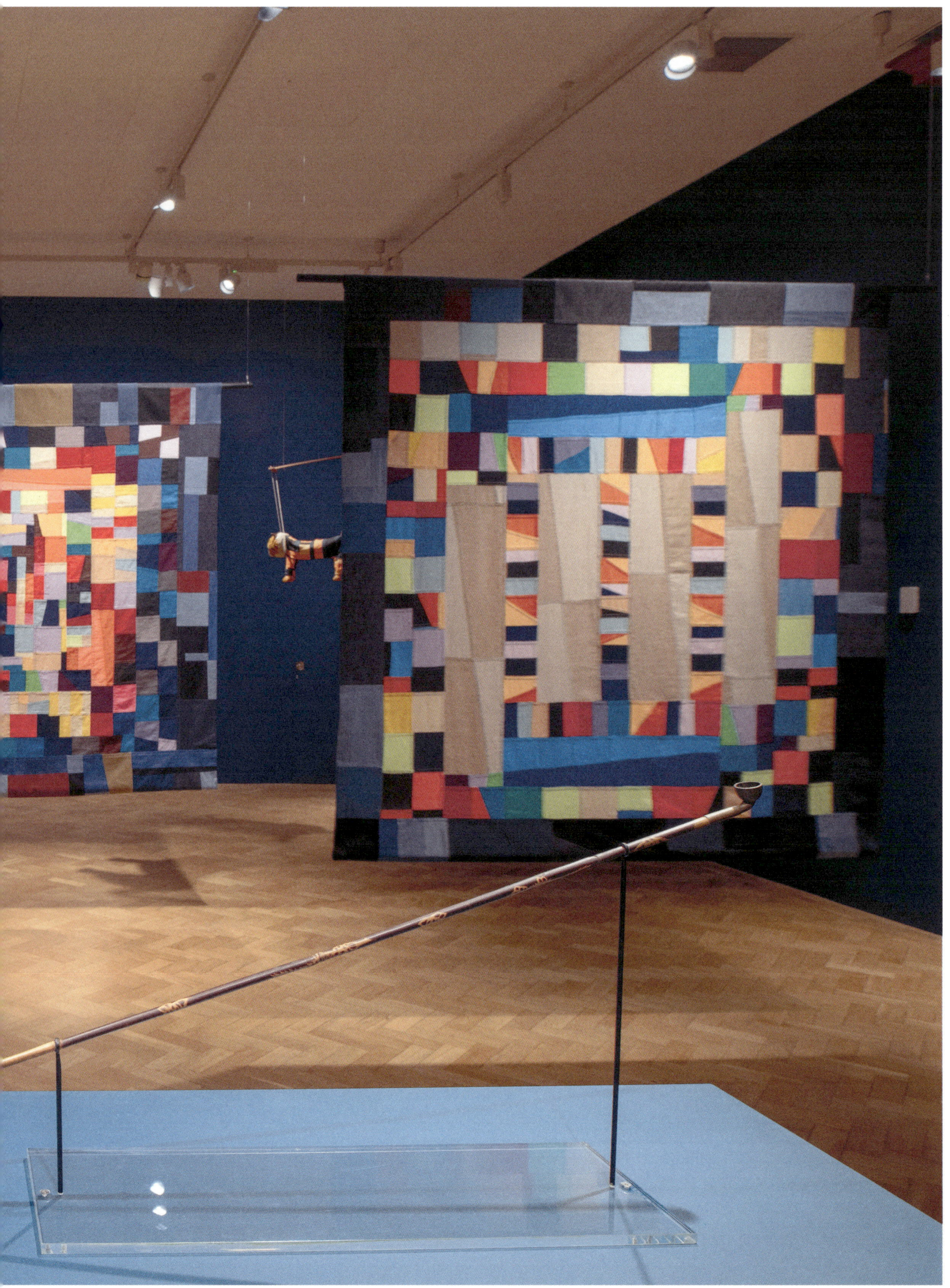

HOMEBOY 3030: *Return the Tiger 2 the Mountain*

Installation views of
HOMEBOY 3030: Return the Tiger 2 the Mountain,
Union Pacific Gallery, London, UK, 2018

Works included:

Bio Enhanced/Hiero Advanced:
The Genius of Gene Jupiter, 2018
Hand-sewn and machine-stitched assorted
fabrics and synthetic hair on bamboo
166 × 170 cm

91 Chyzanthemumz 4 Imsook, 2018
Hand-sewn and machine-stitched
assorted fabrics, mother of pearl buttons,
faux fur and synthetic hair, bamboo
165 × 169 cm

The Re-Up of Yung Yoomi:
Hell Fire Can't Scortch Me, 2018
Hand-sewn and machine-stitched
assorted fabrics, faux fur
and synthetic hair on bamboo
188 × 210 cm

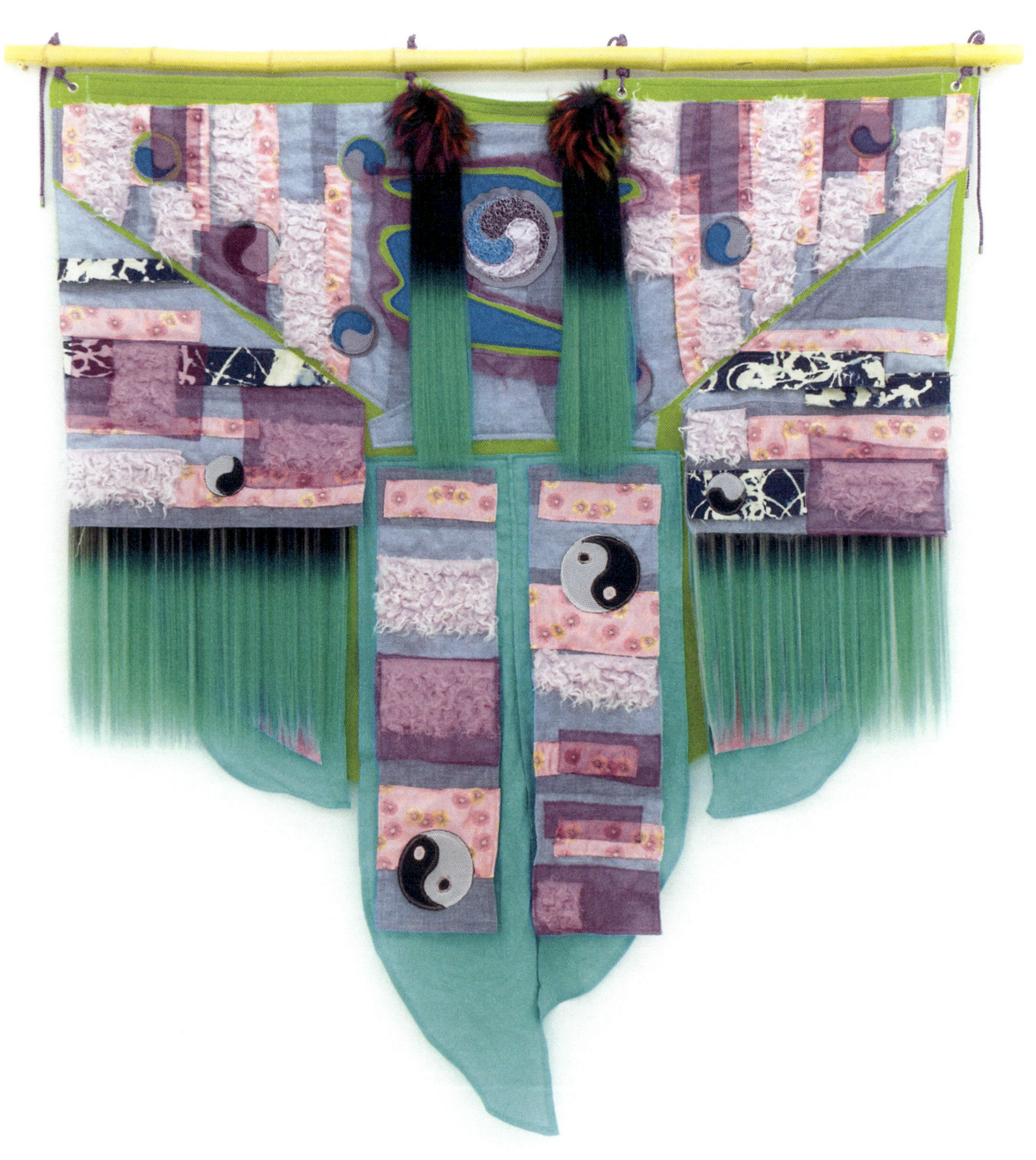

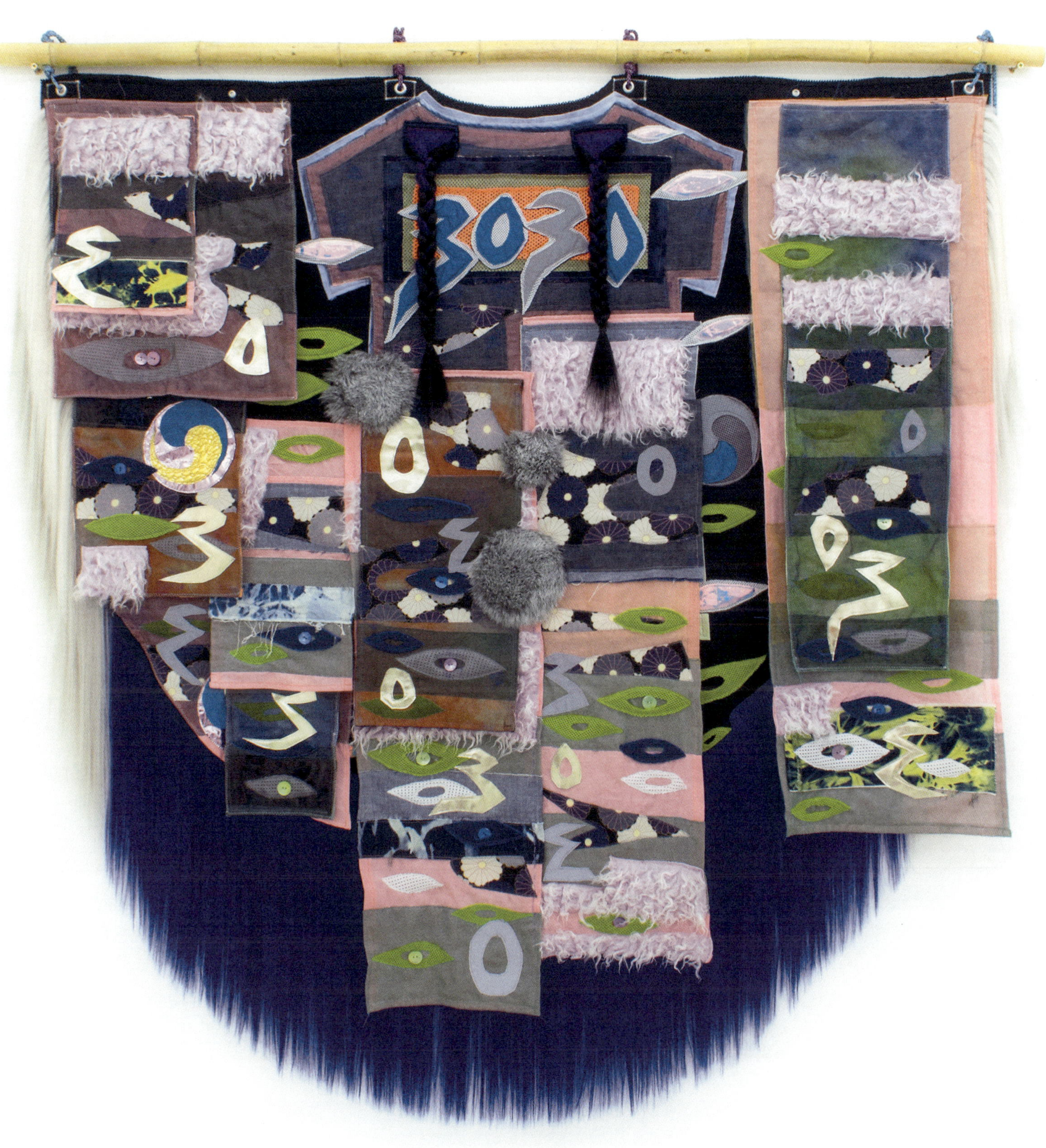

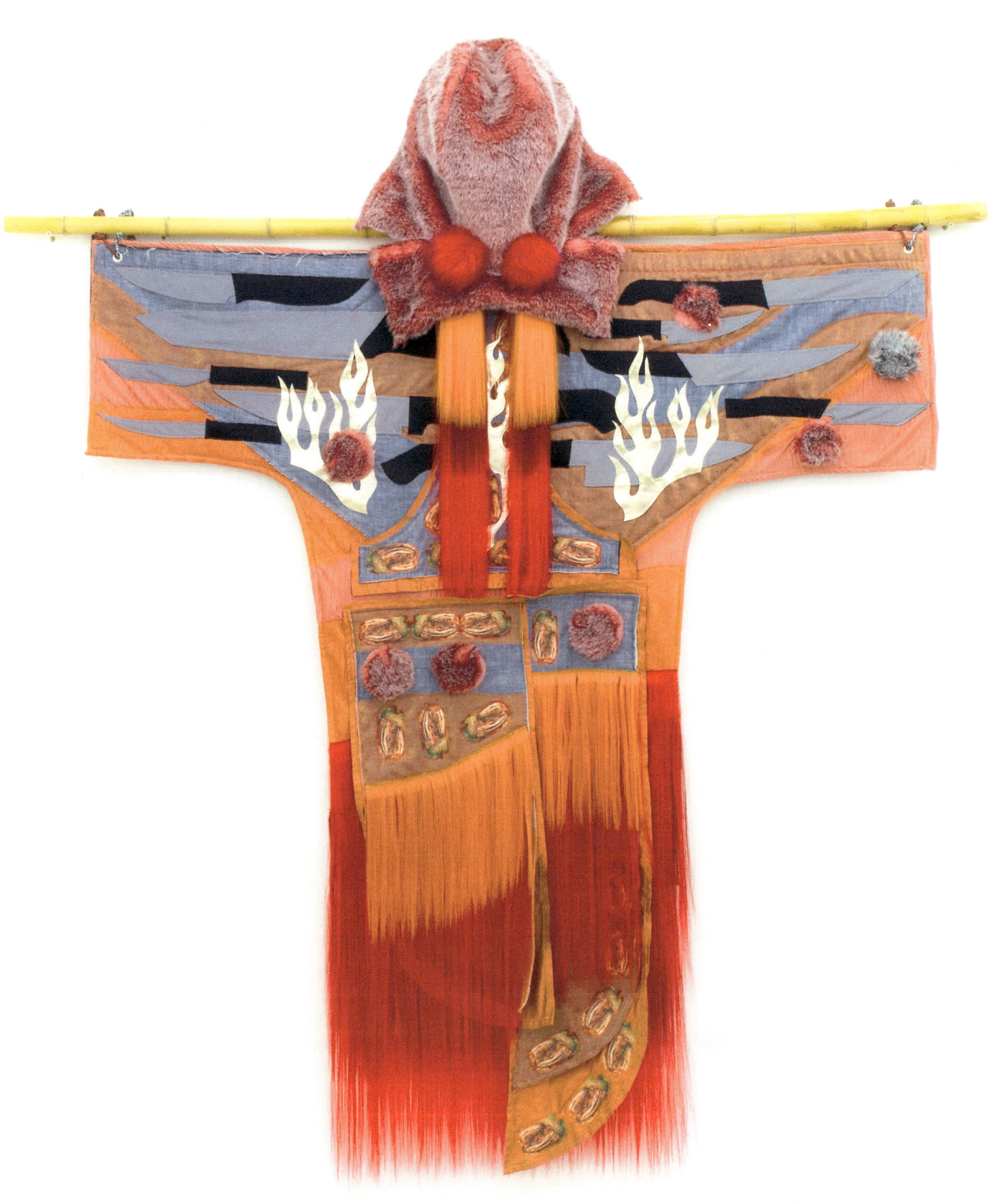

*Child
of Magohalmi
and
the Echoes
of Creation*

Child of Magohalmi and the Echoes of Creation,
portrait of the artist, 2020

Installation views of
Child of Magohalmi and the Echoes of Creation, Tramway, Glasgow, UK, 2019
and De La Warr Pavilion, Bexhill-on-Sea, UK, 2020

Co-commissioned by Art Night, London, UK; YARAT Contemporary Art Space, Baku,
Azerbaijan; Tramway, Glasgow, UK and De La Warr Pavilion, Bexhill-on-Sea, UK

Works included:

*Child of Magohalmi and the Echoes
of Creation*, 2020
Single-channel HD video
50:21 mins

*Barnacles and Kelp Beneath Sea Salt //
An Homage to my Ancestors*, 2019
in collaboration with Benito Mayor Vallejo
Oil on canvas, hand dyed and
bleached denim
330 × 260 cm

*In the belly of our Grandmothers through
the eyes of an Orca (Sojourn through
Saju across the Salish Sea)*, 2020
in collaboration with Benito Mayor Vallejo
Oil on canvas with hand-sewn and
machine-stitched fabrics, assorted buttons,
shells and drift wood
236 × 150 cm

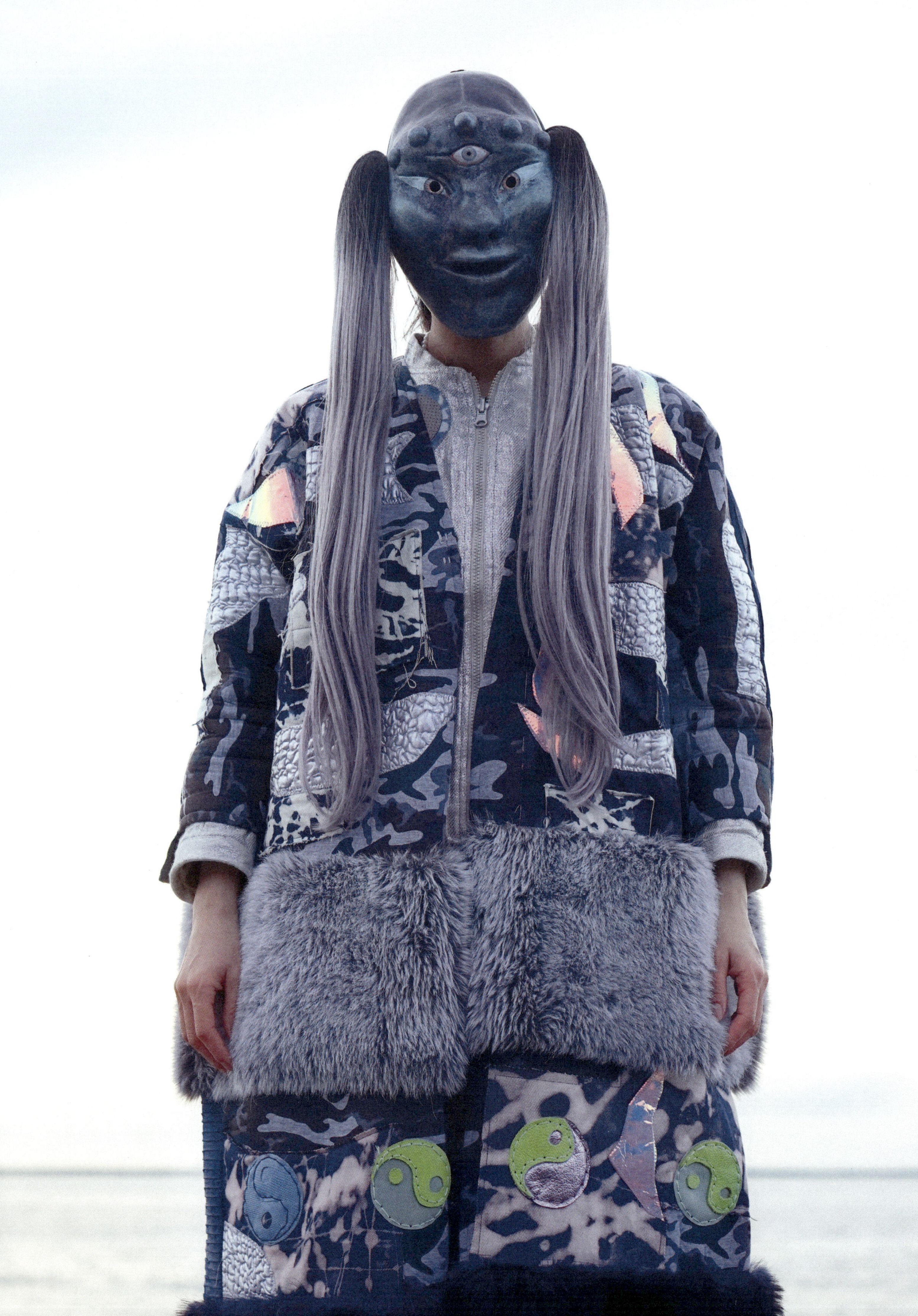

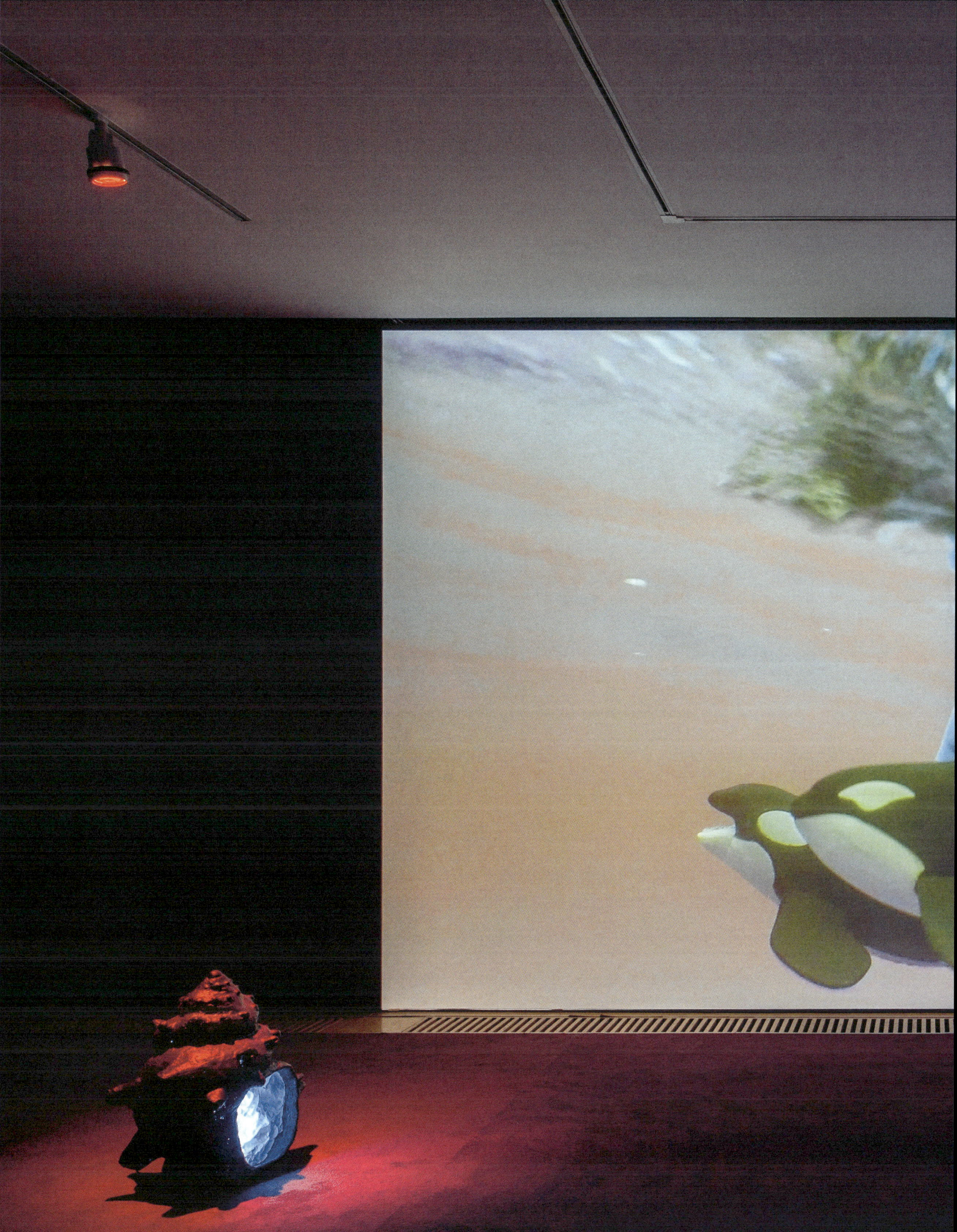

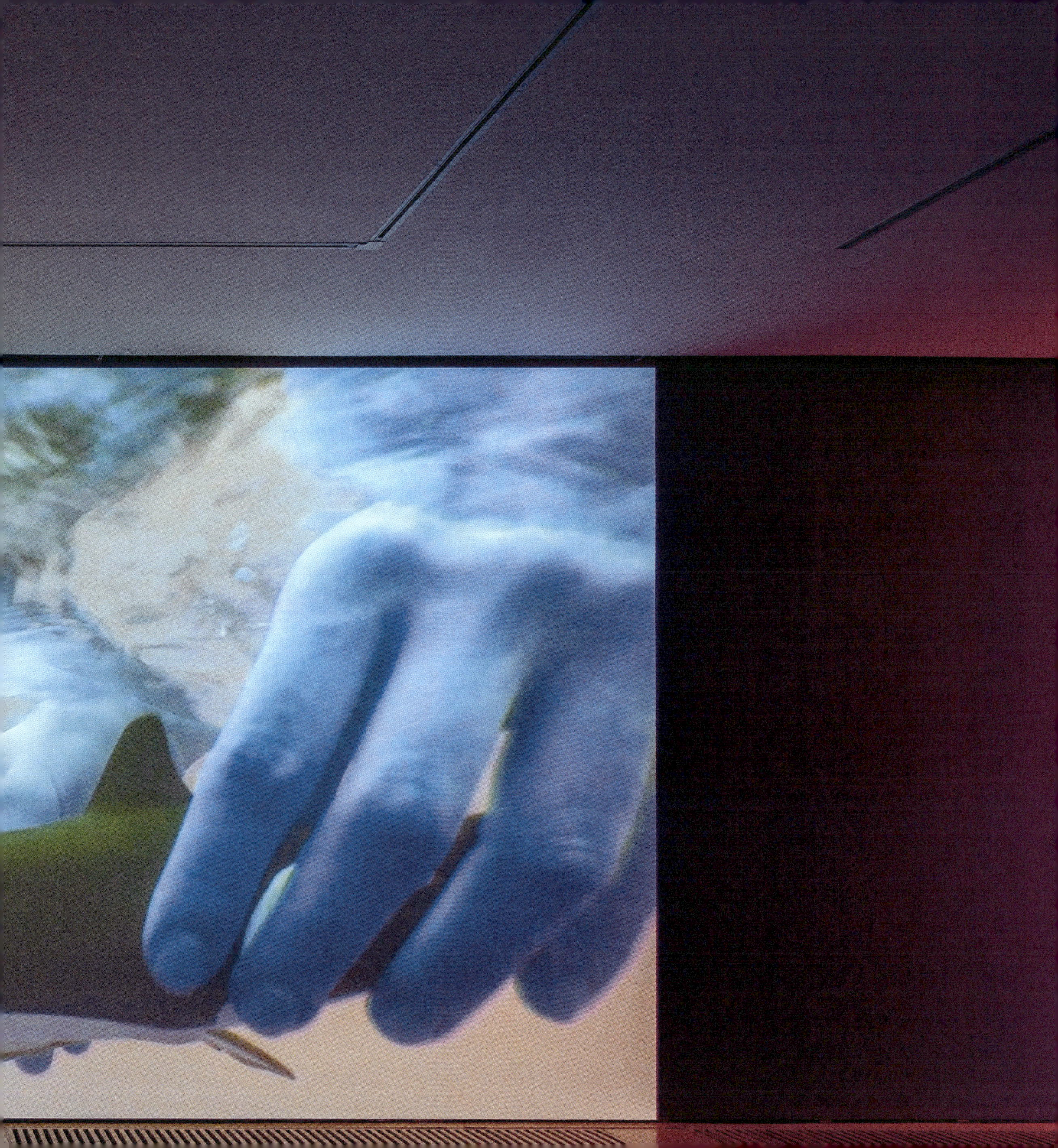

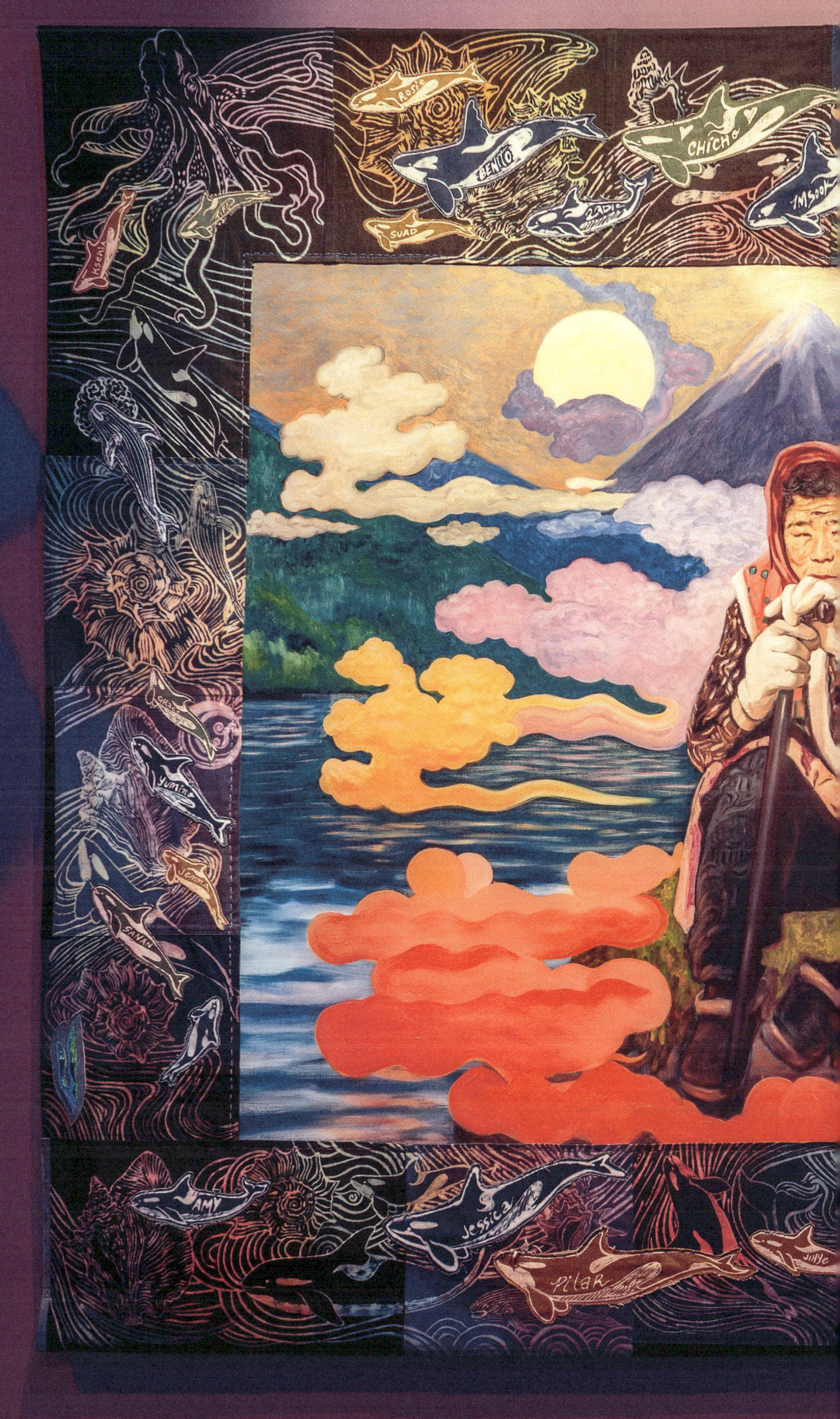

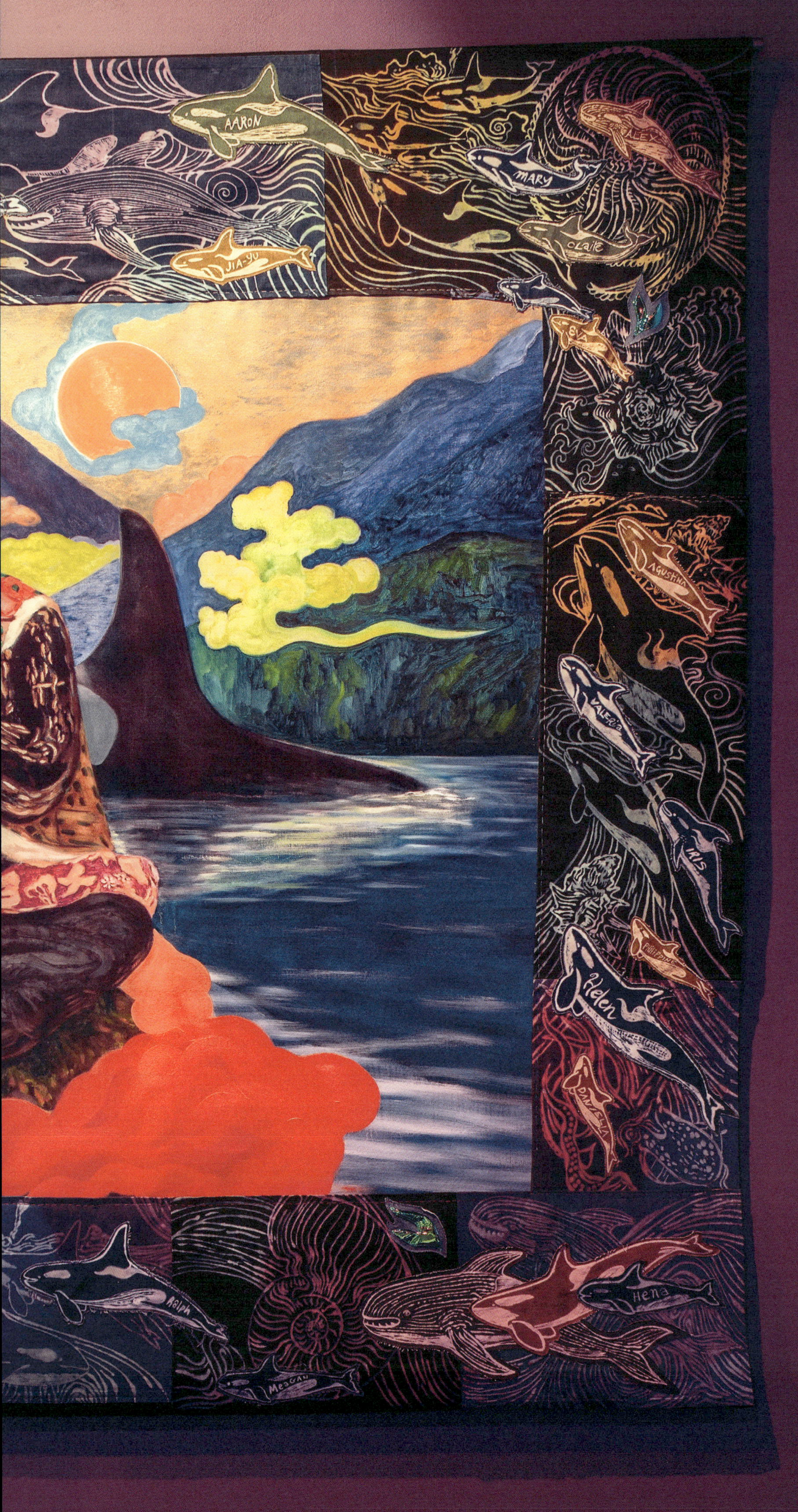

AARON
JIA-YU
MARY
CLAIR
AGUSTINA
VALERI
IRIS
HELEN
RALPH
MORGAN
HENA

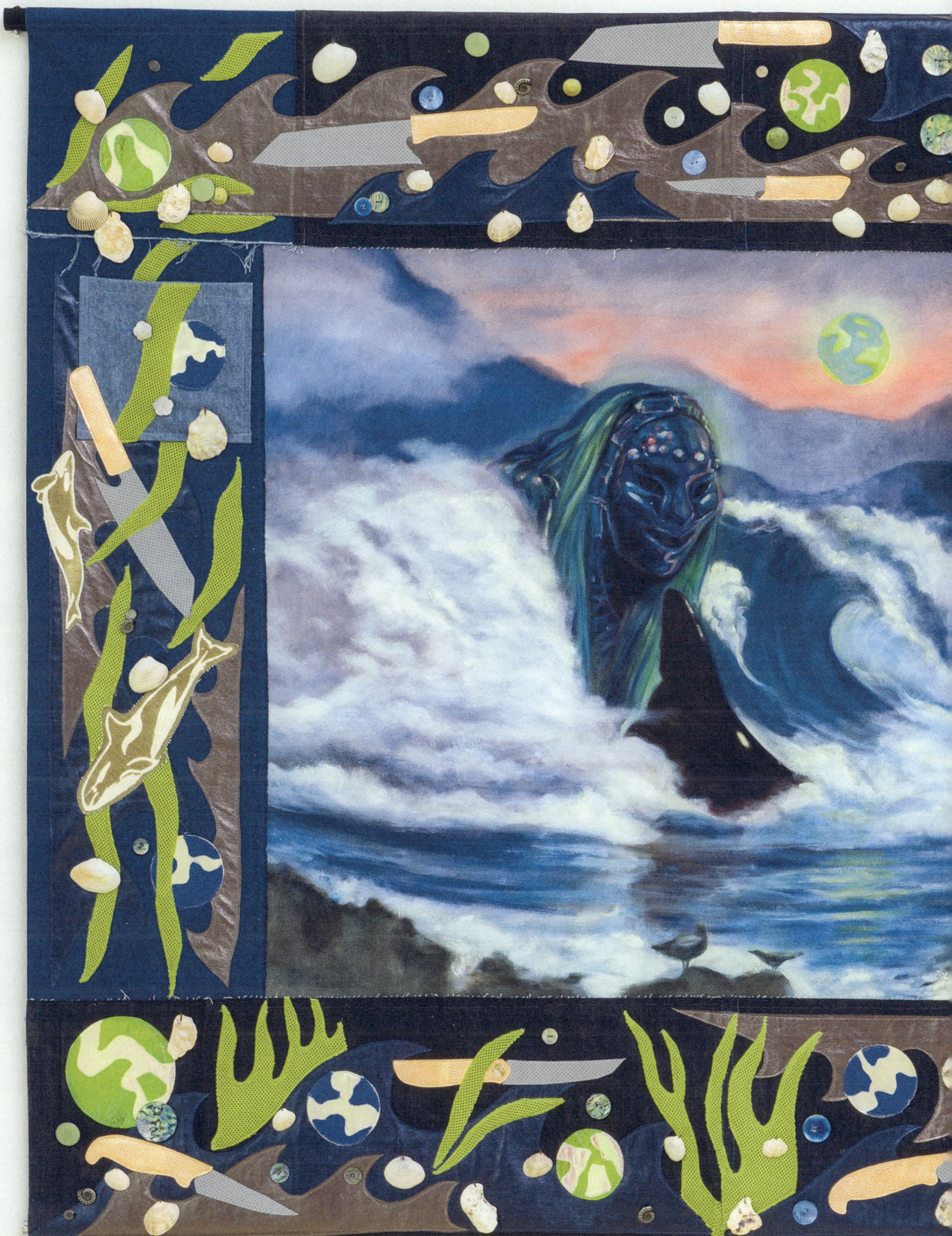

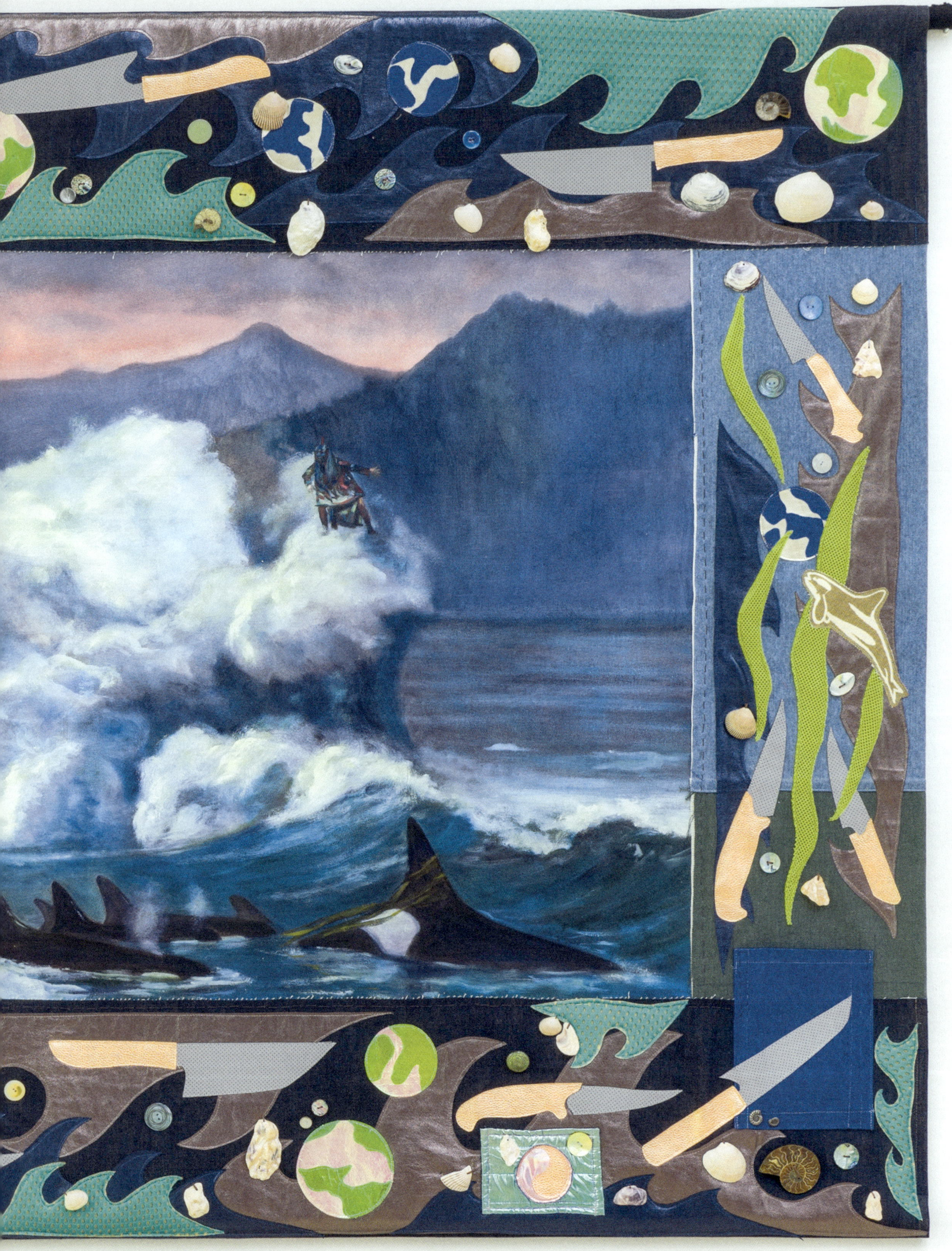

House
Spirits

Installation views of
Hernan Bas & Zadie Xa: House Spirits,
Jessica Silverman, San Francisco, CA, USA, 2022

Works included:

Vancouver Sunset, 2022
Machine-stitched linen and denim
195 × 203 cm

*House gods, animal guides: Halmoni
(Grandmother)*, 2022
in collaboration with Benito Mayor Vallejo
Acrylic on polylactic acid filament,
polymer resin, linen, string and wood
73 × 56 × 56 cm approx.

Seven full moons, 2022
Machine-stitched linen and denim
211 × 208.5 cm

*House gods, animal guides:
Horangi (Tiger)*, 2022
in collaboration with Benito Mayor Vallejo
Acrylic on polylactic acid filament,
polymer resin, linen, string and wood
73 × 56 × 56 cm approx.

Kimchi rites, kitchen rituals, 2022
Machine-stitched fabric,
photo-printed cotton on hand-dyed linen
126 × 37 × 136 cm (when hung)

Princess Bari, 2022
Machine-stitched fabric, photo-printed
cotton, mother of pearl buttons,
on hand dyed linen
159 × 33 × 155 cm (when hung)

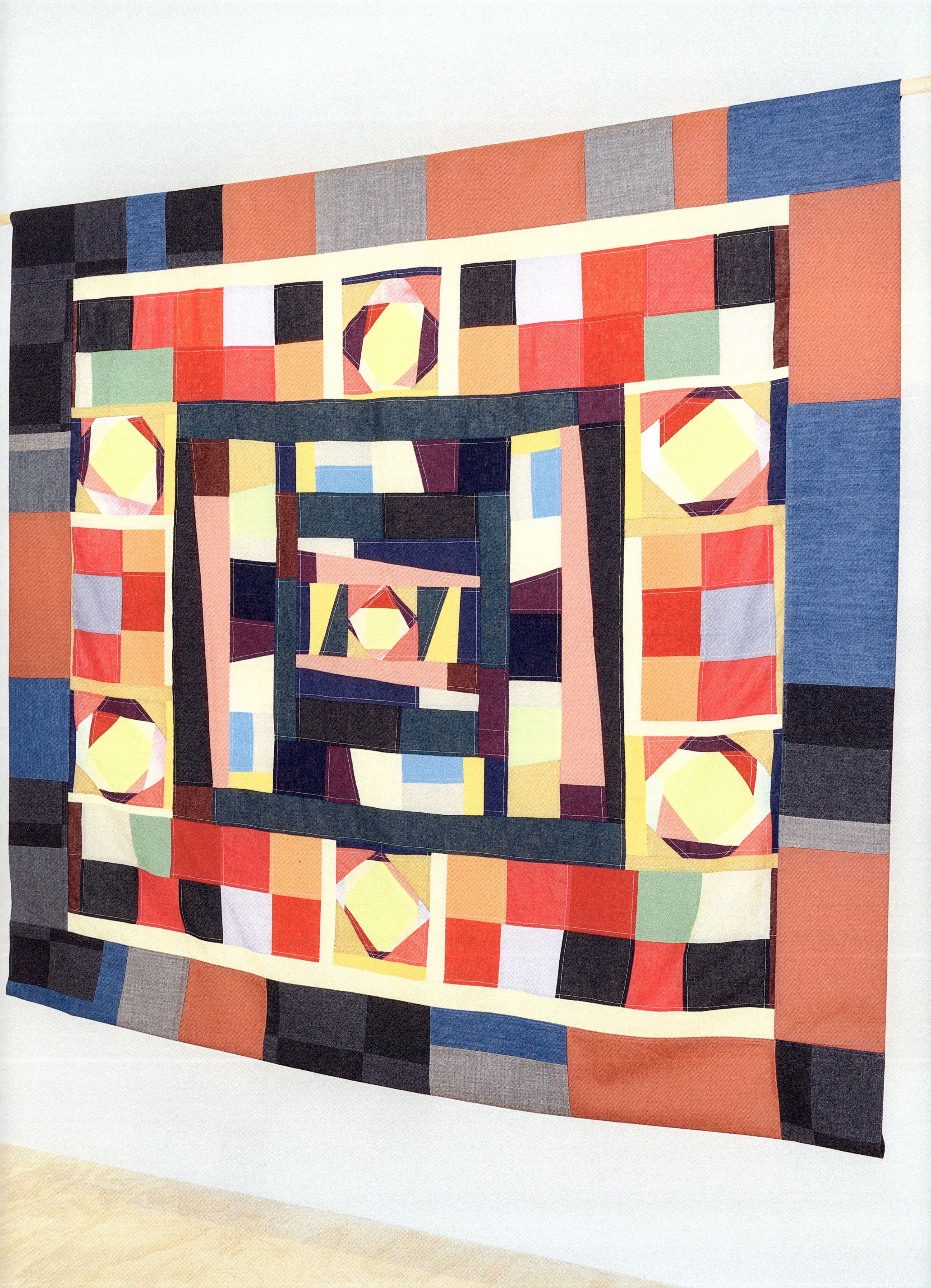

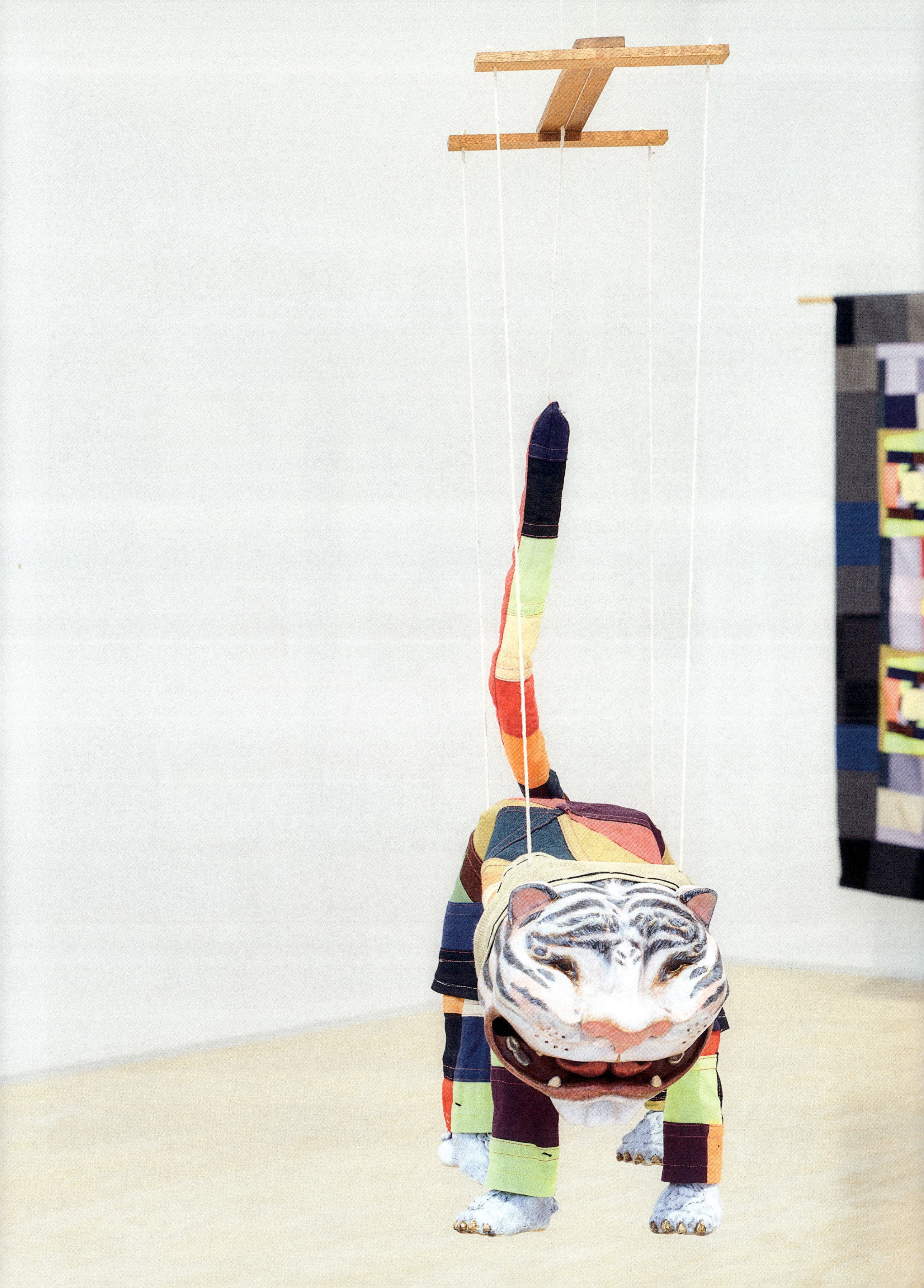

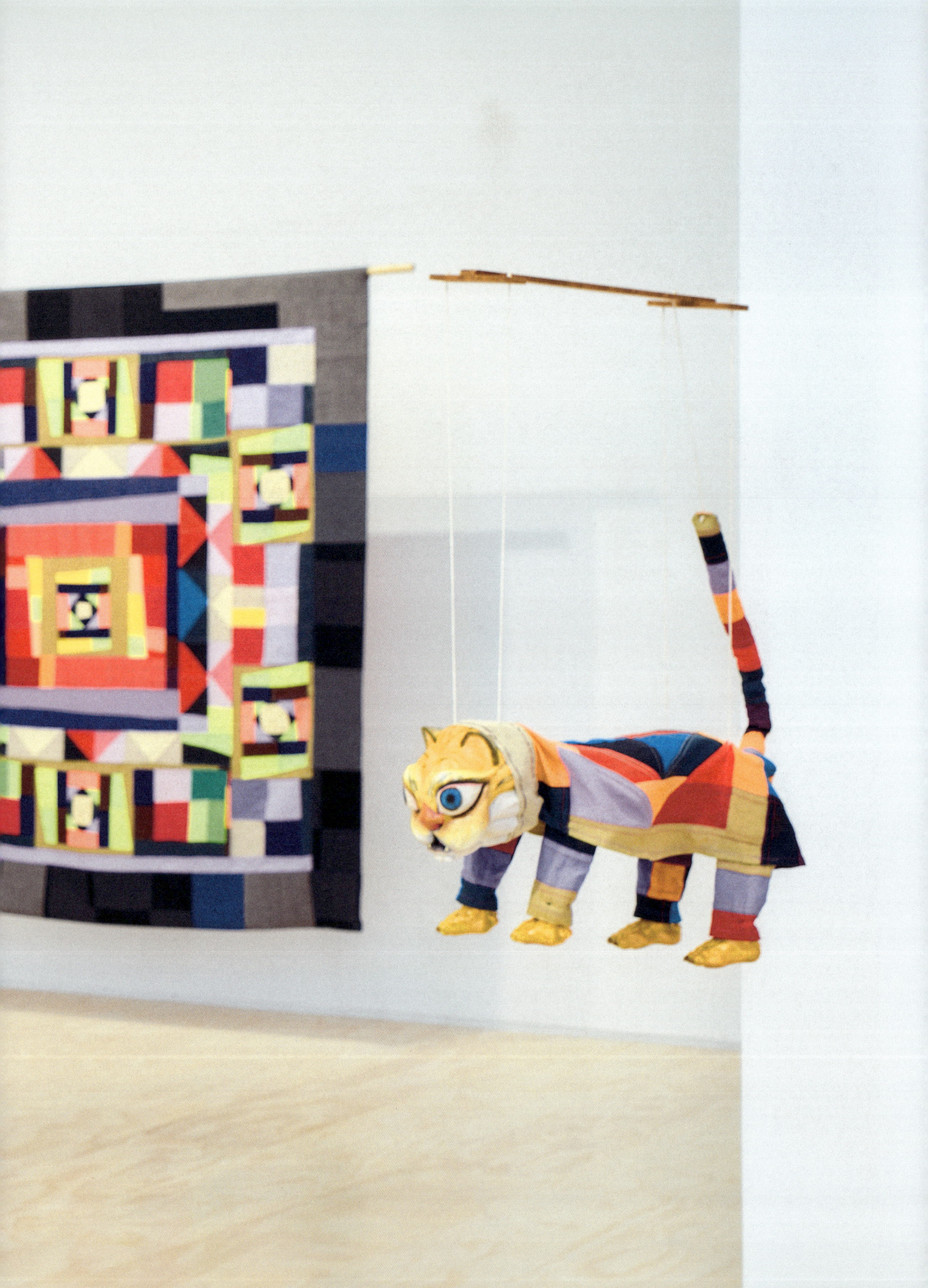

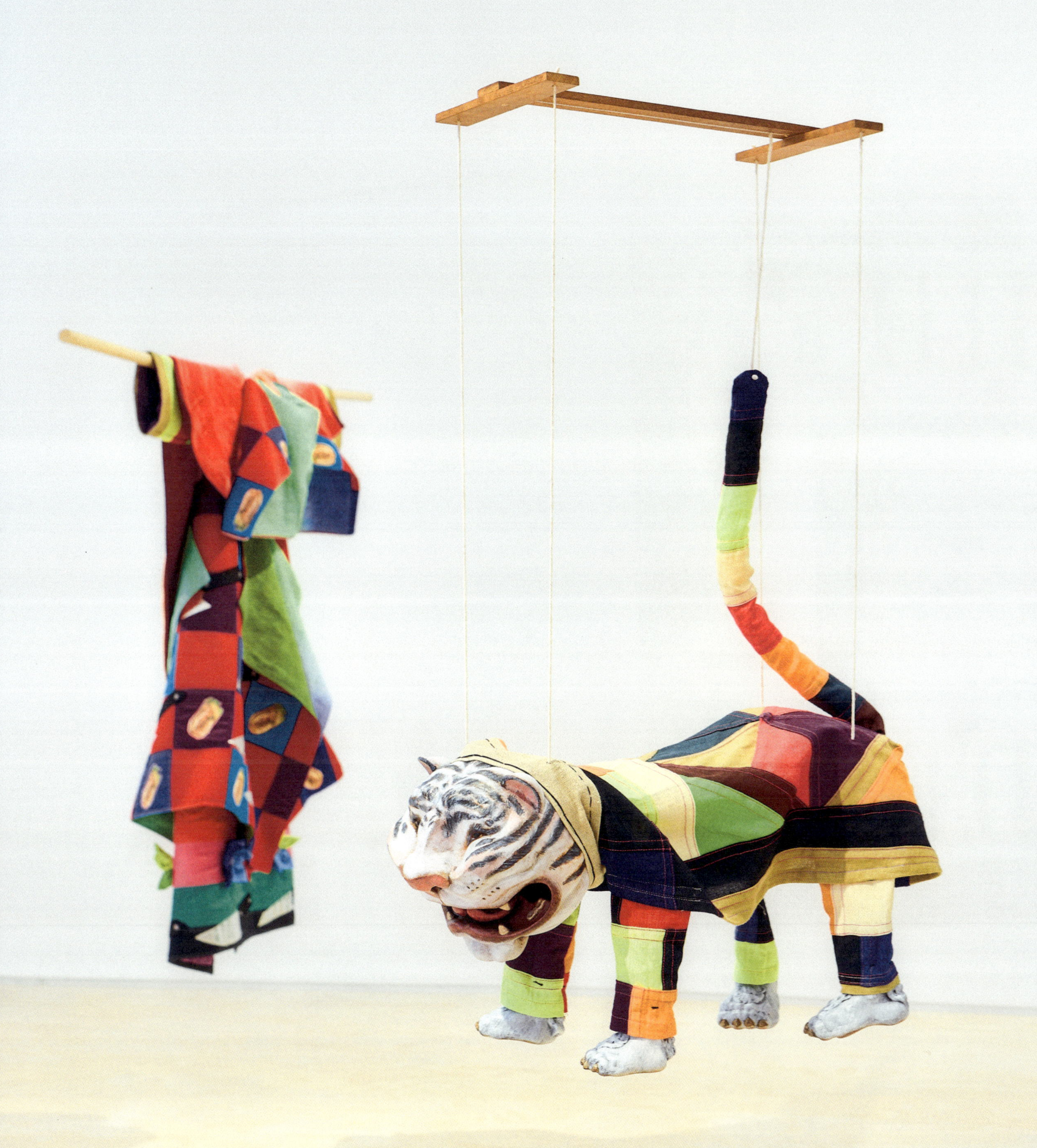

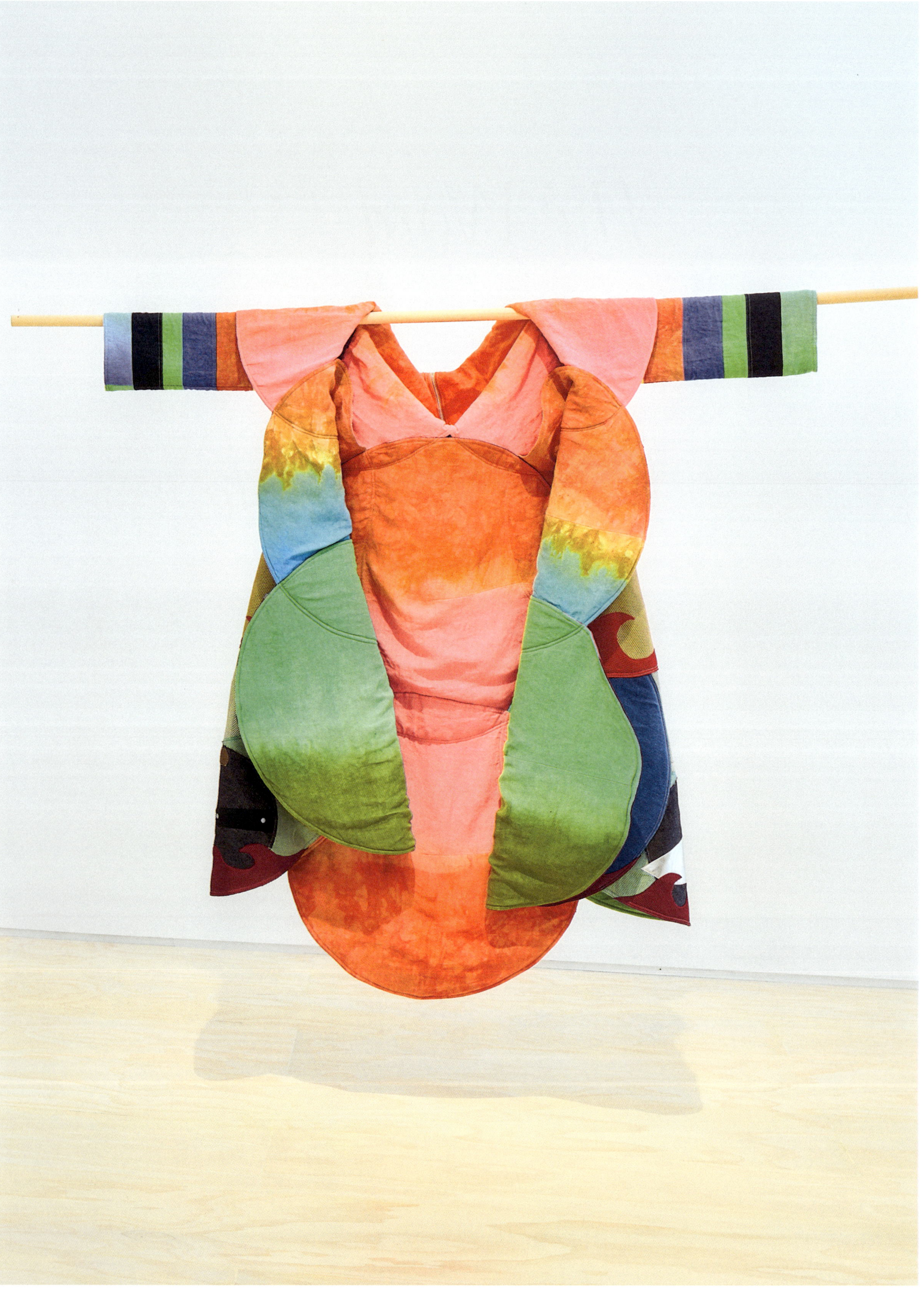

The Word for Water is Whale

The Word for Water is Whale, 2021
in collaboration with Benito Mayor Vallejo
Oil on linen
200 × 400cm

Installation view of
The Word for Water is Whale,
The 13th Shanghai Biennale: Bodies of Water,
China, 2021

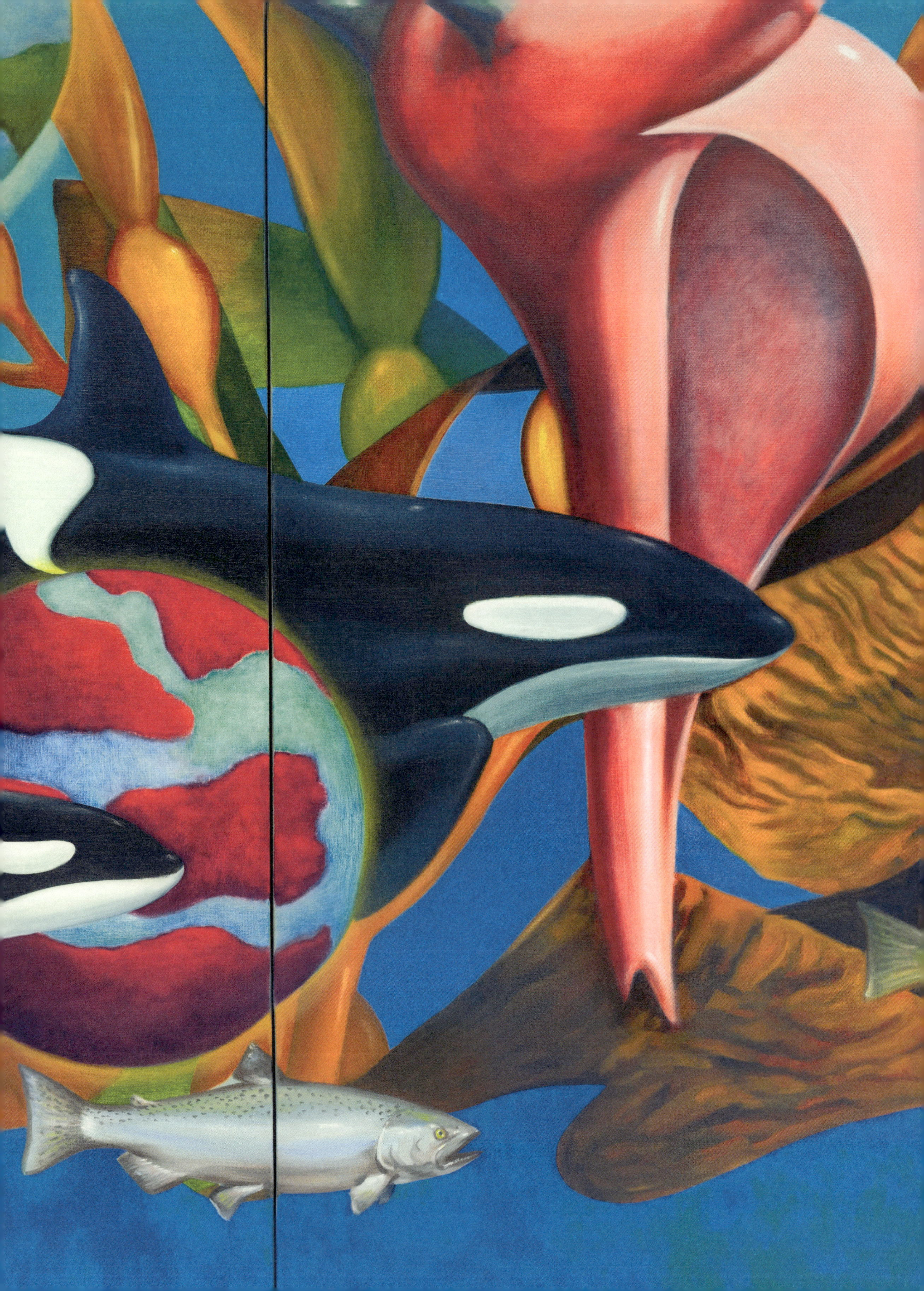

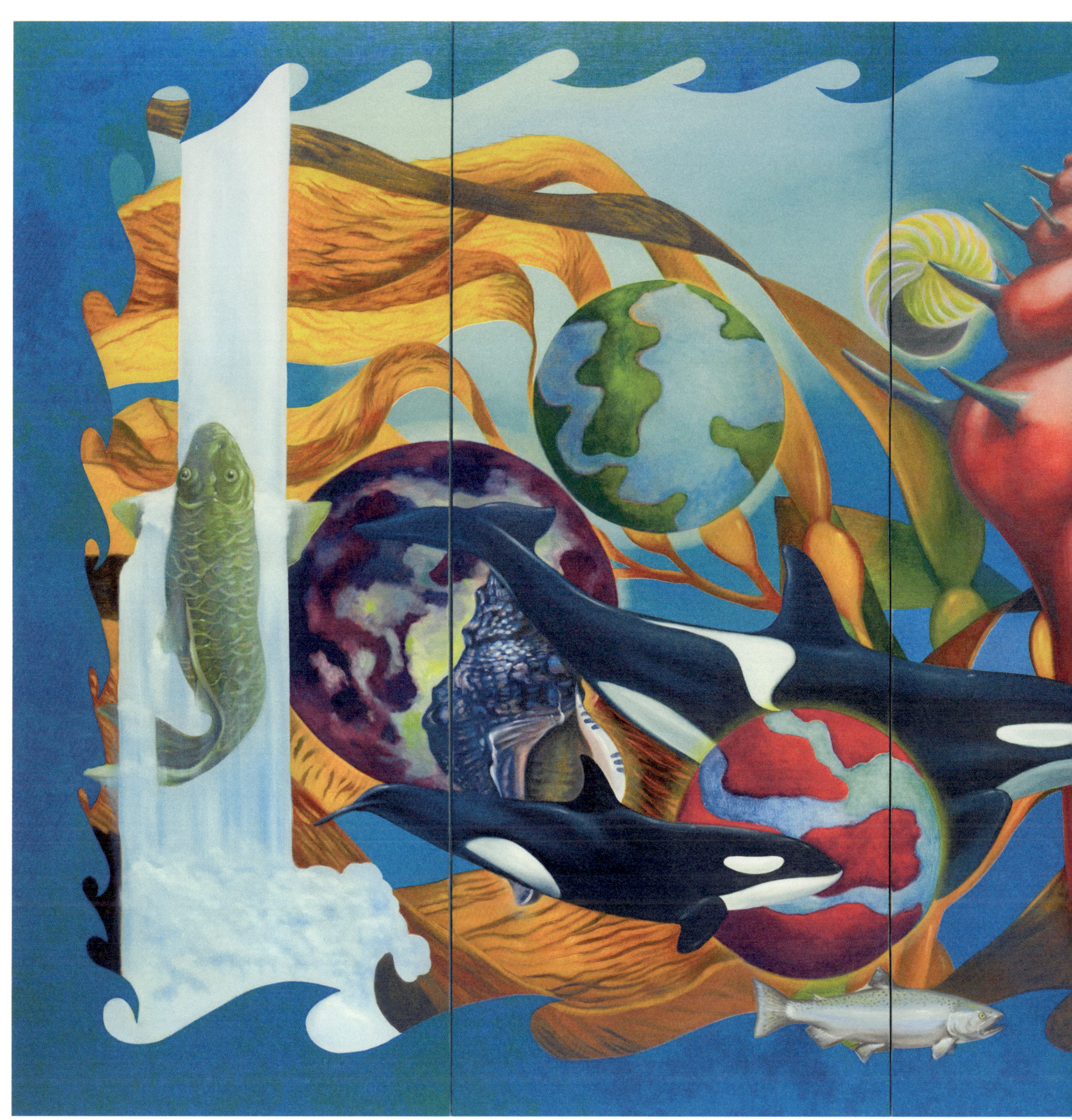

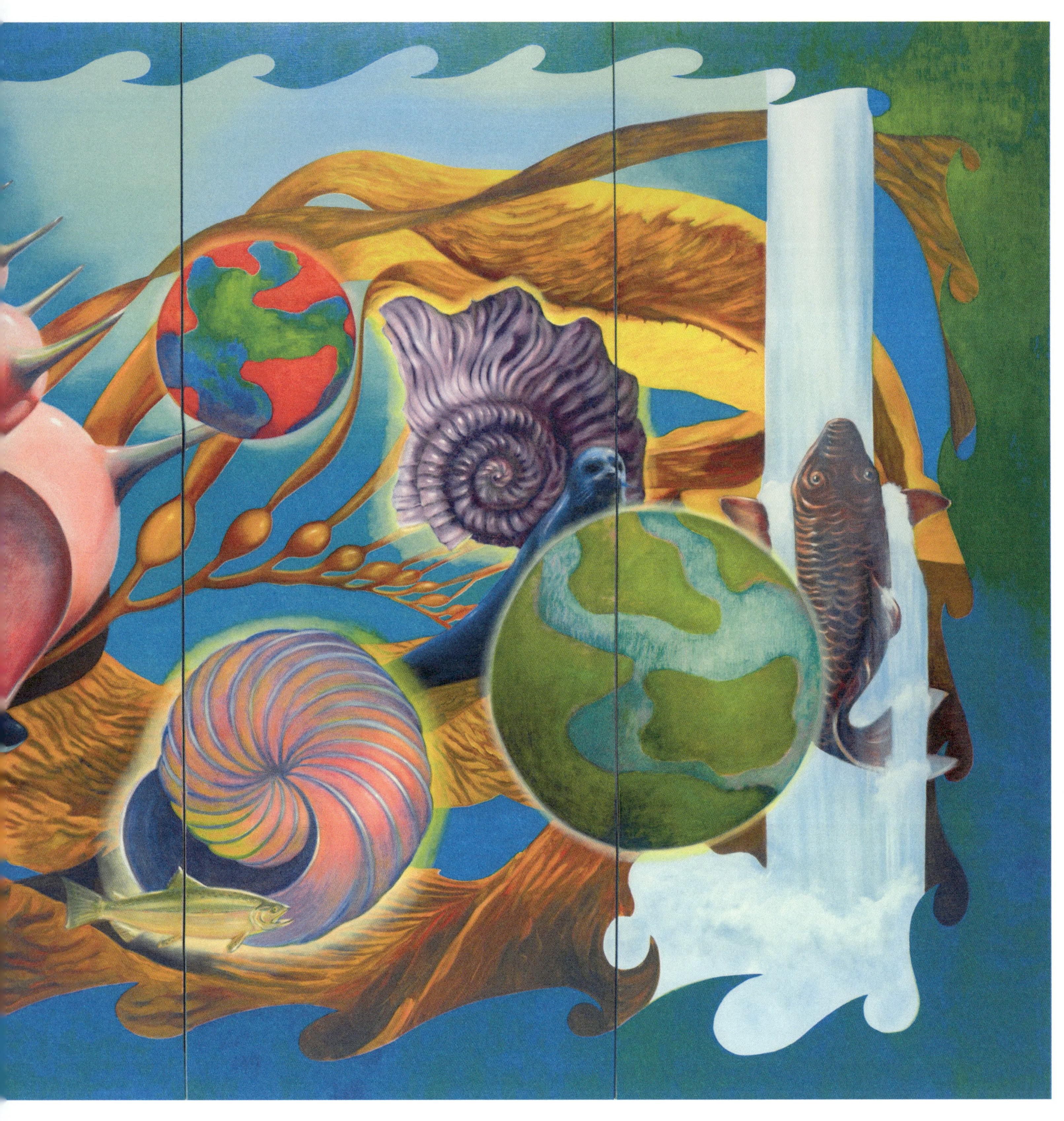

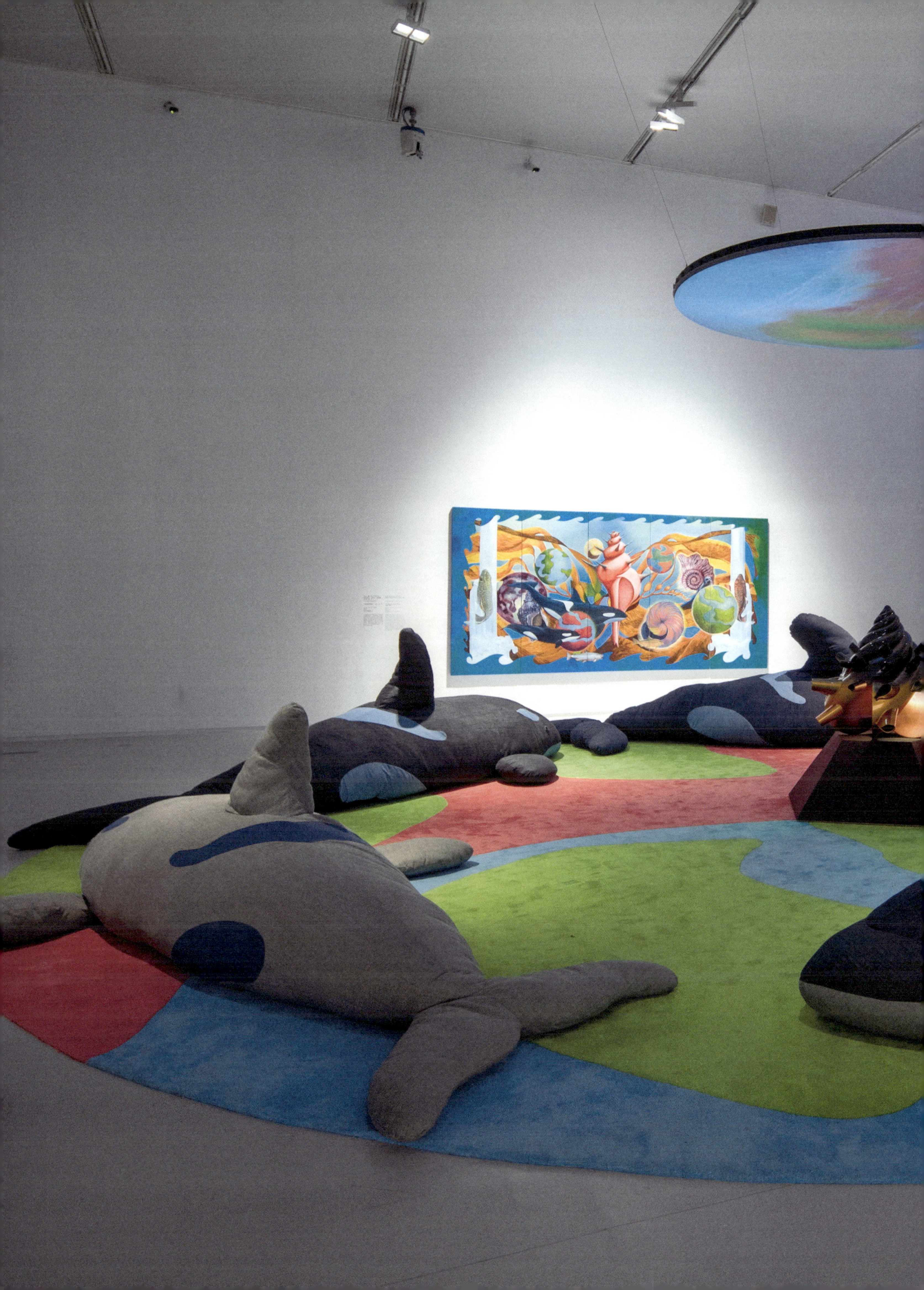

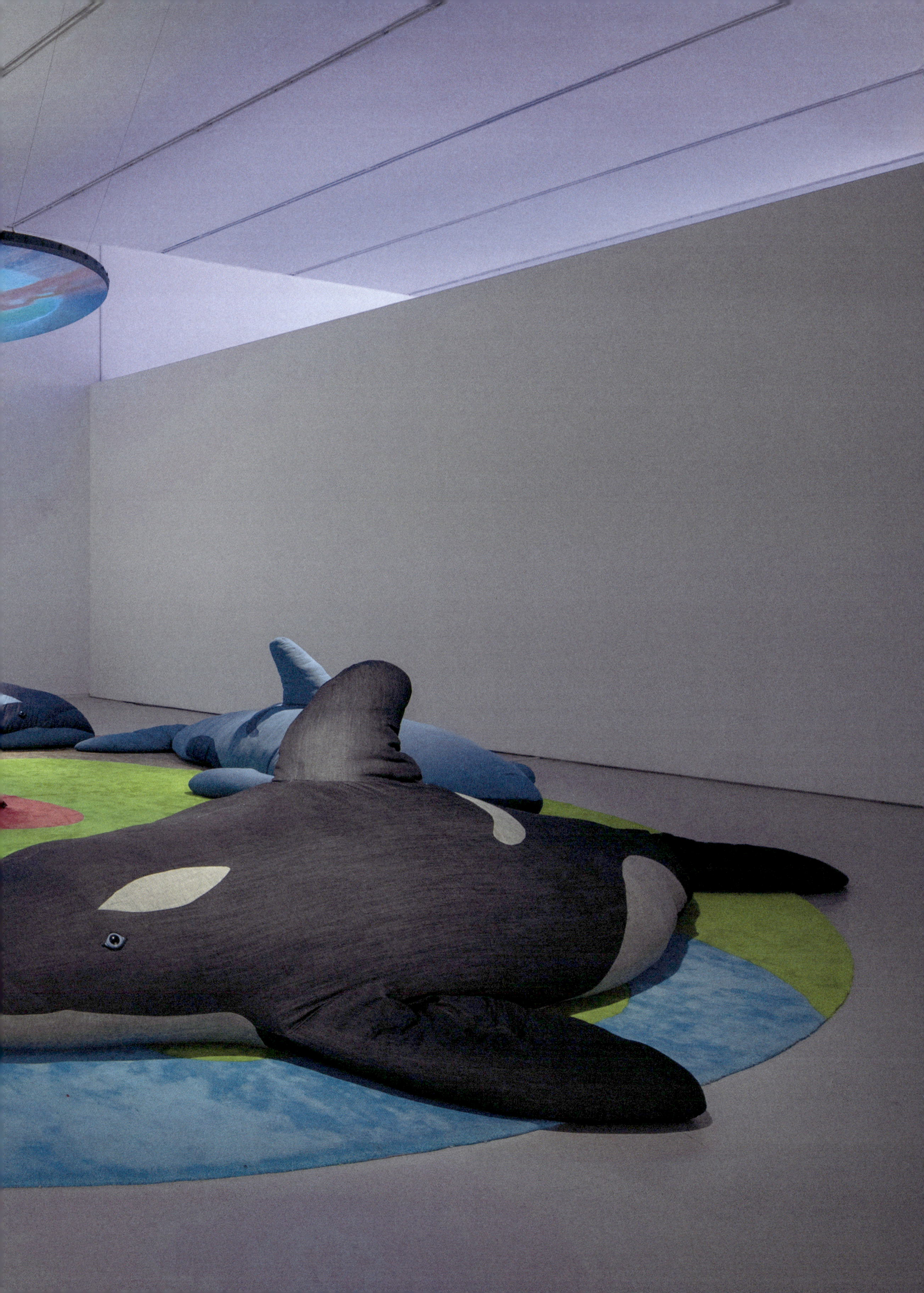

Linguistic Legacies and Lunar Exploration

Linguistic Legacies and Lunar Exploration,
live performance, Serpentine Galleries, London, UK, 2016

Masks by Benito Mayor Vallejo.
Performed by Jane Chan, Eunjun Kim, Soojin Hong,
Joonhong Min and Zadie Xa.
Choreography by Eunjung Kim.

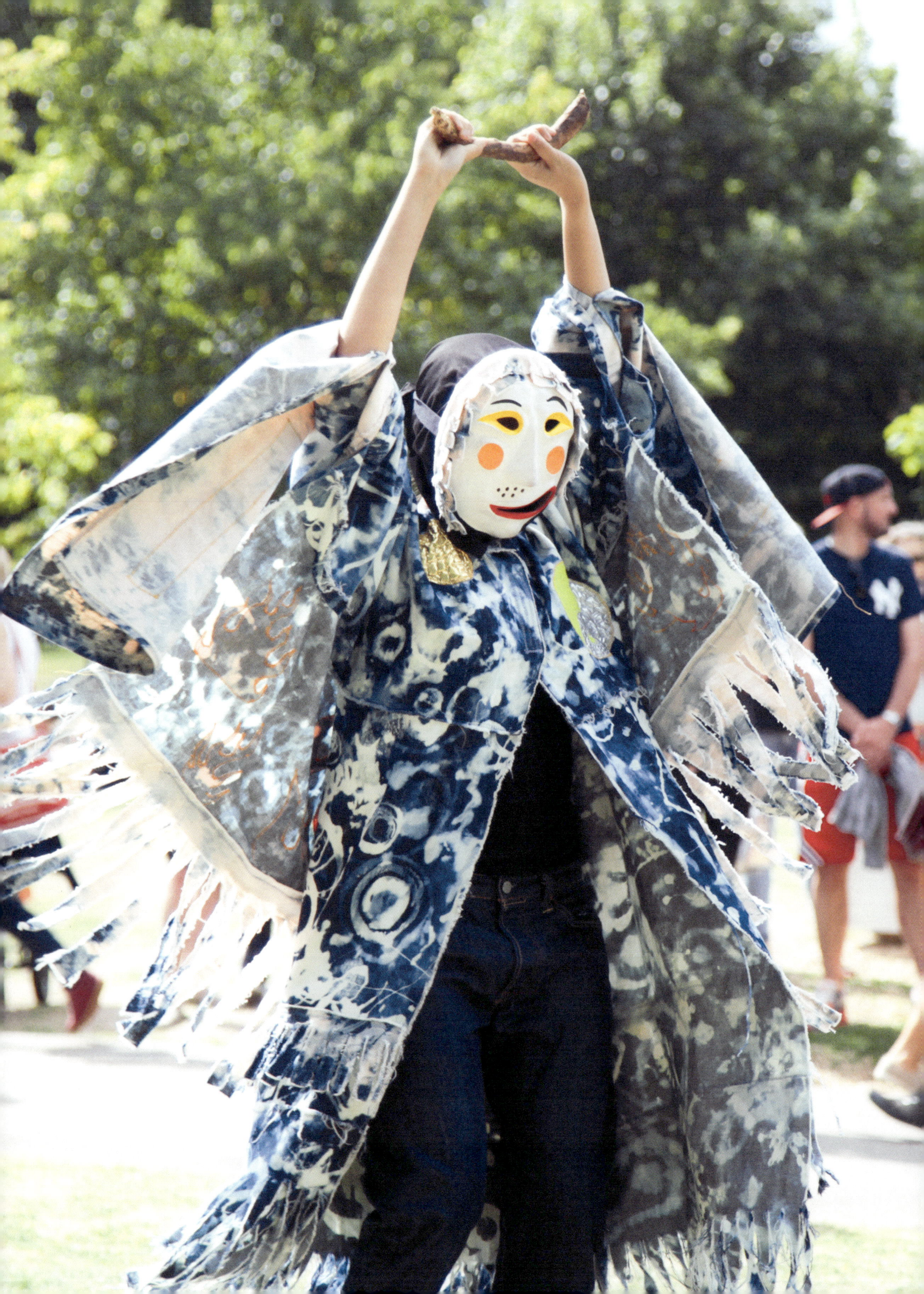

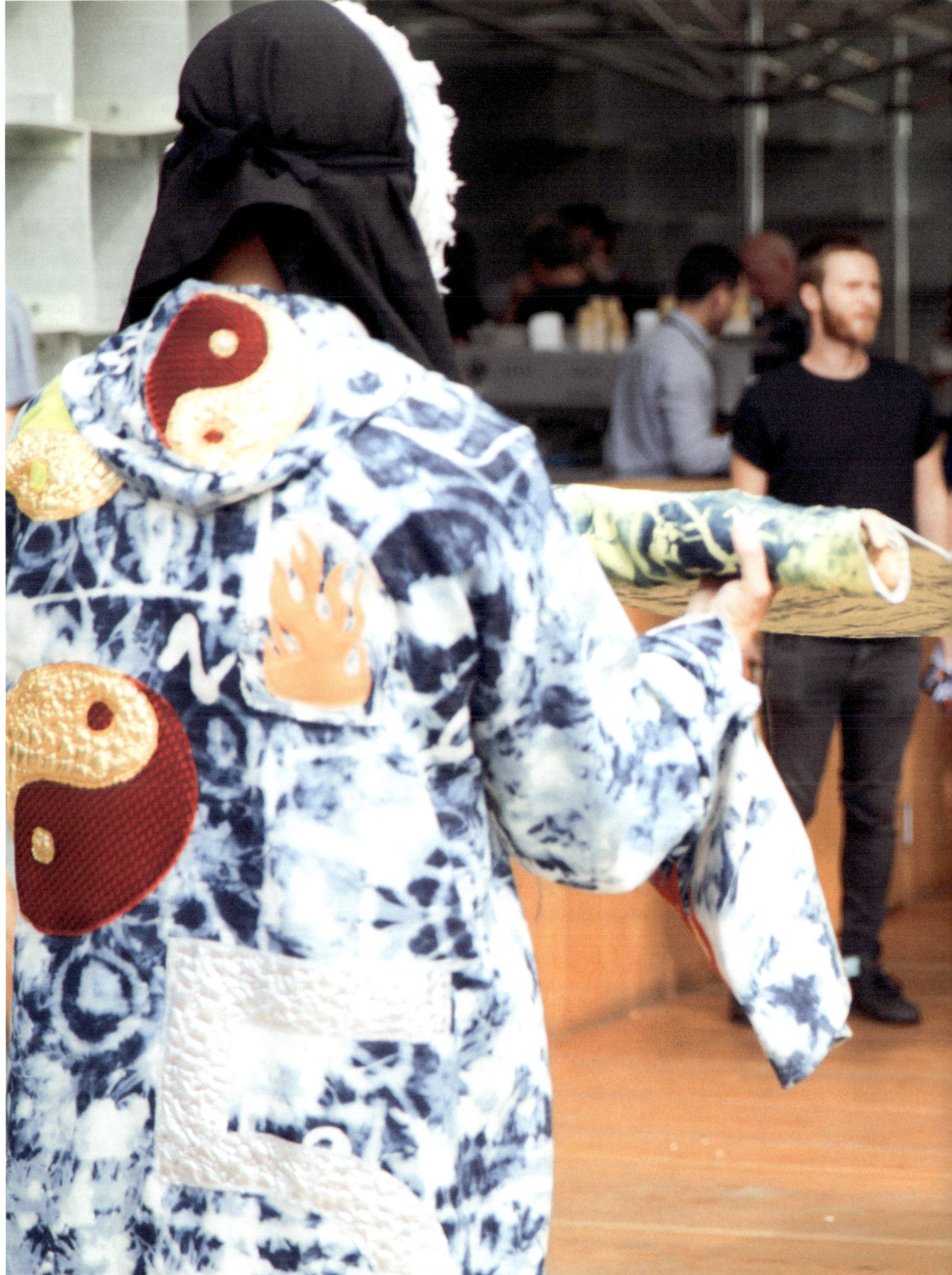

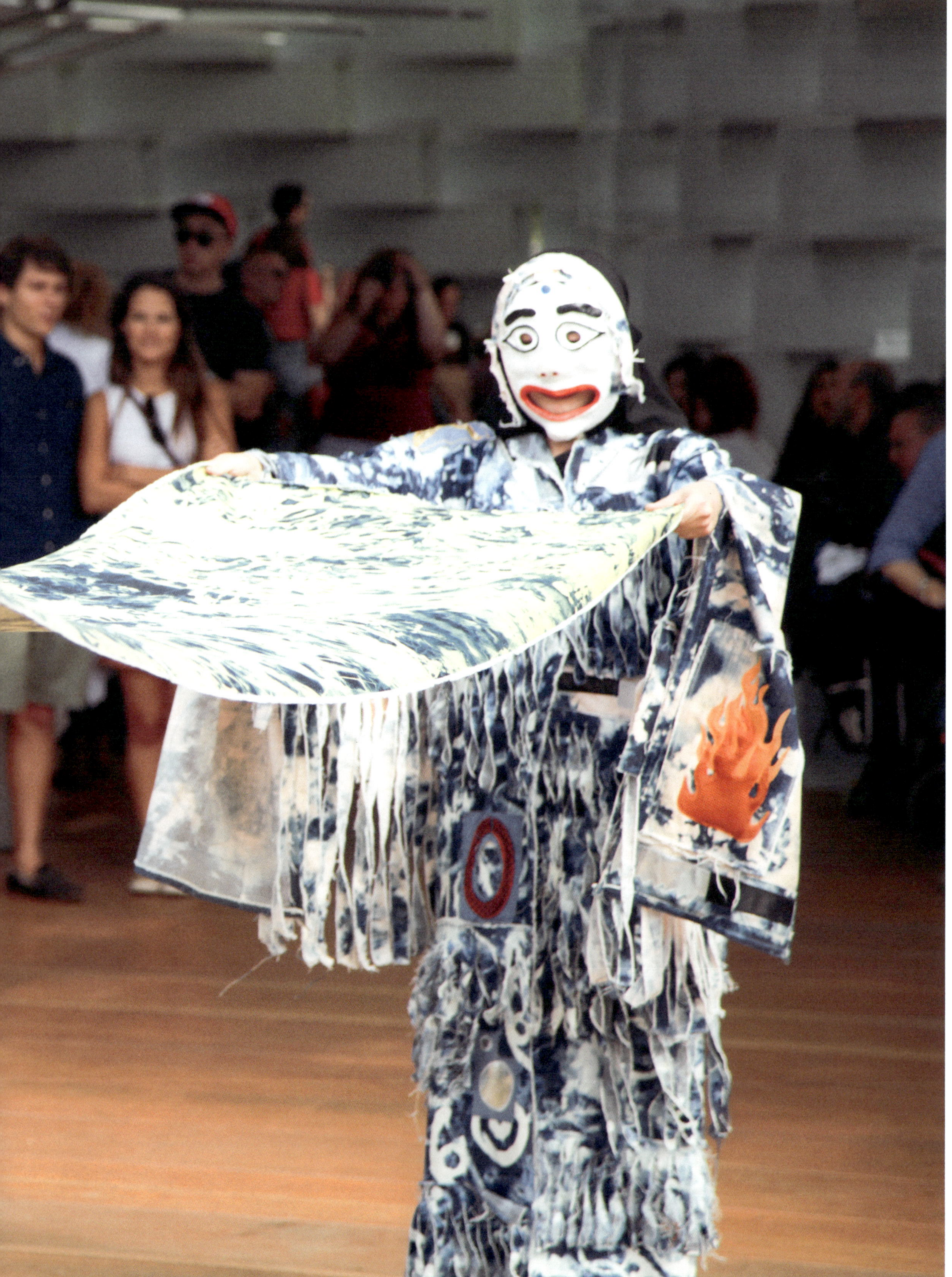

*Five
forms of
mending*

*after
Zadie Xa*

by
Daniella Valz Gen

To remember

I uphold your memory as a precious gift
I search for it and craft it,
trace your footsteps with mine

With my hands I evoke you

I invoke you in my bones
          your memory in my bones
through the movements embedded in my body
          my body, fractal of yours

I carry your memory in the flesh that I am and all I make, you make

I trace your steps
My pace is slow and consistent

I am you and I search for you as I craft memories of you
I return to you
I return to the small task:
This here in front me, my path towards you

I sense you
and I sense behind you the threat of forgetfulness rushing in
clad in steel, armoured to divide me from you

I hold on to your seed
I pour myself into what I do

As long as I move with you, I remember you
As long as I make you, I have you
As long as you move in me, I honour you

I

To make a temple

I have built you a home inside me
I stitched it with my hands square by square
I made a portable altar so I can wear you

My movement venerates you

Every movement of my hands your movement,
a way of communing

Here in this home I weave our intimacy
Here I come to grieve
to offer you my pain and ask for your company

I want to envelop you with something soft

This temple is simple
a square is strong

Here we punch the leather skin
we pierce and cut through
we make a space to remember and we call in for help

Here in this space we dwell together

I find you in the home I made for our grief

II

To contemplate
the passage of time

No light is ever the same and no light can be reproduced

I drink its liquid as its arc engulfs us:
Your dawn my dusk

Wherever your bones lay they are touched by light

I learn to inhale and exhale like the celestials

We wax and wane with the moon
We rise and set with the sun,
together

Here I sit and observe death as primordial seed
and in my longing to hold you and be held by you
there's an unending warmth,
the clarity of belonging to each other

Though I hold the pain of my loss of you deep within me
I pour it in the company of death
I oil your bones to make them shine like the suns they are

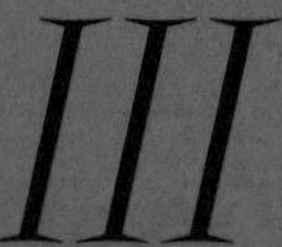

III

With helping spirits

How could I say it all
                even with all my might
without help

I call on the tricksters
overlooked vermin knows of dirt
remembers the corners where evil hides
a vixen in flames knows of shapeshifting

I call on them, I call on the specialists

Small gods find their place in our home

I nourish them and you
we go back and forth turning reciprocity into a feast

Never a burden
Always a celebration

IV

With humility, hospitality

I learn to protect as my duty
as an act of repair

I learn to embody the right story
to become the shaman and the hero
the one that pierces feral tissue

I learn to fish in the right pond
I throw my hook and I catch a ghost
between this life and the afterlife

I hear you ghost, I see you

Once I claim you as part of me
you need haunt no more
you need weep no more

Come find refuge in me
Come find the warmth you long for
Come nest in my body

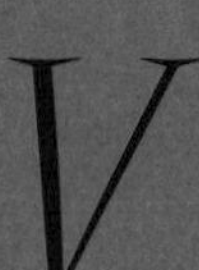

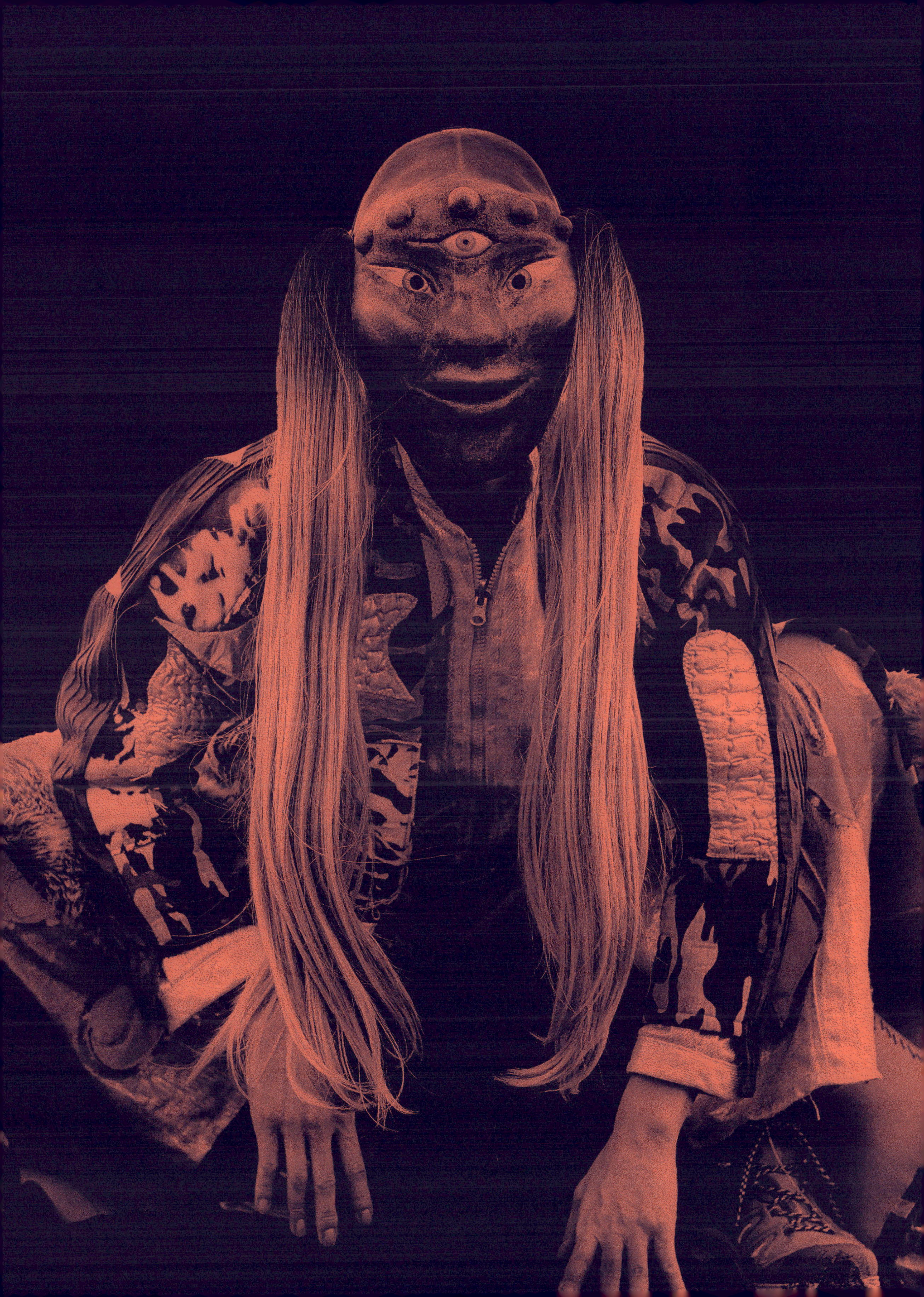

Zadie Xa (b. 1983, Vancouver, Canada) lives and works in London, UK. She earned an MA in Painting at the Royal College of Art in 2014 and a BFA at the Emily Carr University of Art and Design in 2007.

Solo Exhibitions

'Long ago when tigers smoked' (2022), The Box, Plymouth, UK

'Moon Poetics 4 Courageous Earth Critters and Dangerous Day Dreamers' (2021), Leeds Art Gallery, UK

'Moon Poetics 4 Courageous Earth Critters and Dangerous Day Dreamers' (2020), Remai Modern, Treaty 6 Territory, Saskatoon, Canada

'Child Of Magohalmi and the Echoes of Creation' (2020), De La Warr Pavilion, Bexhill-on-Sea, UK

'Child Of Magohalmi and the Echoes of Creation' (2019), Tramway, Glasgow, UK

'Child Of Magohalmi and the Echoes of Creation' (2019), YARAT Contemporary Art Space, Baku, Azerbaijan

'Soju Sipping on a Sojourn to Saturn' (2018), Galeria Agustina Ferreyra, Mexico City, Mexico

'HOMEBOY 3030: Return the Tiger 2 the Mountain' (2018), Union Pacific, London, UK

'The Conch, Sea Urchin and Brass Bell' (2017), Pump House Gallery, London, UK

Performance

Scorpion, in collaboration with Benito Mayor Vallejo (2021), The National Gallery, London, UK

Dream Dangerous, in collaboration with Benito Mayor Vallejo, Jia-Yu Corti and Ophelia Liu (2020), presented with Galerla Agustina Ferreyra, Frieze Live 2020, London, UK

Grandmother Mago (2020), AGO Toronto, Canada

Child of Magohalmi and the Echoes of Creation (2019), Dance International Glasgow, Tramway Glasgow, UK

Child of Magohalmi and the Echoes of Creation (2019), Art Night 2019, Walthamstow Library, London, UK

Grandmother Mago (2019), produced by Delfina Foundation for 'Meetings on Art', 58th Venice Biennale, Italy

Flooded with ICE/Hellfire Can't Scorch Me (2018), commissioned by Hayward Gallery, Southbank Center, London, UK

Irridezcent Interludez (2018), 'DO DISTURB', Palais de Tokyo, Paris, France

Perfumed Purple Rice and Sateen Songs for Sadie (2017), 'GUEST, GHOST, HOST: MACHINE! Marathon', Serpentine Galleries, London, UK

The Sea Child (2017), 'Rehearsals from the Korean Avant-Garde Performance Archive', Korean Cultural Centre, London, UK

Crash Boom Hisssssss. Legend of the Liquid Sword (2017), Block Universe, Somerset House Studios, London, UK

Basic Instructions B4 Leaving (2016), Cafe OTO, London, UK,

Linguistic Legacies and Lunar Exploration (2016), Serpentine Galleries, London, UK

Selected Group Exhibitions

'The Horror Show!' (2022), Somerset House, London UK

'Soy Dreams of Milk' (2022), Blindspot Gallery, Hong Kong

'The Condition of Being Addressable' (2022), Institute of Contemporary Art, Los Angeles, USA

'Flowing Moon, Embracing Land' (2022), Jeju Biennale 2022, South Korea

'Hernan Bas & Zadie Xa: House Spirits' (2022), Jessica Silverman, San Fransisco, USA

'Wonder Women' (2022), Jeffrey Deitch, New York City, USA

'Lee Scratch Perry: The Orbzerver' (2022), MACRO – Museo de Arte Contemporáneo de Roma, Italy

'The New Bend' (2022), Hauser & Wirth, New York City, USA

'Painting in Person' (2021), Castello di Rivoli Museo d'Arte Contemporanea, Turin, Italy

'Sweat' (2021), Haus Der Kunst, Munich, Germany

'Wishbone Vision' (2021), Project Native Informant, London, UK

'Interior Infinite' (2021), The Polygon Gallery, North Vancouver, Canada

'I am a heart beating in the world: Diaspora Pavilion 2' (2021), Campbelltown Arts Centre, New South Wales, Australia

'Bodies of Water' (2021), 13th Shanghai Biennale, China

'Siembra' (2020), presented by Galeria Agustina Ferreyra at kurimanzutto, Mexico City, Mexico

'Feedback Loops' (2019), ACCA – Australian Centre for Contemporary Art, Melbourne, Australia

'Still I Rise: Feminisms, Gender, Resistance – Act 3' (2019), Arnolfini, Bristol, UK

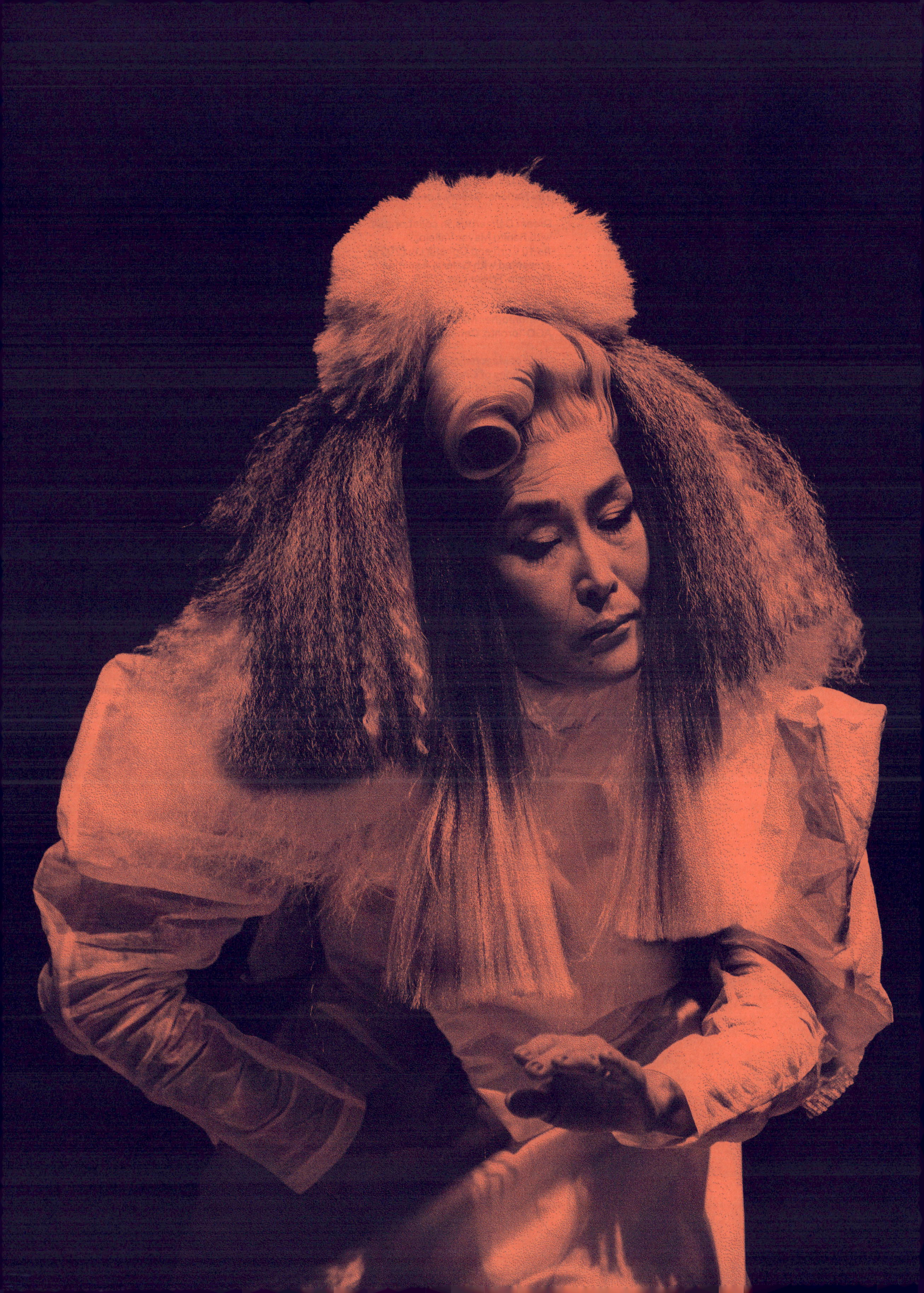

Inês Costa

is Assistant Curator at Whitechapel Gallery, London, where she has worked on various exhibitions such as 'The London Open' (2022); 'Nalini Malani: Can You Hear Me?' (2020–21); 'Carlos Bunga: Something Necessary and Useful' (2020); 'Anna Maria Maiolino: Making Love Revolutionary (2019–20); '"la Caixa" Collection of Contemporary Art' (2019–20) and 'Killed Negatives: Unseen Images of 1930s America' (2018). Recent independent curatorial projects include 'Swayze effect' (2019), Platform Southwark, London; 'Geltung [Validity]: perception of a natural right' (2017), GENERATORprojects, Dundee; and 'IT IS PROBABLY BETTER TO START FROM ZERO' (2016–17), Window Space, London.

Tarini Malik

is Curator at Whitechapel Gallery since January 2022. Previous to this, she was Assistant Curator at the Hayward Gallery (2017–22) where she has co-curated a number of landmark group exhibitions, as well as the first solo presentations in the UK of artists such as Emmanuelle Lainé, Thabiso Sekgala and Igshaan Adams. Previously, she was Head of Exhibitions for Isaac Julien, and Curator on several major international exhibitions with Mark Nash during her tenure at their shared studio (2014–17). She was Research Curator under the artistic directorship of Okwui Enwezor for the 56th Venice Biennale, 'All The World's Futures' in 2015. She has also held curatorial posts at Fiorucci Art Trust (2012–14), Frieze Projects (2013) and Serpentine Galleries (2010–12).

Novuyo Moyo

is an editorial assistant at art-agenda and a freelance writer. She has written for *art-agenda*, *ArtReview* and *Convergence*, the South London Gallery's online platform for critical conversations. She previously worked as an editorial trainee at *ArtReview* (2019–20). Before that, she studied History of Art at Goldsmiths, University of London (2013–17), where she specialised in online platforms and the effect on our digital visual culture and behaviours and is currently completing a master's degree in the same at UCL (2022–23).

Lucia Pietroiusti

is a curator working at the intersection of art, ecology and systems, usually outside of the gallery space and is the founder of the General Ecology project at Serpentine Galleries, where she is currently Strategic Advisor for Ecology. Current projects include the research and festival series, *The Shape of a Circle in the Mind of a Fish* (with Filipa Ramos, since 2018); the opera-performance *Sun & Sea* by Rugilė Barzdžiukaitė, Vaiva Grainytė and Lina Lapelytė (Venice Biennale, 2019 and international tour, 2020–24); the 8th Biennale Gherdeïna, 'Persones Persons' (with Filipa Ramos, May-September 2022,); and the non-profit organisation, Radical Ecology (with Ashish Ghadiali, since 2022). Recent and forthcoming publications include *More-than-Human* (with Andrés Jaque and Marina Otero Verzier, 2020); *Microhabitable* (with Fernando García-Dory, 2020–22); and *PLANTSEX* (2019).

Ana Teixeira Pinto

is a writer and cultural theorist based in Berlin. She is Professor of Art theory at the HBK Braunschweig and Theory Tutor at the Dutch Art Institute. Her writings have appeared in publications such as *Third Text*, *Afterall*, *e-flux journal*, *Manifesta Journal*, and *Texte zur Kunst*. She is the editor of a book series on the anti-political turn published by Sternberg Press. Together with Kader Attia and Anselm Franke, she organised the conference and podcast series *The White West: Whose Universal*, taking place at HKW Berlin, in collaboration with the 2022 Berlin Biennial.

Daniella Valz Gen

is a poet and artist. Their work explores the interstices between languages, cultures and value systems with an emphasis on embodiment and ritual. They're the author of *Subversive Economies* (PSS Press, 2018) and contributor to various art journals such as *The Happy Hypocrite*, *Lish*, *Map Magazine*, *Lux Scotland* amongst others. Recent projects include *Deslices* (2021), Glasgow International; *Howl Sigh Sing* (2022), An Tobar; and *You can call me Horse* (2022), Gropius Bau.

Wong Binghao

approaches art through curatorial and essayistic modes. They constellate contextually specific, conceptually capacious, and emotionally available readings and experiences of art in the hope of building more emancipatory and ethical worlds. Select projects include publications *Indifferent Idols* (2018) and *Charm Offensive* (2019), digital and public programs 'Third Date' (2022); 'Concealer' (2021); 'pillow talk' (2016); and 'We Are Losing Inertia' (2014), and exhibitions 'Good girls go to heaven, Pretty girls go online' (2019) and 'Asymmetric Grief' (2015). They presented their research at 'Gender in Southeast Asian Art Histories: Art, Digitality, Canon-making?' (2019). They are currently C-MAP Asia Fellow for the Museum of Modern Art.

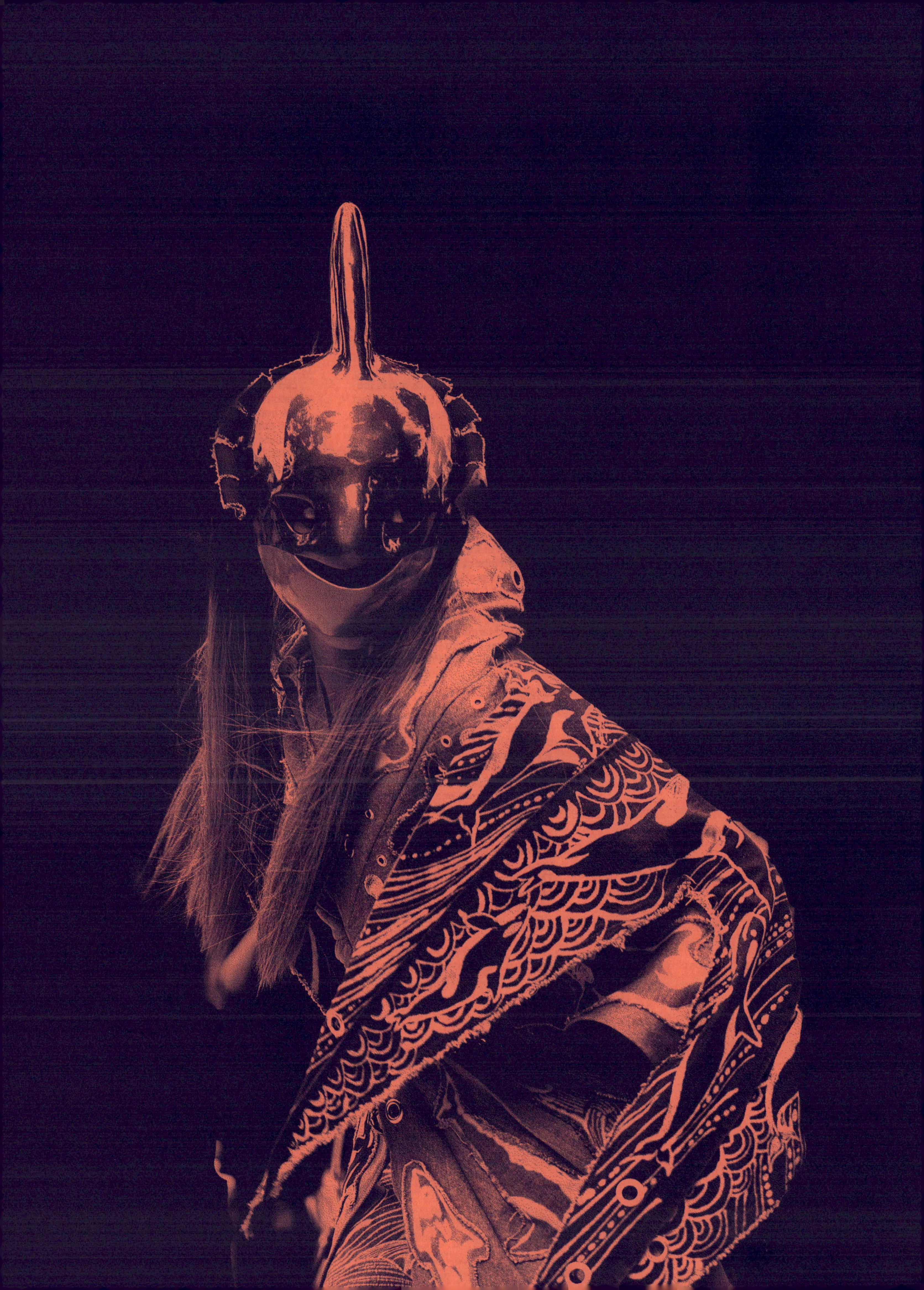

Acknowledgements

Zadie Xa: House Gods,
Animal Guides and
Five Ways 2 Forgiveness
is generously supported by

DIOR

The Whitechapel Gallery
Commissioning Council
Dorota Audemars
Erin Bell
Emilie De Pauw
Heloisa Genish
Leili Huth
Irene Panagopoulos
Nicole Saikalis Bay

Additional support from
The High Commission
of Canada to the United
Kingdom
Nicoletta Fiorucci Foundation
Sanghee Kim

With thanks to
Abbotts Flooring
J&C Joel Ltd

The exhibition's design and
production of the artworks have
been created in collaboration
with Benito Mayor Vallejo.

The artist would also like to
acknowledge Lin Sheng for his
tireless support and assistance
in the studio, Tom Slater
for his work on crafting of the
sound piece, Jihye Kim for
her percussion excerpts and
Manuel Vadillo for designing
the patterns of two of the
exhibited cloaks.

The artist gratefully
acknowledges the support of
the Canada Council for the Arts.

The Whitechapel Gallery would like to thank its supporters, whose generosity enables the Gallery to realise its pioneering programmes.

Towards Tomorrow Champions
D. Daskalopoulos Collection
Michael & Nina Zilkha

Major Donors
Asymmetry Art Foundation
Bloomberg Philanthropies
City Bridge Trust
Clore Cultural Learning Fund
Collezione Maramotti
Max Mara
NEON
Swarovski Foundation

Exhibitions Programme
Aldgate Connect BID
The AKO Foundation
Bagri Foundation
Balice Hertling, Paris
Jill & Jay Bernstein
Christen Sveaas Art Foundation
The Circles of Art
Cockayne Grants for the Arts
Collezione Maramotti
Nicoletta Fiorucci Russo
Gagosian
Sarah & Gerard Griffin
Henry Moore Foundation
High Commission of Canada in the United Kingdom
Hiscox
Galerie Hubert Winter, Vienna
Jayhawk
Karma International, Zurich
kaufmann repetto, Milan, New York
Galerie Lelong & Co.
London Community Foundation
Max Mara
Paul McCartney
Ministry of Culture, Republic of China (Taiwan)
The Norwegian Embassy
The Polish Cultural Institute, London
Regen Projects
Galerie Tanit Munich-Beirut
Tavolozza Foundation
Laura & Barry Townsley
The Whitechapel Gallery Commissioning Council
White Cube
and those who wish to remain anonymous

Education & Community Programmes
Aldgate Connect BID
Art Fund
The Arts Society Westminster
Dorota & Olivier Audemars
Capital Group
Clore Cultural Learning Fund
Paul Hamlyn Foundation
Mayor of London
Phillips
ZVM Rangoonwala Foundation
Alex Sainsbury
Dasha Shenkman
Swarovski Foundation
Tower Hamlets Arts & Music Education Service (THAMES)
The London Borough of Tower Hamlets
The Worshipful Company of Grocers

Public Events Programme
Aldgate Connect BID
GPE
The London Borough of Tower Hamlets
Stanley Picker Trust

Capital Renewal Programme
The Headley Trust
Culture Recovery Fund, Heritage Stimulus Fund – Historic England
The Wolfson Foundation

Whitechapel Gallery Corporate Patrons and Members
Bloomberg Philanthropies
Frasers Property UK
Gazelli Art House
Lisson Gallery
Phillips
David Zwirner

Whitechapel Gallery Corporate Supporters
Aldgate Connect BID
Bloomberg Philanthropies
Burgess & Leigh
Champagne Castelnau
Crozier Fine Arts
FRAME London
Hiscox (Artworks Insurance Partner)
Jayhawk
Max Mara
Collezione Maramotti
Omni Colour (Signage Partner)
Phillips

Future Fund
Mahera & Mohammad Abu Ghazaleh
Sirine & Ahmad Abu Ghazaleh
Swantje Conrad
Mr Dimitris Daskalopoulos
Maryam & Edward Eisler
Luigi Maramotti
NEON
Dominic Palfreyman
Catherine Petitgas
John Smith & Vicky Hughes
V-A-C Foundation
Sir Sigmund Warburg's Voluntary Settlement
Arts Council England
Catalyst Endowment Fund

Whitechapel Gallery Commissioning Council
Dorota Audemars
Erin Bell
Emilie De Pauw
Heloisa Genish
Leili Huth
Irene Panagopoulos
Nicole Saikalis Bay

Whitechapel Gallery Patrons' Chair
Francis Outred

Whitechapel Gallery Global Circle
Elyse & Lawrence B. Benenson Charitarian Foundation
Yan Du
Peter & Maria Kellner
Elie Khouri Art Foundation
and those who wish to remain anonymous

Whitechapel Gallery Director's Circle
Erin Bell & Michael Cohen
Dirk Boll
Pilar Corrias
Aud & Paolo Cuniberti
Julie & Debashis Dey
Rami Kim
Bimpe Nkontchou
Katie & Felix Robyns
and those who wish to remain anonymous

Whitechapel Gallery Curator's Circle
Cherry Cheng
Mark Harris
Marcelle Joseph
Adrian & Jennifer O'Carroll
Ralph Segreti & Richard Follows
Dasha Shenkman
Audrey Wallrock
Oba Nsugbe
Soo Hitchin
and those who wish to remain anonymous

Whitechapel Gallery Patrons
Cedric Bardawil
Keith & Helen Clark
Sadie Coles HQ
Beth & Michele Colocci
Swantje Conrad
Francesca Consigli
Michael & Elizabeth Corley
Xiaochi Dong
Dunnett Craven Ltd
Sarah Elson
Sian Emmison
Belinda de Gaudemar
Joanna & Alan Gomes
James Green
Richard & Judith Greer
Sarah Griffin
Pippy Houldsworth
Crane Kalman Gallery
Marie Krauss
Frank Krikhaar
Gerrit & Tilman Kristen
Anaïs Lellouche
George Loudon
Xi Liu & Yi Luo
Di Luo
Kate MacGarry
Pat Maugüé
Mary E McNicholas
Heike Moras
Jacqueline Nowikovsky
Reine Okuliar
Indi Oliver
Maureen Paley
Dominic Palfreyman
Darryl de Prez & Victoria Thomas
Maria-Cruz Rashidian
Eugenio Re Rebaudengo
Paulina Rider Wilhelmsen
Steve Ruggi & Gilda Williams
Marina Ruiz-Colomer
Jackie Russell
Alex Sainsbury & Elinor Jansz
Cherrill & Ian Scheer
Elisabeth von Schwarzkopf
Henrietta Shields
Matthew Slotover & Emily King
Karen & Mark Smith
Bina & Philippe von Stauffenberg
Nayrouz Tatanaki
Christoph & Marion Trestler
Vanessa Vainio
Samantha Wainstein
Eleanor Warnock
Kimberley Williams
Sharon Zhu & Michael Tian
and those who wish to remain anonymous

We remain grateful for the ongoing support of Whitechapel Gallery Members.

The Whitechapel Gallery is proud to be a National Portfolio Organisation of Arts Council England.

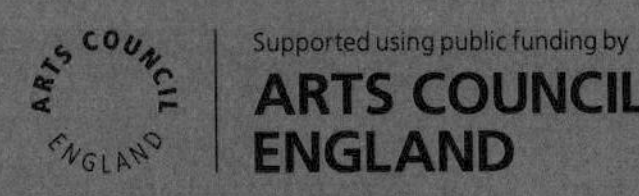

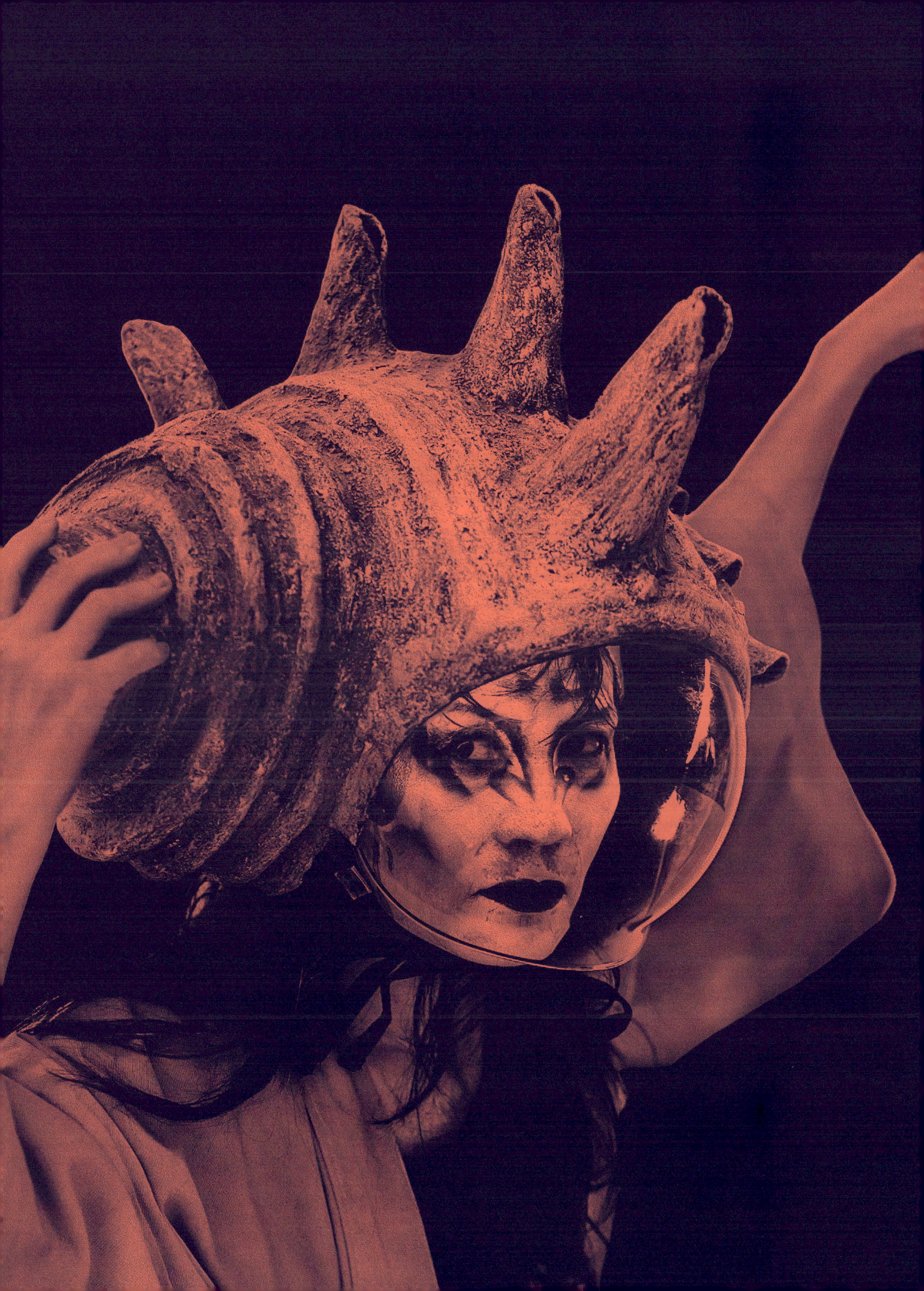

Published on the occasion
of the exhibition
    Zadie Xa: House Gods,
    Animal Guides and
    Five Ways 2 Forgiveness

20 September 2022 – 30 April 2023
Whitechapel Gallery
77–82 Whitechapel High Street
London, E1 7QX
whitechapelgallery.org

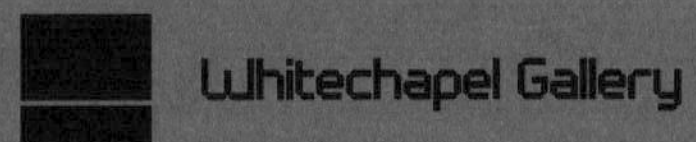

Exhibition

Curator
    Tarini Malik
Assistant Curator
    Inês Costa
Head of Exhibition Design and
Production
    Christopher Aldgate
Gallery Technical Manager
    Alejandro Ball
Installation Technicians
    **Isobel Adderly, David Corbett,
    Paul Cousins, Thomas Mathew,
    Francesca Penty, Jonathan Pinn,
    Clem Routledge, David Spicer,
    Nick Yarroll**
Build
    Sam Forster Ltd.
Lighting
    **Liam Cahill and Sanford Lighting
    Design**
Sound
    Tom Slater

The exhibition's design and
production of the artworks have
been created in collaboration
with Benito Mayor Vallejo.

The artist would also like to
acknowledge Lin Sheng for his
tireless assistance in the studio,
Tang Hong and Xiao Xia for
the additional sewing support,
Tom Slater for his work on crafting
the sound work, Jihye Kim for her
percussion excerpts and Manuel
Vadillo for designing the patterns
of two of the exhibited cloaks.
The sound piece in the exhibition
contains poetic excerpts from
the work of Kim Sowol and Seong
Sam-mun.

Publication

Editors
    Tarini Malik and Inês Costa
Head of Publications
    Francesca Vinter
Copy editor
    Novuyo Moyo
Design
    In the shade of a tree
Typefaces
    **Oroban Hermonthica (Blaze Type)
    Söhne (Klim Type)**
Inner pages
    **Munken Lynx 130 gsm
    Sirio Color Flamingo 80 gsm**
Cover
    Sirio Color Flamingo 290 gsm
Dustjacket
    Dubletta 3251 165 gsm
Printer
    Graphius
ISBN
    978-085488-310-3

First published 2022
by Whitechapel Gallery, London
© 2022 Whitechapel Gallery
and the authors

A catalogue record for this book
is available from the British Library.

Distributed by
    **Thames & Hudson
    181a High Holborn
    London, WC1V 7QX
    Tel: +44 (0) 20 7845 5000
    sales@thameshudson.co.uk**

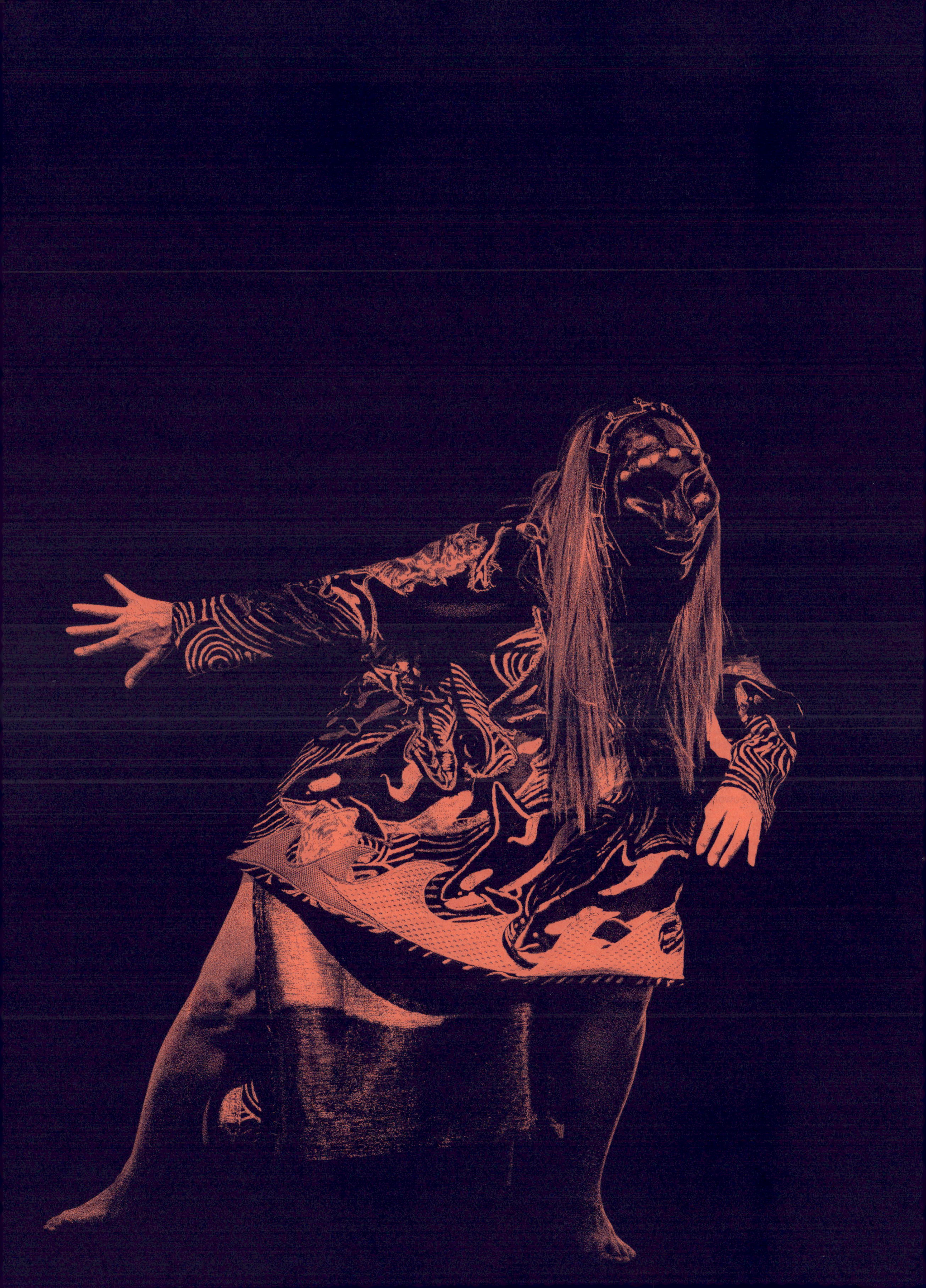

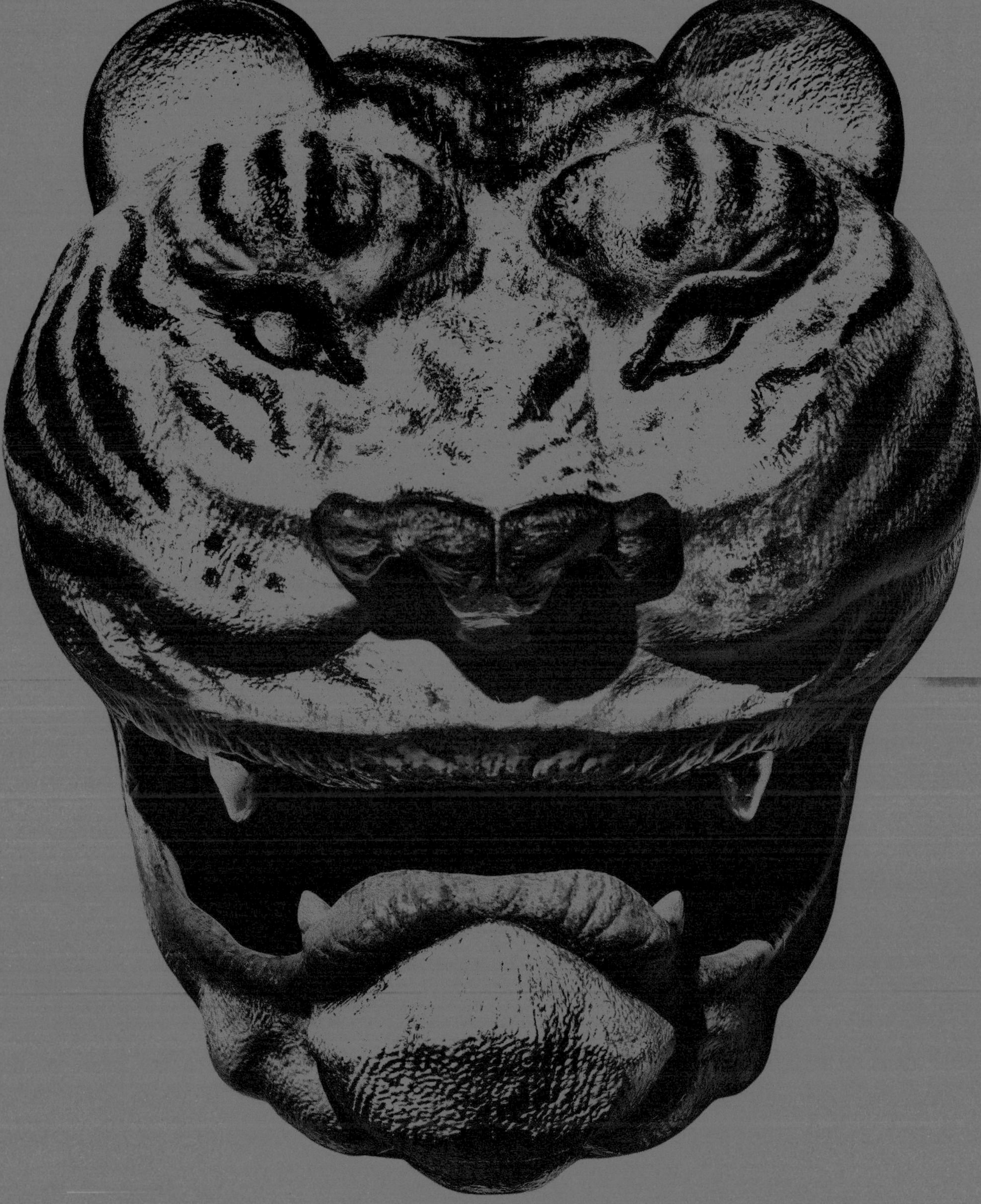

Whitechapel Gallery